Table of contents

Introduction

Today we very often hear the words that everything in this world is invented by man or depends on man. Many phenomena of this world are considered subjective and dependent on our personal interpretation. What is more, it is claimed that even the very concept of nature is wrong and that, in fact, there is no nature! Everything, such people say, is "a social and cultural construction." Nature as such is dismissed. The natural order, the order in the world, is denied.

All this leads to its logical result - faith in God is rejected because where there is no order, there cannot be God. The world is simply a collection of our human fabrications and conventions. Our world is a "social construction." All we need is to live according to our desires; to choose the gender we want; to practice relationships that are unnatural and immoral, and so forth. Therefore, the constructivist approach has its implications in practice, and we see them nowadays.

As a counterpoint to this conception, we will turn to the theological doctrine of natural law. According to the latter, *the world is regulated by a law established by God*. This regulation is intended to help us and the world not fall into a state of chaos. Furthermore, every single thing in this world has its nature, its essence. Although both things are not the same, we can perceive them as demonstrating that there are stable and fixed entities in this world. Man's nature is permanent, at least on earth; genders are permanent; ethnicity and nationality are less permanent and more fluid, but they still can be defined according to objective criteria.

To prove that there is order in the world, we will turn to three central concepts: Logos, or the Word; the Liturgy as a reflection and participation in the divine order and life; and the relation between science and religion as reflecting the essence of the Logos.

The Logos refers to the Greek term "word" and represents the general principle of divine reason and creative order in the world. Natural law, on the other hand, is the moral law that is accessible to all people through reason. Liturgy refers to the ritual and ceremonial practices of the Church.

The thesis expressed in the current work will defend the reality of God by means of establishing natural law, the dignity of the human person, God's beauty manifested in nature, and the fact that faith goes hand in hand with science. By knowing the world, we will know that God is real- although we can never know His nature perfectly.

This work is divided into six chapters. The first chapter is focused on one interesting concept existing in Ancient philosophy and transformed by Christianity: the Logos. Here we will discuss the Stoics' conception of the Logos as a universal Law governing the order in cosmos (the world), as well as the destiny of all people. However, Christianity criticizes this fatalism and explains that Logos does not determine our concrete lives. The Logos is defined in the Bible as having divine essence and being part of God. The Logos descends to earth and incarnates in the Son of God, or Christ. The Logos is conjoined with God. He is the foundation of the world, as we will see by referring to St. Justin, Philo of Alexandria, and Maxim the Confessor.

The second chapter will discuss the problem of nature and natural law and its relation to Logos and morality. We will consider notions like *physis, cosmos, nomos,* as they are perceived by Ancient Greeks and Christian theologians. There is an objective moral order that is based on the natural order of the universe. The Bible teaches that natural law is accessible to all people, regardless of their religious beliefs. The Logos is the Law which rationally and benevolently (since it is the Good in itself) governs the world. The Decalogue is based on the Logos and it is our way to follow the Logos (God) with our deeds.

The third chapter will examine the Liturgy as a means to encounter God. We will demonstrate that there is a divine economy and plan behind scripture, and that the ultimate fulfillment of scripture is a liturgy. This plan is God's work and God's liturgy. Liturgy is the *summum bonum* and it is reached by the Logos. It is our Way to eternal life and it takes us closer to God.

The fourth chapter will now turn to another connection between God and the world- the natural law as a proof for the reality of God. The order of the world, the presence of regularities (or laws) in it indicate the reality of a Creator. This Creator made the world as to prevent the emergence of chaotic states. Thus, we will refer specifically to St. Thomas Aquinas' arguments and Paley's Watchmaker argument.

The fifth chapter elaborates our arguments further. It now deals with science. It is no coincidence that many scientists in the past claimed to believe in both science and God. Science actually led them to God. These were scientists like Einstein, Newton, Arthur Eddington. They believed that the universe is too beautiful and harmonic not to have been created with some purpose, by some Designer. To this belief, we will oppose the chaos theory- the idea that the world does not exist in a stable state; there is no permanent order in nature. Quite the opposite - the world is a system that tends toward chaos, toward disorder. Here we will show the confrontation between these two conceptions and see which one stands up to our logical analysis. However, even the Chaos theory at its core does not posit the existence of "pure chaos"- what we call chaos is simply the lack of enough data and facts.

But our analysis of the problem of nature and the Logos will not be complete without turning to the central problem of our times- the debate between essentialism and a radical wing of social/cultural constructivism. The sixth chapter is focused on a process that we may call *de-naturalization of the world*- there is nothing natural in this world and everything could be changed according to our will and desire (for example, gender, race, ethnicity). We can even become "transhumans" if we want it! Here the conception of Judith Lorber of gender will be scrutinized. We will oppose it to the Christian doctrine that man and woman will always be man and woman; and a family established by a man and a woman is a natural family. Transitoriness does not speak against the existence of nature of things. Gender exists in nature and through nature and we cannot change this fact. This is the approach called *gender essentialism*.

The last chapter of this work will elaborate on the problem of artificial intelligence. Why do we need it? Is there any limit to this development? Is there any risk of AI being declared as a "person"? We will analyze the possible risks and advantages of developing AI in our civilization. As we will demonstrate, we need to be open to this development, but still we have to put moral limitations on it. At the same time, artificial intelligence is perfect proof for the reality of a Creator- there is no intellect appearing by pure chance in this world.

The reader will be right to ask: Do we need another theological and philosophical work on the Logos and natural law? What contribution will such a book have to theology? What should be its practical meaning?

As we stated at the beginning of this Introduction, the debate between essentialists and constructivists is very serious at this moment. It is a pity that most of the debate participants employ rather political arguments instead of philosophical and rational arguments. Thus, the proponents of constructivism are not its defenders because they believe in its philosophy; they are rather politically motivated by their belonging to the liberal camp! If one is a liberal, then one should be a constructivist as well. Here we will attempt to carry out a theological and philosophical analysis to show which approach is more sound. We will also refer to Scripture, but as taken in itself; Scripture is supported by our intellect and experience.

We should also note that some conservatives wrongly believe that conventionalism and constructivism in general, are something immoral. As a matter of fact, both conceptions stem from the anthropocentrism of the Sophists in Ancient Greece. Some things in our world depend on convention (mathematics; Euclid geometry); and other phenomena are constructed (statehood and politics; sport activities; money). But these two approaches are led to their extremes in what we can call de-naturalization of the world. Therefore, the problem lies not with constructivism per se but with the de-naturalists.

We can get to the truth by carrying out an impartial debate, deprived of any political or ideological shades. What we would like to achieve in this work is to understand human nature better, and with this, to understand our world. By turning to the divine Logos, we will see ourselves there.

Chapter I: The Logos

The concept of Logos is among the most important in philosophy. Originally used in the sense of "reason" and "law," later it was transformed into "intellect" and reached Hegel's conception of the Absolute Idea. Without knowing what the Logos is, we cannot properly understand the history of philosophy. But apart from philosophy, this concept is of great importance for Christianity. The Logos is not only reason and law, but also the Word; and the Word is Christ, our Savior. Therefore, here we will analyze the ancient Greek understanding of the Logos, which will be then contrasted with the Christian understanding. Logos is not an impersonal entity that rules the world; The Logos is living and eternal; God is the Logos.

1.1 The Ancient Logos

Summary:

Ancient Greek Stoic philosophers emphasized one moral end of our conduct: to live in accordance with the rules of Reason, or Logos. The Logos was considered a universal law that governs the whole *cosmos*. Real freedom is found only within the Logos; we are free as long as we follow Its decisions. Pain, suffering and pleasure do not exist, but they are rather our own perceptions (or opinions) about given facts.

The ancient Greek word *logos* enjoys a long history. It appears as early as in Homer's works. It is employed by many Greek philosophers afterwards. The word *logos* has plenty of meanings: speech, relation, narrative, reason, law, meaning, notion, word. In the Greek translation of the Old Testament, this word is encountered in the following passage:

Then they cried to the Lord in their trouble,

and he saved them from their distress.

He sent out his word and healed them;

he rescued them from the grave. (Ps. 197:19-10; New International Version).

In addition to this passage, this word occurs elsewhere in the Old Testament. For example, the Ten Commandments of God are called the Decalogue - or, that is, "ten logos." In this case, the word "nomos" is not used, which also means law but more in a political sense. Therefore, the word *Logos* is of essential importance in the ancient Greek language.

We will not do an in-depth analysis of the concept of the Logos here. Certainly, its use in the philosophy of the Stoics is of essential importance to us, because it is precisely this that seriously influences the first Christian theologians. St. John, in his Gospel, also uses the term *Logos*, but already in a different form.

The Stoic school was founded in Athens in the 4th century BC. Its name comes from a special place in the Agora, which is called the Stoa. The most important Stoics were Chrysippus, Zeno, Epictetus, Seneca and Marcus Aurelius. Stoic ethics was developed mostly in the late period – 1st century AD. This is a period of many important historical events in Rome and Greece; a period of instability, uprisings and coups, the transformation of the Roman Republic into an empire.

Stoicism follows Platonic idealism. For Plato, the earthly existence is a reflection of the World of Ideas. The material world is merely a "shade" of this World. Ideas are the only true being; their reflections cannot be held to be real. Of course, Plato's doctrine is much more complex than this dualism, but the truth is that Plato considers this existence as preparation for the true being.

Stoics borrow plenty of Plato's ideas. For them, the material world does not exist per se; it is not independent. There should be a spiritual force governing the whole world. Therefore, we can assume that Stoicism is a kind of objective idealism- the reality is of ideal nature, but it still exists outside our minds.

Today we associate the Stoics with the notion of apathy and another concept they call ataraxia. These are concepts that mean lack of passion, lack of emotions, indifference to the surrounding world. The Stoics developed many different teachings in the fields of logic, ethics, and cosmology[1]. However, here we will pay attention mostly to ethics. Their ethics was extremely well developed and introduced some new ideas that dominated the Hellenistic world at the time of Christ and His apostles.

Stoic ethics rest on the understanding that many of our concepts do not reflect the external world. In fact, many things in our life depend only on ourselves. Our understanding of suffering, for example, stems from a wrong understanding of life. For us, life is something external that happens to us. But the truth is the opposite - our life is what we make of it. If we cause suffering to ourselves, then there will be suffering in our lives; and vice versa.

The question with which the Stoics are primarily concerned is this: how to live well? How to attain to the good? Before them, Socrates and Plato showed that the Good exists as something objective, independent of us. Good is something absolute, it does not depend on our opinion. We do not know enough about Socrates' theory because he left no written works. Plato, however, continues his moral ideas by arguing for the existence of a Supreme Good. This Good is like the sun that spreads its rays everywhere. That is why our main goal is to reach the Good; to contemplate it; to be a part of it. In a sense, this Good is God (though not exactly in the Christian sense).

---

[1] Regarding Stoicist Physics, we can turn to a curious conception: the idea of the eternal cosmic cycle. The world is born, then it grows, and finally it dies in Cosmic Fire. Then it is reborn, and the cycle goes on.

In Plato's time, however, the sophists were enormously popular. It was a movement of private tutors of philosophy and other sciences. They were known for their controversial concepts and the idea that they can defend any thesis. For the Sophists in general, truth, knowledge, and goodness are not absolutes. We will talk later about their relativism, which is very similar to today's moral relativism. Plato himself opposed their moral ideas by stating that the good is the highest moral category. Even if we encounter a lot of evil and suffering in the world, this does not mean that there is no good. But as there is shadow in our world, so there are evils and sufferings.

The Stoics do not go so far. For them, there is no Higher Good or Good that stands above all else. They deal with how we perceive good and evil. For most Stoics, these are not absolutely objective categories. They depend on our perception of them. What does this mean?

Let us imagine that our home has burned down in a fire. Most people will be sad and cry. They will be heartbroken due to the loss of their home. Where will they live now? Will they ever recover what they lost? This is a mere example of a disastrous tragedy that could happen to anyone.

However, a Stoic would say this: fire is something objective. Indeed, our home is no more, it ceased to exist. But is this the most important thing in our life? Should we be sad? Should we be broken after this evil? A Stoic would say: We should not be sad because sufferings, or what we call evils, are a part of our life. They exist and we cannot remove them. Disasters, diseases and death are here and we cannot completely protect ourselves from them. This is human destiny - to go through various calamities and suffering. The real problem is: should we take them so deeply?

Here the Stoics introduce their concept of *ataraxia*. It is a state in which nothing external affects us. Whatever happens to our home, family, and other things we believe to be vital, should not make us concerned. How we will react to it is only important - if we get excited every time, then we will suffer. Suffering results from being unable to control our emotions and passions.

And yet, what does this have to do with our subject - the Logos? How does it appear in the teachings of the Stoics? The concept of Logos is very important with them. The Logos is the World Reason. He rules the whole world (everything that exists). The Logos rules rationally, not emotionally. He has nothing to do with the capricious Olympian gods. He is impersonal - he does not feel sympathy for anyone, nor does he feel hatred. The Logos just puts things in order as they should be. The order in nature is reasonable - there cannot be anything better than it.

Researcher Philip Mitsis notes that the foundation of Stoic ethics is the idea that we should be indifferent, accepting everything with equanimity. It does not matter if it is joy or sadness: "The wise man is completely unafraid, no matter what sorts of external threats he may face, since everything important to him is internal and under his own control" (Mitsis 262). There is nothing important in our lives except life itself. We must live in harmony with the Logos, with the Universal Reason. Then we are good, we are righteous. We cannot influence his decisions; neither prayers nor rituals would change anything (this is an onslaught on Greek mythology). Even the gods obey this universal law.

It is a mistake to rebel against the decisions of the Logos; any attempt we make to assert some illusory freedom of ours is pointless. We are free only to the extent that we obey his decisions. There is no such thing as absolute freedom: "If we follow the path of the sage, we will mold our beliefs to the rational structure of the universe and will thereby avoid the tendency of lesser minds to rail against what is and must be the case" (Mitsis 265). The strong man does not resist the Logos, but listens to it, obeys it.

Here comes the question of the nature of things. For the Stoics, as for most ancient Greek philosophers, nature is something unchanging. Everything has its own nature, its own essence. It is determined and defined by this nature. Nature is something objective; nature is indifferent to us. She does not deliberately make us suffer. We must live in harmony with the nature of things - houses burn or are flooded; people get sick and die; the earth sometimes shakes in the process we call an earthquake; etc. These are all natural states, and we have to accept them as such.

And here the Stoics may be answered directly thus: Is it not true that it is in our nature to strive after happiness (as Aristotle says) or after pleasure (as Epicurus says)? In that case, we have to consider only those interests of ours.

As we have already shown, for the Stoics joy, sadness, pleasure are subjective states. They depend only on my perception. If I consider the fire in my home as something natural, then I will not suffer. I will be glad to be alive and my family is alive. Pleasure is a good thing, but when we become accustomed to pleasure, we also experience suffering more strongly. If we do not pay attention to pleasure, our suffering will be more moderate. That is why the Stoics believe that everything is only in our mind, in our perception - and how we will feel depends on this perception.

Thus it appears that the Stoics adhere to a sort of rationalism. As Philip Mitsis explains it, "rationality is a defining feature of nature which we begin to see as something that shares this uniquely valuable trait with us, but in a more perfect form. This more perfect form of rationality turns out to be the rationality of nature which itself is a divinely provident logos" (Mitsis 261). In short, nature itself is sensible; reason is not a purely human trait. There was reason long before us and there will be even after us. Reason is completely objective, in contrast to the Sophists' view that nature is impersonal and irrational.

Thus it turns out that living in harmony with nature is the highest good, the *summmum bonum*, for us. Nature is good, and good is in the nature of things. We should live our lives as dispassionately as possible. This observation about the Stoics is also confirmed by the words of Diogenes Laertius, an ancient historian of philosophy: "Living in agreement with nature comes to be the end, which is in accordance with the nature of oneself and that of the whole, engaging in no activity wont to be forbidden by the universal law, which is the right reason pervading everything and identical to Zeus" (Diogenes Laertius, quoted by Mitsis 258). It is our moral duty to strive for such a life. Of course, this is not absolutely achievable, but it remains our moral ideal.

Here we will not deal with the philosophy of the Stoics in more detail, but we will turn to the brightest representative of this school - Epictetus. Epictetus was an enslaved Greek. In this capacity, he reached certain philosophical (particularly ethical) insights. This is the reason he is also sometimes called the philosopher-slave. It is no accident that he deals with moral issues such as freedom, suffering and death. These were problems already addressed before him by the Roman thinker Seneca, but Epictetus brought more clarity and systematicity. If one wants to know more about Stoicism, then Epictetus' *Discussions* is a must-read.

This work contains brief reflections on various matters related to our feelings and emotions, with everything that can move us. In a calm tone, without arguing in absentia with anyone, Epictetus presents his concept. We must be wise and strive for a state of calmness, of the absence of passions and emotions. Above all existing laws stands the law (*nomos*) of life, about which Epictetus says the following: "But much before this law is the law of life, that we must act conformably to nature. For if in every matter and circumstance we wish to observe what is natural, it is plain that in every thing we ought to make it our aim that neither that which is consequent shall escape us" (Epictetus 73).

We must seek only the natural, only that which is in the nature of things. This is a universal task - not only for philosophers, but for all people. It does not matter what the capacity of the mind is, you can live in harmony with the nature of things. Epictetus here denies (albeit indirectly) Plato's concept that only philosophers can contemplate the Good, or Highest Good. To this elitism, Epictetus opposes his idea of general accessibility of knowledge and wisdom.

Epictetus continues with his idea of the law as follows: "And what is the divine law? To keep a man's own, not to claim that which belongs to others, but to use what is given, and when it is not given, not to desire it; and when a thing is taken away, to give it up readily and immediately" (Epictetus 146). We should concern ourselves only with what is ours - both internally and externally, in the material aspect. We should think only about our life, about what depends on us. At the same time, taken in their external aspect, these words mean that we should not strive for anything foreign - foreign things, foreign women, foreign fame. We should not envy, be jealous, steal. All this is not ours. What the gods (Epictetus does not express a firm belief that they exist; they are rather a metaphor) have given us, we must keep as much as we can. At the same time, we should not "cling" to our things - they are only temporarily ours, they are transitory in their essence.

In some places, the enslaved philosopher also mentions God as the one who guides our destiny: "Dare to look up to God and say: Deal with me for the future as thou wilt; I am of the same mind as you art; I am thine: I refuse nothing that pleases thee: lead me where thou wilt" (Epictetus 148). This is very reminiscent of Christianity, although Epictetus was not familiar with Christian doctrine. I am totally dependent on God - which in Epictetus' case means Logos, nature, universal law. Let the Logos do with me what he decides; I accept his decision, his will. Yes, Epictetus is not talking about the Christian God here, but it is not difficult to interpret this passage as leading to Christian moral doctrine. A Christian accepts the will of God; so must we do with the Logos.

Suffering and pleasure are not sent to us by the Logos intentionally. Or if so, we do not know the reason for it. Why do some people suffer more than others? It is not within our mental capacity. Perhaps the Logos has reasons of its own. He puts things in order somehow. Perhaps sufferers rejoice afterwards, and vice versa – maybe those who are mired in pleasures afterwards suffer? Plato (in his work *The Republic*) explains all this by the fact that our evil deeds affect us in the future and we suffer because of them. Furthermore, Plato believed in the afterlife and that everyone would get what they deserved (although Plato also allowed for reincarnation). After all, justice always prevails and we cannot have a good and peaceful life if we are unjust and unvirtuous.

The opinion, or perception of things, is what really worries us. The problem is only us! The scary things, the disturbing events are only in our mind and nowhere else. That is why Epictetus gives the following advice: "Then, when the appearance (of things) pains you, for it is not in your power to prevent this, contend against it by the aid of reason, conquer it: do not allow it to gain strength" (Epictetus 280-1). Suffering must be rejected; we do not have another choice. Trying to resist only makes us more vulnerable. What is more: frustration leads to more frustration, to anger, to aggression. We must stop this series of emotions in time; then we will preserve our personality from the unwanted consequences of anger, self-pity, and disappointment.

Epictetus describes the greatest Greek epic - the *Iliad* - as a series of events that are indifferent in themselves. All great and shameful deeds there exist only in our opinion, in human perception of them: "So then all these great and dreadful deeds have this origin, in the appearance (opinion)? Yes, this origin and no other. The Iliad is nothing else than appearance and the use of appearances" (Epictetus 81). Therefore, we should not be excited by such events.

At the same time, the slave philosopher explains that we should be grateful to the gods (or Logos or God) for our lot. We should enjoy what we possess and have in our life: "In the name of Zeus and the gods, any one thing of those which exist would be enough to make a man perceive the providence of God, at least a man who is modest and grateful" (Epictetus 45). The following words cannot but remind us of the Christian teaching on modesty and gratitude. As Epictetus writes, we can sing the following hymn to Zeus: " 'Great is God, who has given us such implements with which we shall cultivate the earth: great is God who has given us hands, the power of swallowing, a stomach, imperceptible growth, and the power of breathing while we sleep' " (Epictetus 46).

These words are striking- one could see Christianity there! However, the fact is that Epictetus does not reflect much about gratitude. His theory is not reminiscent of Gottfried Leibniz's "best possible world." Stoics, in general, do not show much optimism. But their goal is not that either - the optimist is a person who is still "clung" to the world, cannot get rid of earthly emotions and passions. To be an optimist means that I still desire something, strive for something. I judge that a thing is good in order to strive for it. And things in themselves are indifferent - ἀδιάφορα, adiaphora. Therefore, we can be neither optimistic nor pessimistic!

This completely rejects the accusations that the Stoics are pessimists and view the world and all phenomena in it negatively. A Stoic will simply watch life go by without making remarks, criticizing or discussing the problems of others. The Stoic will neither dwell on the problem of the glass being half empty or half full. He will simply state that it does not matter how full the glass is. Whether people think I am optimistic or not, it does not matter to me and it will not affect my life. I will not be swayed by the criticism of those who accuse me of pessimism. Not a few people today are interested in how others judge their actions and words. The Stoic does not need this - he turns only to himself for judgment; because we are all capable of judging whether our actions are right. Unlike Plato and Aristotle, the Stoics are confident that all people could make rational decisions and be guided by the Logos.

Here comes the criticism of the Stoics. We cannot help but find weak points in this philosophy, especially its moral teaching. These weak points are as follows:

1. It is a philosophy of indifference. We only look out for our own interests without caring about other people. We live in a society, don't we? How can we isolate ourselves from it?

2. The existence of the Logos is a metaphysical assumption, but it cannot be easily proved. What is this impersonal power that has nothing divine in it and does not appear to us? Why does this power not communicate with us, why does it not try to send us messages (e.g., through prophets)?

3. It is a philosophy of resignation. Whatever happens, we must not resist. Anyone can insult us, hit us and treat us unfairly; we should not react.

Instead of the Stoics, we can respond to these criticisms like this:

Answer 1: We can still live in society and be a family. However, the best society is based on the principles of the Logos. It follows the Logos and does not deviate from it. When we all follow this universal law, we will all feel good together.

Answer 2: The Stoics' Logos is entirely rational, it is the Reason itself. We cannot think that he can mystically appear to us and talk to us. There is no need for that; we have a particular impulse within us that leads us to the Logos.

Answer 3: Resignation is a matter of personal judgment. Resignation from what? From passions and emotions, from possessions, from experiences? If one man kills another, he will be punished by the Logos. There is a way of retribution. If a natural disaster happens, I cannot prevent it. I can only help people save themselves. Stoicism does not deny the possibility of helping. And yet, we must help so that we do not "cling" to passion, do not get too carried away. Even our love should be moderate.

According to Philip Mitsis, the interpretation of the term "nature" here is wrong. As he says, "Many philosophers have warned that such Stoic thoughts are untimely, not only because they are dangerous to one's own humanity and one's relations to others, but because they are deeply mistaken about our relation to nature" (Mitsis 266). But these critics start from the point of view of relativism. For them, "nature" is a vague concept. It depends on my point of view. These philosophers criticize not Stoicism, but the approach itself, which we can call essentialism. For essentialism, things have a nature of their own that is stable and unchanging.

But why not accept the existence of a universal law? As we will demonstrate later in this work, the existence of natural laws shows that the Stoics have some right after all. There really are immutable laws in the universe! It does not matter what we call them. Of course, the Stoics speak more in moral terms - the Logos governs our destinies and directs our affairs. That is why our decisions need to follow it!

Stoicism perceives the world as an orderly, harmonious cosmos. Everything in it takes place out of necessity – or, as the Logos decided is necessary. There is little room in this world for spontaneity, for chance. *Our freedom is rooted in turning to our nature and living in harmony with reason*, i.e., with the Logos.

1.2 The Logos as the Living Word

Summary:

The Christian conception of Logos sheds new light on it. The Logos is the Living Word. It is eternal and it is part of God. Through His Word, God created the world, as the first Christian theologians held- Philo, Justin, Clement. We will also discuss Maximus the Confessor's notion of Logos and how to attain to it. Our analysis will conclude with an interpretation of St. John's Prologue to the Gospel.

When Christianity began to spread, Stoicism was already an established philosophy. Not a few thinkers supported its moral views. Only Platonism had a stronger influence in that period - mainly through the emerging Neoplatonism (Proclus, Porphyry, Plotinus). There is no way that these two schools did not influence Christian philosophy, which at the beginning represented an attempt to defend Christianity from various attacks and accusations. It was extremely important to show at the outset that there are points of contact between the teachings of Christ and the ancient Greek and Roman thinkers.

Stoicism attracted the first Christian thinkers because they saw various similarities between the teaching of Christ and that of, for example, Epictetus. Christ preached peace and tolerance; abstinence from passions and extremes; respect and love for other people. But the Son of God also stated that we must love even our enemies! It is very easy to find a parallel with Epictetus, according to whom we should feel neither strong love nor strong hatred.

The fate of Christ can also be explained through the philosophy of Stoicism: the Logos, or God the Father, willed, based on his rational choice, to send his Son to earth. Christ suffers and is killed by men - but this is not something that has absolute value in itself. Such suffering is temporary, transitory. It is rewarding and meaningful. From Epictetus' point of view, Christ's self-sacrifice would be a bit strange (but then again, Epictetus was not aware of the concept of Original sin). And yet, Christ would serve as an example of the strength of the spirit, of the strength of man who submits to his destiny.

Stoics, however, did not believe in an afterlife, or at least did not show profound conviction in it. For Epictetus, for example, it is important how we will live here on earth without thinking about the afterlife. This is a huge difference from Christianity. However, let us not forget that Stoicism was a school of philosophy, not a religion. That is why suicide was considered normal by both Seneca and Epictetus. Sometimes it is necessary, so the Stoics justify suicide. This is how the life of the Roman philosopher Seneca ended - because of fear of political persecution. For him, it was a dignified death. For Christianity, however, this is a mortal sin, because no one has the right to kill either another person or himself.

Looking at the first Christian philosophers, who we also call apologists - because they defended Christianity with reasonable arguments - we see many concepts from Greek philosophy. And this is not surprising - the Greek schools of philosophy existed until the 6th century, when they were officially disbanded and banned. We find Greek philosophical ideas in philosophers such as Philo and Clement of Alexandria, Justin Martyr, Origen, Irenaeus of Lyon, and later in the three great Cappadocians - Gregory of Nyssa, Gregory of Nazianzus and Basil. We find fundamental concepts in Maxim the Confessor elaborated a little later. In Augustine, we already find a serious reworking of Greek philosophy and a distancing from it, which practically opens the period of patristics. But Augustine no longer has the task of defending Christianity from the rulers of the Roman Empire - he rather fights for the principles of Christianity to be clarified against the background of various heresies.

The first of the authors we will consider now is Philo of Alexandria. He wrote just as Christ's apostles were beginning to spread His teachings. Hence, Philo is a contemporary of the Acts of the Apostles, though not a direct witness. Philo gives the Logos a serious place in his philosophy. According to him, the Logos is a kind of instrument through which God creates the world. According to the researcher Jiri Hoblik, "The blending of various influences can be seen in the fact that Philo's concept of the Logos, influenced not only by the Stoics and Plato but also by the Bible" (Hoblik 248). Thus, we cannot say that Philo was an entirely Christian philosopher, but we must bear in mind that the Christian doctrine at that time was not yet clarified, and many principles were barely elucidated.

Philo drew ideas from some Greek thinkers and the Bible (as a Jew, he could read the Old Testament in the original). As Hoblik notes, "these biblically motivated considerations demonstrate the universal activity of the Logos, but on the other hand Creation no longer looks like the direct work of God as described in the Book of Genesis. Perhaps we are seeing here the influence of late Platonic philosophy" (Hoblik 252). In short, Philo does not take the Bible literally, but attempts to interpret it as having a symbolic value. He looks for various messages in the Old Testament that point specifically to God using a mediator(s) in the act of creation.

Here we must note that Philo's understanding does not coincide with the Christian understanding of the Logos as the Word, as the Son of God. The Logos is rather a cosmic power: "The Logos is a rational cosmic power, although unlike the Stoics, the Bible does not speak of the elements and materiality" (Hoblik 264). The Logos is a sort of mediator between God and the world. Although he is not God in himself, he still has a relationship with God and to some extent is divine: "In correspondence with Old Testament and Stoic thought, Philo's Logos is an active Logos. It represents God's thought aimed toward manifestation" (Hoblik 256). Through it, God manifests himself and we can perceive Him.

This notion is not bizarre in any way, nor is it absurd. It is quite reasonable to assume that God created the world using Thoughts, Ideas as a tool. Ideas are a very important element in Platonic philosophy as well as in Neoplatonism. They are models by which the world is formed. Here the Logos seems to merge with the Ideas into one whole - it is completely intelligible, perceptible only through the intellect. The Logos is necessary as that which directly acts upon matter.

In Philo's works, the Logos is not identical to the power we see in the Stoics. Philo sees it rather as an agency that assists Creation. For the Stoics, the Logos is a force that governs and regulates the world and our lives. It is vital to understand that God does not create the world entirely in a mystical way, but He first "plans" the world in His mind, then allows the Logos to realize, to materialize this plan, this design.

Here we should pay attention to two more statements of Philo, which are based on the Old Testament. According to Philo, the covenant between God and man is realized by the Logos: "We may assume that what the Bible calls a covenant established by the Lord with Abraham, Philo understands as a commitment that the Logos creates between God and Man" (Hoblik 258). The Logos is a law, but why not accept it as an agreement or a contract? Since the Ten Commandments are called the Decalogue, why not say that the covenant itself is realized and based on the Logos?

The other interesting fact based on the Old Testament is the theory of miracles. The Logos, as Philo claims, is holy. As Jiri Hoblik claims, "The holiness of the Logos is also visible from the fact that it is manifested through wonders. It was the Logos that in chapter 3 of the Book of Exodus appeared to Moses in the burning bush" (Hoblik 263). Then, the Logos possesses some mystical side - which already shows some difference from the concept of the Stoics. It is not an element indifferent to us. However, Philo does not understand that the Logos helps and supports us, that he loves us.

Another important Christian philosopher of the early Christian era developed ideas similar to those of Philo. This was Justin Martyr, who lived a little later. Justin is interesting in that he finds his way precisely in Christianity. Before that he was a philosopher who wandered without hope. Christianity helped him find the right path. Curiously, he considered Christianity to be the highest form of philosophy.

Prior to Justin, other philosophers also sought God but they did not find the right way. There were some things that hindered them. And this is quite understandable- not all Greeks had an idea about the Bible. We could claim that they did not manage to get to the whole truth, but only to a part of it. For example, Socrates and Plato were very close but did not catch the whole truth about this world and the world beyond. Thus Justin developed his concept that the pagan philosophers also arrived at the truth through the Logos - it is universal, universally accessible to all. And so, in a sense, some philosophers before Christ were also Christians!

Justin's thesis that the Greeks should not be called pagans only because they lived before Christ is impressive. Even before the coming of the Son of God, there were Christians on earth! This is because Reason, or the Logos, revealed itself to them all. The Word exists eternally, it does not appear with the coming of Christ to earth. Therefore, it is entirely possible that the Word was accessible to the Greek philosophers as well. Therefore, Christian philosophy is not completely different from Greek philosophy- this is what Justin tells us.

In his First Apology, Justin speaks of demons, which he claims were rejected by Socrates and other Greek thinkers. The following quote is very important: "For not only among the Greeks did reason (Logos) prevail to condemn these things through Socrates, but also among the Barbarians were they condemned by Reason (or the Word, the Logos) Himself, who took shape, and became man, and was called Jesus Christ" (Justin 428). Here we see that the Christian understanding of the Logos was already formed clearly enough, in contrast to the works of Philo.

But why does Justin claim something that seems inadequate in historical sense and from the point of view of Christian doctrine? How can we say that Socrates and Plato were Christians?

At the beginning of the 2nd century AD, Christianity was still persecuted. Little was known about it. Christians were accused of various sins - that they cause deliberate fires, that they commit crimes, that they "disrespect the gods" and even that they feed on children! The first Christian philosophers (because theology was not yet developed) had to show the logic and rationality of Christianity. They did not emphasize mysticism, as Tertullian would do a little later. It was crucial for them to demonstrate that all the principles of Christianity had already been outlined in the works of various philosophers, and that Christ does not say anything fundamentally novel that we do not already know. This is because the Word is only one and it is eternal.

And yet, Justin's words do not mean we should regard Socrates and Plato as Christians. They both came close to the truth, but not quite. And we should not blame them for this - they did not have the opportunity to know that Christ would come to earth. But this is a very delicate topic, which is considered by various theologians: who exactly has the right to salvation and what will happen to the souls of people who lived before Christ. It is important to remember that the Logos exists for everyone - just as the Stoics believed. The Word, the Reason, the Logos are here, before us, and we only have to reach and understand them.

Justin also seriously contributed to developing the Christian concept of the Word. As he states, "Christ is the first-born of God, and we have declared above that He is the Word of whom every race of men were partakers; and those who lived reasonably are Christians, even though they have been thought atheists" (Justin 474). The word "reasonably" in Greek looks like this: *meta logou*, i.e., according to the Logos. With these words of his, Justin demonstrates that the Logos is present in each of us, and we should not oppose the Christian philosophy to the Greek philosophy. Of course, there are Greek philosophers who were criticized by the first apologists, but the Stoics and Platonists are not among them.

We will now turn to another researcher of early apologists. This is Patrick Mwania, who claims the following concerning Justin: "According to Justin, human mind participates in the truth through the action of the Logos which sows seeds of the truth in all mankind" (Mwania 191). He explains how Justin argues his point of view on the universality of reason: "Justin introduces the notion of Logos Spermatikos. He conceives that the Logos acted as a sower of truth before his Incarnation" (Mwania 192). Our laws and principles discovered by us are due to the work of the Logos: "In one part of the second Apology, Justin puts it succinctly that 'all the right principles that philosophers and lawmakers have discovered and expressed they owe to whatever of the Word they have found and contemplated in part (karta meros)' " (Mwania 192).

Therefore, *anyone who lives according to the Word should be considered a Christian.* It does not matter whether he realizes this or not, or whether he lived before or after Christ's coming to earth: " 'Those who have lived in accordance with the Logos (meta logou) are Christians, even though they were called godless' " (Mwania 193). Therefore, Christians should not enter into arguments with Platonists or Stoics - they are all on the same side.

Here Justin arrives at the idea of salvation. Yes, Plato and Socrates will not be saved by being baptized- because they were not; they did not attend church service and did not know about Christ. But, on the other hand, there is another way to save them. According to Mwania, "Those who lived before Christ and observed the Law will obtain salvation not through the cultic practices contained in the Law, but in virtue of the eternal and /universal principles that are present, even if partially, in the Law" (Mwania 193). This means that we should not look strictly at Judaism: "Jewish religion stands a privileged place in the Christian dispensation of salvation" (Mwania 193). Even if the Jews do not recognize Christ, this should not lead to hatred towards them or neglect.

And yet, Christians should not be proud either. Only because they are Christians does not automatically make them superior to others. It is God who saves through his grace: "This full revelation of the Incarnate Logos is not a merit that Christians could claim; it is actually a gift, a grace" (Mwania 194). God's Grace finds us alone; we do not know how this occurs. Only God knows and we should not be proud or boast ourselves.

Of course, the tone of the first apologists is rather conciliatory. They do not wish to come into direct conflict with the authorities, as well as with the worshipers of the pagan Roman religion. We should not take this in an absolute sense - that indeed, many pagans were actually Christians because they stand close to God. Only God can solve this problem; if He decides to save them, it is entirely His decision. But today the Church believes that only members of the Church will be saved.

The idea of a universal mind through which we reach God is not something new or strange. God is certainly Reason itself and Wisdom itself; but we must note that God stands above the rational, above the intelligible. His Mind is not like ours; yes, our intellect resembles His intellect, but their content and abilities are different. God sees and knows everything while we are limited. Therefore, it is wrong to think that we can reach God only through our reason. This is also the mistake made by Philo, Justin, and other of the early theologians in the first centuries AD - they overemphasized the role of reason in general (not just the Logos).

Philo and Justin love philosophy, particularly when it has common points with Scripture. For them, philosophy is also a path to God, but still this path cannot exist without Revelation. Plato is not to blame for not having access to the Bible; but his ideas are close to Christian ones- this is what Justin thought. Indeed, here one sees the ambition of the first theologians not only to justify Christianity, but also to lend a hand to other thinkers. It is a kind of ancient tolerance that shows how open Christianity really is to other cultures.

Another similar theologian, who lived after Justin, was Clement of Alexandria. Mwania remarks regarding Clement: "He bases his argument on a theory of a natural notion of God which is common to all people universally, according to which people can know God through the use of human reason" (Mwania 195). This natural concept inborn in our reason points to God, insofar as we can find various traces of God in our world - both in ourselves and in the world around us. But, again, we must repeat, God is not reached by a rational path alone, and this is what is missing from the first apologists (with the exception of Tertullian). And such was their task - to protect Christians from persecution and to convince the authorities of the Roman Empire of the legitimacy of their faith (without emphasizing that it stands above other religions).

By the 7th century, apologetics as a genre of Christian theology had already disappeared because Christianity officially dominated the Eastern Roman Empire (by this time the Western Roman Empire had already been disintegrated). There was no need to go into tolerance mode toward other religions and explain how important Plato and Socrates are to Christianity. Indeed, Plato was still mentioned, as are some Neoplatonists, but over time they no longer had such influence. Over time, the respect toward Greek philosophy almost disappeared. It was rediscovered in the 12th century with the works of the Arab philosophers.

In this setting, the concept of Maximus the Confessor, one of the most influential theologians of the East, appeared. He combines the rational with the mystical, pointing out that God must not only be understood, but also experienced and felt. Typically for Byzantine philosophy, Maximus relied on some Ancient Greek sources but did not put too much stress on that.

Here we will consider only one work of St. Maximus - this is the work called *Difficulty* 10. In this work, he outlines his thoughts on contemplation through which we can know the whole world and attain to God. It is a process consisting of five levels. Maximus states the following: "In addition to this, taught by creation, we shall know the meanings [logoi], that is to say the ultimate meanings that we long to know, and connected with them the five modes of contemplation" (Maxim 109). Here the word *logoi* means some meanings; the meaning for which something was created. But it is not difficult to perceive these words also as pointing to the essence of things; because meaning is also part of the essence of a thing.

Mystics, or contemplatives, are able to combine all these meanings into one. As Maximus the Confessor puts it, "they gather together the above-mentioned forms of contemplation into the single meaning that, by the different forms of the virtues, fulfills the spiritual cosmos at the level of mind." They gradually reach the Logos, which stands above all these individual meanings: "They impart them to themselves, passing through all the logoi of beings and those of the virtues, or rather with them passing to the one who transcends them, being drawn up to the [ultimate] logos, that is beyond being and goodness" (Maxim 113).

Eastern theology is more mystical than Western, and this is seen in the works of such men as Maximus, John of Damascus, and Dionysus Pseudo-Aeropagite. All three emphasize the need to know God in a mystical way, i.e., a path that stands above the senses and above reason. The following words of Maximus perfectly express this philosophy: the people who manage to look at the world, which is governed harmoniously by the Logos, "they discover what is perceived through the senses, and what is understood and what is universal, everything contained in everything and turning by the exchange of the individual qualities of each" (Maxim 132). In a word, they see that the world exists in unity, and individual differences are temporary and immaterial. The laws of the world are attainable and each of us can understand them, and through this we will also understand the reality of God.

The role of Original sin should not be underestimated either. It has distorted our sense of truth and prevents us from coming to a better knowledge. This is noted by researcher Andrew Louth, who observes the following concerning St. Maximus: "There is also a kind of obviousness about the idea that rational beings, logikoi, should be able to understand the logoi of creation, but that, cut off from the Logos, because of the Fall, the logoi of creation are now obscure to them" (Louth 65). We are naturally inclined to seek and find the truth, but this is now difficult because of the sin of Adam and Eve.

St. Maximus is convinced that natural law and written (positive) law are complementary; they do not contradict each other: "The natural law is like a book, and the written law like another cosmos" (Louth 68). The Logos is universal and omnipresent. We reach it through contemplation. But we must bear in mind that the Logos is Christ himself, the incarnate Son of God. That is why *there is no Logos apart from Christ*! We should not perceive this universal law as something impersonal, unrelated to us. There is no way to understand the Logos without turning to the Crucifixion and Resurrection of the Son of God!

Original sin caused many troubles to mankind- the appearance of diseases, death, imperfection; but it also led to something more terrible - the disintegration of the Oneness, the appearance of parts and fragments in the world. The world is no longer one after this Sin. As Louth notes, "Instead of holding in union what is divided, it has been the cause of separation of what is united. The universe is now characterized by fragmentation, disintegration—the corruption leading to death" (Louth 71).

This is an interesting thought that is somewhat unusual for Christianity. Christian theology assumes from the beginning that God created the whole world gradually, within six days. This in itself means that the world never existed in unity![2] Maximus' statement that there are different levels of being that we reach through the five levels of contemplation is no accident either. This hierarchy shows that we can reach God gradually and not suddenly as most mystics think.

Interestingly, Maximus' view of multiple levels of being does not automatically lead to the proof that God stands highest in the hierarchy. We find such an argument in many theologians, for example, in St. Thomas Aquinas - namely, that the presence of degrees of being means that there is a highest degree, and this is precisely God. However, Maximus does not have this goal - he is more concerned with the problem of attaining to God and how to overcome our distance from Him. The reality of God is unquestionable to St. Maximus, and therefore he sees no logic in engaging in discussions about this reality. What is crucial is to know how to attain to God.

As we will see later, St. Maximus developed his concept of the liturgy, which reflects precisely the different levels of being and the cosmic hierarchy. In this concept, as Louth writes, Maximus combines various ideas such as: "The movement between God and mankind in the Incarnation, ascetic struggle leading to contemplation as a healing of divisions within the human person and the cosmos, the liturgy as celebrating the mutual encounter between divine self-emptying and human deification" (Louth 74). The harmony of the cosmos will be restored when we return home to our Creator, who loves us infinitely. But there is a long way to go until then, and we must purify ourselves so that we are worthy of this return.

Hans Ur von Balthasar, the renowned Swiss theologian, offers more insights on Maximus' theology of the Logos. As von Balthasar notes, Maximus introduces the idea of knowing God through nature. This takes place via a process of contemplation, through which

---

[2] Christian theology claims the world is one whole; however, the idea of a possible defragmentation of the world after Original sin is not present in Scripture.

the mind ascends to the divine. The Swiss theologian remarks that "Through the contemplation of nature…, the wise person acquires a natural knowledge of God, of his righteousness, wisdom, and goodness, and this knowledge is in the true sense a kind of 'vision', 'contemplation' " (von Balthasar 291). This law, we can say, governs "the body" of creation; and the Biblical law governs the "soul" or "spirit" of the universe.

There are two other laws that are analyzed by Byzantine theologians. The second law is the law of Scripture. Maximus posits both of them at opposite poles; they can complement each other (von Balthasar 291). Somehow, they even contain each other (the biblical law is part of natural law, and natural law is contained within the biblical law). The third law is the law of Christ. It unites these two laws and the final synthesis is implemented (von Balthasar 291). Thus, we see here something of a kind of Hegel's dialectics, but not entirely. Maximus speaks of complementing each other rather than of fighting or struggle.

Natural law is present in our souls; it is an internal law: "The natural law, engraved in the hearts of all men and women, forces us to recognize the unity of human nature in all individuals, to reverse the fragmentation and alienation of men that has its origin in sin" (von Balthasar 298). This law makes us feel part of one big family, the family of mankind. On the contrary, "the written law is … a law of fear and, so, a law of obedience demanded from above" (von Balthasar 298). Both laws are needed to direct our spiritual and intellectual efforts to the Creator.

However, the New Testament brought another law: the law of Christ, which is "the unique and universal law of creation" (von Balthasar 291). The law of Christ synthesizes the previous two laws into one, and now we have the conception of love and grace as the new law, the universal law of the universe and life. Therefore, all proper efforts to observe and know God through contemplation of nature are impossible without love and grace: "The contemplation of nature … can be genuinely and fruitfully carried out only in the light of grace" (von Balthasar 298).

Maximus' theology employs some insights taken from Greek philosophers, but it transforms it as to be able to offer a proper conception of God and the universe (*cosmos*). The universe is organized in hierarchical order and we need to ascend gradually to know God. Love and grace have their place in this conception.

However, all these topics would not (most likely) be present in Christian theology if it were not for the Gospel of John. This Gospel contributes enormously to the understanding of the essence of Christ, who is not only our Savior, but also the very Word, Reason, Wisdom. What can we learn from this Gospel and why is it so important?

Unlike the other three gospels, John's contains fewer biographical facts about Christ's earthly existence. St. Evangelist John emphasizes the spiritual dimensions of the earthly incarnation of the Son of God. John proceeds from the position that Christ is the Word (Logos) and as such, He is consubstantial with the Father. This is an idea that appears distinctly in John, although we can see it (to a lesser extent) in the Old Testament and in the Synoptic Gospels. Together with the Logos, we also find in him a serious emphasis on the problem of truth and knowledge. That is why we sometimes call this Gospel "theological," although we could also name it "Gnostic"- from the Greek word for knowledge - γνῶσις, *gnosis*. The reader should not confuse this word with the Gnostics, who are an occult-heretical movement that offers an "alternative" to Christianity. For the Gnostics, Christ is only a "great teacher" who has nothing to do with the son of God. But *gnosis* and Gnosticism are not the same. *Gnosis* is the real knowledge.

And now, for John, the Logos is unique in its character - it is not an impersonal force, but a Person; moreover, it is one of the Three Persons of the Holy Trinity. Christ is the Son of God, but also the Truth, and the Life, and the Way, and the Knowledge, and the Good, and the

Light (John 8:12; 14:6). Christ is our Way to God; no one can reach God without Him, without our Savior.

This can be taken in many different senses - Christ is the Son of God and will judge us on Judgment Day; but also, we must follow the teachings and works of Christ and believe in His divinity. Our salvation from sin is also an important issue that is touched upon in these words - that Christ can save us and forgive us. But is there anything more logical than that Logos, or Word, should be our Way to God?

Of course, we should not miss another extremely important idea of John - God is love. We all live in God through love, and we can all hope for salvation because of His love. Love appears in the Word, although they are not the same. But the relationship between Truth, Good and Love is very interesting. Without Truth we cannot be good; and if we are not good, we cannot reach the Truth.

God sent his Son because He loves us (John 3:16). He does not want us to continue living in sin. Original sin had to be atoned for. Through His painful death, but also through His miraculous Resurrection, Christ proved that He is the Son of God. He proved that there is hope for us all. The Word was here, on earth, among us; incredible as it is, God came down to men!

This is what the beginning of the Gospel of John looks like:

> In the beginning was the Word, and
>
> the Word was with God, and the Word
>
> was God.
>
> He was with God in the beginning.
>
> Through him all things were made;
>
> without him nothing was made that has

been made.

In him was life, and that life was the

light of men (John 1:1-4; New International Version)

And here is the first verse in the original Greek language: "ἐν ἀρχῇ ἦν ὁ λόγος, καὶ ὁ λόγος ἦν πρὸς τὸν θεόν, καὶ θεὸς ἦν ὁ λόγος", John 1:1). As we see, John writes specifically about the Logos, which the traditional Latin translation of the Bible translates as the Word; but there is also a certain conception behind it which distinguishes John from the Stoics. Of course, the Logos could also be translated in another way; why was the term "Word" chosen as the correct translation? Could there have been another, different translation of this passage? Would that change the message of St. John the Evangelist?

It must be said that the translation in languages other than Latin uses the Word as well. This also applies to translations directly from Greek and not from Latin. In the Slavic languages, for example (Polish, Russian), we see the same translation again. This means that there is a consensus among all translators: the best and optimal translation of the Logos is this one. Any other translation (law, speech, knowledge) would narrow the meaning of the word Logos and thus divert us from the idea of St. John. Christ is the Living Word who speaks before us and who lives among us. But also, the Word is the Idea by which God creates the world. We have already seen this concept in Philo and Justin - God does not create the world directly, all at once, but rather uses an "instrument" to help him accomplish this Act. God first creates the world in his mind, and then through the Logos, He materializes this "project" or "design."

If this Gospel had been written by a Stoic, then we would have conceived of it as expressing the Law or even Destiny. But the Word is something different from the Logos of the Stoics - the Word is Truth and Knowledge, our Way to God and Salvation. Therefore, the translation of the word *Logos* as the Word is correct. The phrase "In the beginning, there was the Law" would confuse us - we would wonder if this law is in the legal sense or not? The Word is a much broader concept than the Law, although the law is a part of the Word.

Hence, it is no accident that John begins precisely with the Word. He does not describe the birth of Christ; John speaks philosophically about the essence of Christ, of the Son of God - and this essence is the Word, Speech, Reason, Knowledge, Law, Language, etc. The Word became one among us: "The Word became flesh and made his dwelling among us" (John 1:14). Therefore, this Logos, contrary to the teaching of the Stoics, does not stand far above us; he is with us, within us, and lives for us!

In another sense, the Word also means the Teaching. These are the true words that lead us to salvation. In chapter 8, we read the following: "To the Jews who had believed him, Jesus said, 'If you hold to my teaching, you are truly my disciples'" (John 8:31). Christ is also our teacher; He educates us how to live rightly, how to know God, how to relate to life beyond death. The Living Word speaks to people, and they have the unique opportunity to hear His words, record them and spread them. Yes, those were unique times!

Another important figure in our understanding of the Logos is St. Paul. He reflects on the problem of life and death, of the spiritual death, of the life beyond earthly existence. We find an interesting connection between the Word and Life in his Epistle to the Philippians where he remarks the following:

> Do everything without complaining or
>
> arguing,
>
> so that you may become blameless
>
> and pure, children of God without fault in
>
> a crooked and depraved generation, in

which you shine like stars in the

universe

as you hold out the word of life—in

order that I may boast on the day of

Christ that I did not run or labor for

nothing. (Philip. 2:14-16)

God is the Life and the Word is Life; if we follow and listen to the Word, we shall *live*- i.e., we will be here forever! Not obeying and not listening the Word would ensue in the opposite- eternal death!

But this should not be taken as a claim that the Word has an independent existence. It is not a separate God; it is not some divine entity that stands above us and has always existed before us. Not only is the Word alive; not only does it help us to move toward salvation. Christ should not be considered a separate God or a separate divine entity! This is a very dangerous heresy that existed in the first centuries AD. That is why the Council of Nicaea, as well as several other councils after it, shaped the understanding of Christ as having *one essence* with the Father. Christ should not be understood as another God, something like one of the three gods of Hinduism's Trimurti- Brahma, Vishnu and Shiva. The relationship between the Father and the Son is a mystery, but it is a fact that they share one and the same essence, although only the Son can come down to earth because of His dual nature - divine and human.

Some critics believe that the idea of Christ as the Word is an "invention" of John the Evangelist. According to them, he was strongly influenced by Stoicism and Platonism, and that is why he decided to incorporate this notion into his Gospel. Why, for example, does Christ not say "I am the Word"? Instead, He declares, "I am the Way, the Truth, and the Life"

(John 14:6)? This criticism is not sound because it is based on a wrong interpretation of St

John's Gospel, and now we will show why.

As we read Scripture carefully, we see that the facts say otherwise - in the Old

Testament we find mentions of the Word as a part of God. Hence, this is not an exceptional

idea or something "invented" by St. John. Such a mention, for example, we see in Isaiah, who

says in the name of the Lord:

> "All men are like
>
> grass, and all their glory is like the
>
> flowers of the field.
>
> The grass withers and the flowers fall,
>
> because the breath of the Lord blows on
>
> them. Surely the people are grass.
>
> The grass withers and the flowers fall,
>
> but the word of our God stands forever"
>
> (Is. 40:6-8)

Here we clearly see a reference to the Will and Wisdom of the Lord. The Word in this

case points to His Wisdom. God has laid down a certain Law, which we must abide by. But

this is a wise law, and not a mere will of God. Therefore, in this case it is about the Covenant

between God and man, as well as His law. But this Law is part of God - therefore, it must be

the Son of God.

We see how the Stoic concept of the Logos was transformed by Christian theologians.

This is no longer the same understanding of the Logos; it is not that impersonal Logos that does as it pleases. The Stoic fatalism is absent here with its assertion that the Logos has the right to decide our fate and we must accept it without rebellion.

We can formulate the main differences between the two conceptions as follows:

1. For the Stoics, the Logos is impersonal. It is simply a powerful agency that can be thought of but not seen or touched. The Logos does not have personal feelings, emotions, or attitudes. On the contrary, according to the Christian understanding, the Logos is a Person (Christ). We cannot think of the Logos in another way.

2. For the Stoics, the actions and decisions of the Logos are incomprehensible to us. The Logos decides what to do according to his own will. We cannot hold it accountable for its decisions. On the contrary, for Christians, the Logos acts on our behalf and with the purpose of leading us to salvation (although this salvation depends to some extent on us as well). Most of the actions and words of the Logos can be interpreted according to Scripture.

3. With the Stoics, the Logos is abstract and transcendent; it never appeared in this world. According to Christians, the Logos was already on earth, among men. Logos exists in reality, it is not a fiction. Many people witnessed this miraculous event.

4. Stoic teaching leads us to resignation. Stoics aim to comfort suffering people by suggesting that suffering is not real. They, to some extent, marginalize human personality. For them, resignation and passivity are our only virtues. Christianity does the opposite - it gives us hope for salvation and eternal life. Suffering is real but temporary. Our personality is much more than our earthly being.

5. For the Stoics, the Logos is rather a Law that governs the world independently. We cannot exercise any influence on its decisions. For Christianity, the Logos is the Living Word that teaches us how to live and to seek God.

From these five points, we can easily conclude that the Christian teaching about Christ is not based on Stoicism. There is some remote connection here, such as the idea of the Logos as a universal law; but if we compare Epictetus's works with the Prologue of John, we see vast differences. And all this, bearing in mind that Epictetus lived later than John.

As we have already noted, Philo and Justin argue in favor of a clear and inextricable connection between Greek philosophy and Christianity. For them, it is not important whether a person is a Christian, but whether he follows the Logos. Thus it turns out that some people can be Christians without formally belonging to the Church. But this understanding of theirs is a consequence of the danger of persecution; as apologists, they justify the Christian faith by arguing that most people are actually Christians without realizing it. Philo, Justin, Clement, Origen, Irenaeus, and the other early apologists did not aim to dispute or deny Greco/Roman philosophy entirely. This was not the right time for that, so they had to work on the dialogue between pagans and Christians. But over time, things changed and Christian theology moved away from Greek/Roman philosophy.

Therefore, the fact that Christian theology uses a term that existed in Greek philosophy since the time of Heraclitus is no proof that the theology is simply an addition to pagan philosophy. St. Evangelist John simply uses a word that has existed for a long time, but changes its meaning - the Logos is not only God, but he is also the instrument through which God creates the world. This is already the meaning missing from both the Stoics and Plato, and it is an important deficit- the idea of Creation is not found in Ancient Greek philosophy, with few exceptions. Even Plato, who stands perhaps the closest to Christian theology, does not admit the reality of a true, powerful and personal God. For Plato, the world was created by a Demiurge, or a demi-God.

Therefore, we cannot accuse St. John Evangelist of inventing a different meaning of the Greek word for Logos. The truth is that Christ has always been the Living Word; and this will never change. The Stoics were unable to grasp this truth due to many reasons. It is a main principle of the history of mankind that history progresses slowly and plainly, thereby revealing more and more about God and our relationship with him. We could feel sympathy for their attempt to understand Logos and to define it in moral context- for, Stoics' ethics is based on this conception. But our progress had to move forward and this took place with Christ descending to earth. This new picture of the world is clearly expressed in the Gospel of St. John- the only one that we may call theological, for its profound analysis of Christian theology.

The Logos is not entirely mystical, it is not completely hidden. On the contrary- we cannot help but think that the Logos itself appears to us and invites us to grasp it. In contrast to all mystics that claim the Truth and the Reality are hidden to us, we should agree that all rational creatures should be provided with the capacity to attain to the Logos. The Logos is open to everyone; of course, some of its accidents (properties) are hard to grasp only with our intellect. But generally, no one is prohibited from being in touch with the Logos, with Wisdom, with the Truth. We are invited to participate in this divine mystery and to understand- both with our reason and our heart- what is Wisdom, what is truth and what is Life.

1.3 Conclusion

All further analyzes of the Bible are now based on the understanding of St. John, as well as St. Paul. They both give direction to the interpretation of Christ as the Living Word.

Stoicism had its role in the development of the concept of the Logos. We might say that to some extent Philo is right - since the Word is universally accessible, some philosophers before Christ should have had access to it. But the Stoics only partially reached the Living Word. For them, Logos is simply a law that governs the cosmos, without it being personified.

There are some differences between the Greek conception of the Logos and the one developed by Christianity. One can note that for Greeks, the Logos is more of spontaneous nature; it makes decisions regarding our lives but without explaining logically why it does so. This is because Greeks perceived the cosmos as a harmony of rational and irrational, law and chance, randomness and necessity. For them, the Logos was divine and not divine at once; it could not be called god because it was not a person; and still, it was divine because there, according to them, is nothing superior to it.

This is only our introduction into the topic of the Logos. We saw how this notion emerged and how it developed over the centuries. The reader should know that similar notions emerged also in India and China- for example, Tao as the universal Way. However, Tao, according to the Chinese understanding, is more of dialectical nature- it is good and bad at once, day and night at once, finity and infinity, life and death, rationality and irrationality, and other dichotomies of such nature. Thus, the Greek perception of the Logos stand closest to the Christian one.

Even the first fathers of the Church were not certain on how to define it precisely. It took several centuries for Christian theologians to be able to understand the notion of the Logos better and to incorporate it in their works. As we see, even nowadays it is not an easy job to grasp what is Logos, what is the Word- even though we have access to all possible definitions of this entity.

But besides being the Living Word, the Logos is also the Good and the Law. In the next chapter we will subject to our analysis the connection of the nature of things and natural law. In what way does our morality derive from the Logos, from the Living Word? Is ethics based on natural concepts, or it is rather elaborated in a positive way, i.e., according to human wishes? This is what we need to find answers to in what follows next.

Chapter II: Natural law, Logos, and Morality

We have already understood the origin of the word *Logos* itself. We discussed the similarities and differences between the Stoic and the Christian conception of the Logos. Now we will turn to another crucial connection - that between the Logos and the natural law. These are two notions that are often used by Christian theologians.

Is it easy to define the word "nature"? What is natural law, then? What is the opposite of nature? Is there such a thing as a "nature of morality"? Is there "unnatural morality"? What about the Old Testament and the New Testament? We will deal with these problems in the current chapter.

2.1 Definition- Nomos, Physis, and Cosmos

Summary:

Nomos is another Greek term that is perceived rather in its social and political aspect as a law. *Cosmos* is an ordered world existing in harmony. *Physis* is the Ancient Greek conception of nature. Greeks believed every thing on earth has its own essence, or nature. *Physis* is tied to the notion of *nomos*- both of them indicate there is order in the world and there are natural states of things. On the other hand, Protagoras argued that everything is a product of a convention. Thus, he opposed the conception of *physis*.

We must be very careful when defining ancient Greek terms. The Greeks did not always mean what we think nowadays. In their civilization, there was no direct opposition between nature and convention. There were rather various intermediate degrees between these two things. Convention can also be based on nature, and nature can have a relationship with convention.

What do we mean by "convention"? It is the agreement between people regarding given norms and rules. For example, mathematics is a convention, to some extent. It does not exist as an object in nature itself. Mathematics is a way to describe nature using our minds. But animals, for example, cannot be mathematicians - they do not have the capacity for it. Euclidian geometry is partly a convention, and partly objective reality. It is an ideal model that allows us to describe and predict certain spatial relations on earth. However, it lacks a third dimension, which means it cannot be absolutely realistic. Thus, the theory of Euclidus is a mixture of objective reality and convention.

The very word "convention" is usually associated with agreement between people. This means that without people, there is no convention, no consent or agreement. In this way, convention is opposed to nature as something that does not depend on conventions. Nature is enforced on us; and convention is produced by us.

Among the first philosophers to talk about nature and conventions were the Sophists and Aristotle. For them, this was a vital issue - is our society the result of a convention between people, or is it based on our nature? Can society change? Is there a "natural form" of government? Which authority derives from nature?

Here we will turn first to a researcher of Aristotle and his account of nature. In his article "Physis and Nomos in Aristotle's Ethics" (2005), Thornton Lockwood argues that things are not so simple in Aristotle. He defines nature in a different way, therefore we should not approach it simplistically. Let us see what Lockwood has to say now.

Aristotle talks about nature mainly in his works on ethics and politics. According to him, in ethics we can talk about nature, but nature itself is not the basis of morality. Our virtues develop over time as a result of something like "habit." We are not born good, but become so by practicing our virtues. As Lockwood notes, "Aristotle insists that ethical virtue arises through the habitual repetition of ethically good actions, and thus no one is good or virtuous by nature." However, this does not exhaust Aristotle's position: "At times Aristotle appears to use nature to justify normative claims. Thus, in the Ethics Aristotle distinguishes between natural and unnatural pleasures, and he claims that what is truly good is that which is pleasing by nature to the spoudaios or excellent man" (Lockwood 23).

As we can see, things are a bit complicated here. On the one hand, Aristotle recognizes the superiority of nature - there are such pleasures that are natural. On the other hand, he does not consider virtues "natural" because, according to him, they are developed. This is logical - none of us are born absolutely good. A child makes mischiefs, it is naughty. It acts in a way that we do not conceive of as moral. However, does that mean the child is bad? No, all parents and adults in general are patient with children. They know that children cannot learn good manners immediately. A child needs time to learn how to behave properly. Education and upbringing take some time.

But here the reader will object: education is one thing, virtues another. Yes, upbringing is a long process, but the virtues themselves are "embedded" in our souls. A child has a concept of good and evil; yes, it is often driven by the "pleasure principle" and it tries to manipulate the adults based on the fact that it is a child. Everyone coddles it, protects it, etc. But the child knows that there is good and evil! Also, all children show kindness - when they hit another child and the latter starts crying, they regret what they did. Therefore, virtues are part of our nature!

This objection is logical, but not entirely true. Babies, for example, may hit both people and animals (even in some cases they could do harm). To them, this is a game. They see nothing wrong with it. Gradually they learn that it is not good to hit other people. Is a baby a bad person? No, it is simply not taught virtue. It takes time, as we said. Yes, a little later the baby will grow up and know that it is not acceptable to do harm to other people.

That is why we can agree with Aristotle. Virtues themselves are not inborn; but the knowledge of good and evil is inborn in us. It is part of human nature. Therefore both theses are true: *nature is the basis of morality, and at the same time it is not the basis of virtue.* It is in our nature to be moral beings; but we are not born with a ready knowledge of morality.

And now, someone asks: how come we all have the same morals? How come altruism, love, and charity are virtues for all of us? Then, after all, morality has a common ground. Where does morality come from?

Here, Aristotle offers the most straightforward explanation: morality has to do with pleasure and pain. We all seek pleasure and avoid pain. It is natural in so far as it affects all living things. Not only would man react to pain, but a dog would do the same. As Lockwood explains, "Aristotle claims that 'nature appears to avoid what is painful and to aim at what is pleasant'; 'all things love and choose existence (to einai)'·, 'life (zôê) is good by nature... it is itself good and pleasant...'; and 'natural' desires are those common to all humans" (Lockwood 26).

This position is not very different from the Epicureans, according to whom we should aim at pleasure; and later Spinoza would repeat Aristotle's words and explain that morality is based on the difference between pleasure and pain. It is quite normal for all beings to avoid pain. It can be said that this is the common basis of morality - it is founded on the instinct of survival. But, as we shall see a little later, this is only the basic level of morality. It also has a superstructure - these are our spiritual needs and values, which are not based on the pleasure principle.

Thus, it turns out that for Aristotle, nature is the usual, the normal, and the customary. That which occurs often and in almost all people should be considered nature. On the other hand, however, for him this condition becomes a moral ideal, and this is a serious mistake. As Lockwood notes, "Julia Annas have claimed that sometimes Aristotle confuses nature in the sense of what is usual with nature in the sense of an ethical ideal" (Lockwood 26).

Hence, our virtues must be developed; we must be persistent in our efforts to practice these virtues. A person is virtuous not because she/he was born virtuous, but because she/he constantly practices and demonstrates these virtues. We cannot just rely on doing good from time to time. It is a great mistake to be proud and to think that we have already become virtuous and no more effort is needed. For the rest of our lives, we must practice these virtues, otherwise they would simply cease to exist.

Aristotle is moderate in his analysis of nature and its relation to the virtues. It does not reach extremes such as we see today, for example, in the denial of any relationship between man and nature (or the idea that man is what he thinks he is, not what he really is). We are good or bad according to our merits, according to our deeds: "Aristotle famously notes that ethical virtue is not by nature since it requires habituation and that virtue cannot be a dunamis or capacity, since we are not called 'good' or 'bad' according to things we receive from nature" (Lockwood 27).

It is true that we are given some qualities by birth, and this can be taken as the manifestation of nature in us. But people should not be defined in terms of these qualities because this is rather the result of chance: "Although characteristics which humans possess in the sense of 'mere nature' are not without value, people are not blamed or praised for such qualities, and such qualities do not necessarily result in virtuous actions" (Lockwood 27). For example, a man may be born physically strong. His height is the result of a natural endowment (or genetics, as we would say today). But will this man be brave? It is not always like that. Courage is developed and practiced over time. Therefore, we should not immediately define this man as "brave" without his proving it; his height and physical strength alone mean nothing, they are not virtues. They are "tools" through which a man can show his courage better. Not every strong man is brave, and vice versa.

This understanding of Aristotle is very rational. We should not judge people by their inborn qualities. Only because a person is strong or attractive does not mean that person is virtuous. It is no accident that in Ancient Greece, they introduced the moral ideal of *kalokagatia*, i.e., a good, beautiful and clever person. It is not enough just to be outwardly attractive; you must also be internally beautiful, i.e., virtuous.

In another sense, however, the word "nature" is associated with adherence to some final goal, or the "proper functioning" of a person. Here comes another conception of Aristotle. The eye follows its purpose and then it responds to nature. As Lockwood states, this meaning concerns "...the good functioning or end of a human being. Thus, when Aristotle claims that man is a 'political animal' or a 'household animal' by nature, he indicates the conditions necessary for the good functioning of an individual" (Lockwood 27). This means that a person must function in a certain way that Aristotle considered natural. For example, a philosopher must do philosophy; an engineer – to deal with construction; a builder- with building, etc. This account is reminiscent of Plato's idea of dividing society into classes, each of which is exclusively concerned with one thing - for example, the guards only guard and wage wars, but do not participate in power or taking care of children.

All this refers to the Greek term *physis*. But what to say concerning *nomos*? This word usually means positive law, or a law that is enacted by men rather than by the gods. Here Lockwood explains: "Aristotle means by nomos what we mean by 'law,' viz. a general (perhaps even universal) norm promulgated by a nomothetês or law-giver... Thus, Aristotle famously claimed that 'the law is reason without desire'" (Lockwood 29).

Laws are something necessary for a state, according to Aristotle. Without them, a society cannot function. But do laws derive from nature? For the ancient Greeks, many laws had their basis in nature. It was quite natural for the Greeks to have a division of upper and lower classes; inequality was seen as normal, as was it with slavery. We see that there are strong and weak physical people, therefore there must be rulers and people to be ruled.

We should not fault Aristotle and Plato for their understanding that inequality arises from nature. These are the facts as they appeared in 5th century BC. Such were Greek societies at the time, as were Persia, Egypt, and later Rome. Even Greek democracy did not look like what we imagine it to be. Democracy in Athens is expressed in the concept that a group of citizens have the right to solve various problems together, instead of being done by one person (ruler, tyrant). It does not mean that all people in Athens were equal - slaves, women and children had no political rights (and slaves had no rights at all, they were seen as property).

Perhaps Aristotle is wrong that inequality is entirely natural. As Lockwood notes, "Aristotle also uses the term nomos, and more specifically, the adjective to nomikon, to mean that which is 'customary,' 'conventional,' and that which appears to be opposed to nature" (Lockwood 30).

The last point makes things much more complicated. It turns out that *nomos* derives from nature and is the result of convention at the same time. How can we explain this contradiction? Is it possible for something to be both natural and conventional at the same time?

Here we come to the understanding of what is custom, a tradition. Customs often arise from nature but are modified over time. Through his concept of custom, Aristotle manages to overcome the contradiction that we pointed out above. This was also noted by Lockwood, according to whom: "The sense of nomos as 'custom' points to Aristotle's central way of interrelating mere nature, law, and nature as an ethical ideal, namely, through his account of ethical habituation." Custom is formed on the basis of nature, but it changes gradually with time. The customs of the ancient Greeks were different from the customs of Aristotle's contemporaries. Thus, custom is a natural thing, inasmuch as it is the result of a long tradition. It is now accepted by society and considered normal. But it has already deviated from its original basis, so in a sense, it has already moved away from nature.

An example of this idea can be body language - raising one's hands when the police arrest a criminal. Who needs this gesture? Today it has a symbolic value, but it comes from the ancient tradition of showing that you do not have a weapon on you. This is a tradition that is present in all nations and civilizations, in all historical eras. It can have some modifications - for example, showing only your palms, or showing your hands, not exactly raising them. But this tradition is still here, and even our universal greeting (with waving hands) can be seen as derived from this old custom.

Bowing is another tradition that can be explained through nature. Today it is considered a symbolic gesture, and in Southeast Asia the bow is even used as a greeting. Bowing arose from the idea that the ruler had the right to take his subject's life. By bowing, the subject places his life in the hands of his ruler or master. It is a kind of convention that calms the relationship between master and subject so that unnecessary conflicts are avoided. But this ritual or custom also has a natural basis - it is related to our desire to preserve our lives. By bowing, the subject confirms the fact that he accepts the authority of his master and thus preserves his life. In Shogunate Japan, for example, bows played a central role in etiquette—refusing to bow or bowing incorrectly resulted in immediate death penalty for the disobedient. But all this is just a tradition that comes from a convention, from an agreement between people.

How do we include morality here? In many cases, the convention also defines the moral regulations in a society. But it is a convention that is also based on nature. As already mentioned, our nature dictates that we should avoid pain and should strive for pleasure.

According to this, various moral rules were formulated - not to steal, not to kill, to help. These moral rules are actually natural, not positive (i.e., they are not simply invented by the lawgiver). However, we can additionally say that nature is a moral ideal that we should follow. Thus, for example, altruism is natural, therefore it will be part of our moral ideal. We must always follow it in our actions.

Aristotle argues with the Sophists, who took a more radical position on morality and law. Most sophists denied that norms derive from nature. For them, our moral and legal norms are someone's invention, without any reasonable basis. As Lockwood argues, the Sophists oppose nature and convention. He also notes the following: "Whereas the Sophistical interlocutors set up a false dichotomy between invariable nature and variable customs, Aristotle claims that both nature and convention are variable" (Lockwood 32).

It turns out that change in itself does not mean that something is "fiction"; but it is normal for norms based on nature to change. We will see this notion in Christian theology as well. This is a false dichotomy, a false division, into which the sophists try to get us. Therefore, this researcher claims that Aristotle's position "transcended their opposition of phusis and nomos' " (Lockwood 34). We cannot divide the world simply into nature and convention; these two concepts are interrelated and sometimes difficult to distinguish between them. As we have seen, for Aristotle *convention is based on nature*, and on the other hand, *nature alone cannot make us virtuous*. This is why Lockwood puts it that "Aristotle's opposition to Sophistical thought in his ethical-political philosophy finds its locus classicus elsewhere than the nature/convention Antithesis" (Lockwood 34).

The truth is that nature is essential in our lives, but it does not regulate all relationships in society. However, we can rely on nature as a criterion for what is (sometimes) good: "Aristotle at times appears to base normativity on nature because nature provides guidance about what is wrong without specifying in turn what is right" (Lockwood 35). As already mentioned, this can be something like the pleasure principle (Freud), only formulated in a simpler way. Our morality is related to nature, yet our values are, to some extent, the result of agreement. Society and the state exist to protect us from the "law of the jungle"; therefore, we cannot leave ourselves entirely in the hands of nature. It is necessary to have specific goals to be realized through our virtues. These virtues do not exist absolutely, as Plato thinks. Rather, they exist only in a practical context. One of their main goals is to preserve and contribute to society.

Plato's position is a little more specific. For him, the problem is that people are unaware of the temporality of this world. Our material world is simply a reflection of the World of Ideas. The latter cannot be called nature in so far as nature is associated with something material or created. On the other hand, the World of Ideas is nature insofar as nature is what defines our being. Each person belongs to a common Idea of humanity. Thus, we are not men by ourselves apart from this idea; we are human because we conform to this idea of "manness."

According to the philosopher and theologian Clement Webb, Plato set out to oppose the relativists and atheists of his time. These were people who followed, for example, Democritus and believed that the world consists only of atoms, i.e., of material particles. According to Webb, "The atheists whom he is criticizing he represents as insisting on the priority in the universe not of Spirit or Reason but of φύσις and Τύχη, Nature and Chance. To these alone they trace the existence of the elements and their combinations and of the heavenly bodies" (Webb 87).

We must mention, however, that Democritus was not a materialist in the sense we call Holbach or Marx materialists. The ancient Greeks looked for the beginning of the world in various elements, but for them the material and spiritual beginnings were inseparable. Most philosophers believed in an afterlife- that the soul outlives the body in some way. Rather, Plato opposed those who considered nature to be entirely material.

Sophism was a serious challenge for Plato as well. During his time, different concepts of law, the state, and morality appeared. Sophists such as Callicles and Gorgias, as well as Protagoras, appear in his dialogues. As Webb describes the situation, "Not only is Religion a matter of custom or law, the law and custom of different states prescribing the worship of different gods, but moral distinctions are no less conventional than religious doctrines; the true life according to nature is that of Might not of Right" (Webb 89).

Thus it turns out that nature is a wild force, not the source of justice and wisdom. But Plato disagrees with this. Why must nature be full of injustice? Such a way of thinking is incorrect. Nature is always just, and this is so because nature is actually the correspondence of the World of Ideas. Nature reflects the Ideas in itself.

As Webb notes, true religion for Plato is a kind of cosmology. It is an explanation of the origin of the world, as well as of the connectedness of all souls in one World Soul. Religion is deeply connected with morality as well. However, Webb claims that this view of Plato's is a kind of naturalism, and it places religion in a position dependent on nature: "This religion was not the less a Naturalism because it was involved with errors concerning the system of nature which the later progress of the natural sciences have exploded; and being Naturalism the connexion of Morality with it was forced and precarious" (Webb 135).

The heavenly bodies, according to this cosmology, reflect the World of Ideas. For Plato, the universe is still connected with the Ideas. His religious concept is, to some extent, polytheistic, insofar as it recognizes the heavenly bodies as (demi-)deities. As Webb claims, "it was established for Plato himself by means of the conception of the good Soul of the World, which caused the orderly revolutions of the heavens, and by that of the position assigned to the Sun as the child and image of the Good" (Webb 135).

In the *Protagoras* dialogue, there is an interesting view analyzed by Plato (through Socrates). The dispute there concerns virtues and politics. Can all men learn virtue? Can all people understand politics? Here Protagoras (as represented by Plato) tells a myth according to which all men are endowed with the same political and moral faculties. However, Socrates disagrees - not all people can learn morality. This is possible to achieve by few!

On the other hand, the myth of Protagoras refutes another idea expressed by the sophist Glaucon - that each person can construct his own morality, and that morality should only be for the benefit of the individual: "Glaucon's opposition rests on a conception of human nature as ultimately egoistic, and he sees morality … as a mechanism for inhibiting the full development of the individual... The Protagoras myth, by contrast, presents human nature as essentially social" (Taylor 17).

Threfore, Plato generally rejects the Sophists' ideas about morality. This means that nature is something real, we cannot simply reduce it to the individual. It is not true that everything depends on us; or, as the real Protagoras (not the dialogue character) declares, "man is the measure of all things." If man were the measure of all things, then we would have to deny objective reality and say, "Only what is in my mind is reality." Both Plato and Aristotle seriously oppose this thinking. But we must bear in mind that nature and convention are not complete opposites after all!

Here comes another interesting Greek philosopher who is mistakenly called a materialist. We will look at his ideas through the prism of C. C. Taylor, who defines the concept of *nomos* in the following way: " 'Usage' renders nomos, from the verb nomizein, to have a usage or custom. Nomos is ho nomizetai, what is customary or enshrined in usage. The term is normally contrasted with phusis, literally 'nature' " (Taylor 1). On the other hand, the term *physis* "in this general contrast is simply the abstract noun for how things are independent of human thought or belief. A related sense of nomos is 'norm,' or more specifically 'law' " (Taylor 1).

Democritus was among the first philosophers to note a possible difference between objective reality and human opinion. We know his theory very well: that only atoms and emptiness exist in the universe. But in addition, he elucidates another idea that affects epistemology: "In contrast to atoms and the void, which exist in reality, independently of how things appear to human beings or how they are believed to be, sensible qualities such as colors and tastes exist only nomô(i)" (Taylor 2). This means that some sensory qualities are subjective and do not depend on reality.

Obviously, this assertion is not entirely true, according to what we know today from physics. But Democritus could not have known that there is a wave spectrum and that what a color looks like depends on the wavelength. His thinking is based on the idea that to one person, a color is red, and to another person it is burgundy. People have different sense of taste as well. For one person, a given food has one taste, and for another person – a different taste (for this reason, one person will like it, and the other person will not like it). One person hears better than another; a given house seems big for a child, and for an adult- small. All this comes down to personal opinion – this is what Democritus offers us.

Shortly before him, the philosopher Empedocles expressed a similar idea, as Taylor states: "Democritus (like Empedocles) thus makes explicit use of the contrast between reality and convention (or belief) in the context of physical theory, not in a moral or political context" (Taylor 3). This applies to our knowledge - part of it is subjective, and another part relies on objective reality. Both Empedocles and Democritus thus describe the cognitive process as a combination of sense data (which is subjective, according to them) and concepts or thought processes (which are objective). They introduce the idea that there are opinions or personal judgments about some things that cannot be dismissed as too subjective.

Unfortunately, not much remains of Democritus' works - his texts were later destroyed. Thus, we are left with only this famous passage which deals with the essence of the universe. That is why Taylor explains that "We should avoid concluding from this single fragment that, in general, Democritus uses the singular nomos to refer to positive law specifically" (Taylor 5). In this case, *nomos* can be a law or a convention, as well as a personal opinion. But we cannot say with certainty that Democritus opposes the nature of convention. What is evident in him is the attempt to show that not all our knowledge is completely objective.

The concept of nature changes over time. Ancient or Greek philosophy refers to nature as what defines our personality, what guides us to our purpose in life. But what happens to this concept when it is defined by medieval Christian theologians?

2.2 God and nature- the proper sphere of natural theology

Summary:

Our short analysis goes on with some reflections on the history of the idea of natural theology. What is its scope and what is its relation to God? How do we distinguish it from natural philosophy? We will refer to some works by Alister McGrath, Clement Webb and Ünsal Çimen.

The ancient Greeks saw nature as an unchanging entity, but they also saw that nature defines us. We are the people we are because we have such and such a nature. The craftsman is such because he has such a nature. The soldier has the nature of a soldier, etc. We can say that this approach is called *essentialism* - the essence defines the person, not the other way around.

In that historical period, nature and culture were not seen as opposites. Our culture reflects nature and even more - it reflects nature. The world is a collection of what has existed for centuries and what man creates and produces. But man in himself was not considered isolated from nature. Man was seen as one element of the *cosmos*; but we can also say that man is also a small cosmos - or microcosm, as the ancient Greeks believed.

With Christianity, the idea of the creation of the world appeared. Greek mythology explains the existence of the world with the action of various deities - the earth, the sky, and then other elements that were seen as deities. This process is not exactly a creation, but rather a symbolic explanation of what we see with our eyes. The act of Creation in the Bible is different - it can neither be well described nor well understood by our intellect.

From the idea of the reality of One Creator, theology logically arrives at an approach we call natural theology. This is an approach whereby we can discover the image of the Creator in His creation. By describing and understanding the world, we will be able to reach the Creator - not only to His existence but also to His Attributes.

Here we will turn to Alister McGrath's 2017 book that deals with natural theology. This type of theology, according to him, "can broadly be understood as a process of reflection on the religious entailments of the natural world, rather than a specific set of doctrines." This approach or process contains a variety of views: "It can be undertaken from a variety of viewpoints, secular and religious, and has no 'essential' core, other than an engagement with the question of the relationship of nature (including the human observer) and the divine or transcendent" (McGrath 7). Indeed, it is possible to approach it from a non-religious point of view, for example that of Francis Bacon. However, we must bear in mind that Bacon does not openly express any atheistic position.

As McGrath notes, we can find traces of natural theology as far back as Ancient Greece: "For the Ionian philosophers, a natural theology interpreted the world as an ordered whole – that is, as a kosmos – and therefore was, at least to some degree, transparent to the human intellect" (McGrath 12). This remark shows an important quality of this type of theology: that it starts from the world and analyzes the world in which we live. It does not begin with the premise that God is real and that He created the world; rather, the opposite takes place- departing from the world, it reaches God. But the reality of God here is not a dogma nor an axiom. It is a conclusion.

Today, we think that natural theology is entirely the work of Christianity. However, it turns out that this is not the case. As McGrath explains, "The Latin term theologia naturalis ... was coined in the pre-Christian classical world to describe a general mode of reasoning which ascended from the natural world to the world of the gods" (McGrath 12). Obviously, the very term "theology" points to an understanding of the divine presence in the world. But this does not necessarily mean that a theology similar to the Christian one existed in Greece. It is rather a desire to understand the world through the divine. Moreover, in Greece there was no belief in One God, therefore this natural theology also existed in the context of polytheism.

Hence, this researcher notes that natural theology is not a concept that has been used continuously in one sense for the past 25 centuries. What we call that today actually appeared in the late Renaissance. According to McGrath, "The general acceptance and wide use of the term theologia naturalis within the western theological tradition is actually a relatively late development, and reflects the influence of Sebonde's Liber naturae sive creaturarum" (McGrath 13).

As Clemens Webb remarks, in Sebonde's opinion, all we have access to this natural knowledge: "The knowledge of 'the book of the creatures or book of nature… is necessary, natural, and fit for every man; by means of it he is enlightened both as to himself and as to his Maker, and as to the whole duty of man as man' " (Webb 294). Sebonde was harshly criticized for his dismissing of theology; at any rate, he was among the first to put stress on natural theology as a way to grasp the divine.

Before Sebonde, no clear definition of this conception existed. The main task of Christian theology is to describe and understand God on the basis of the description we find in Revelation, in the Holy Scriptures. As we will see in one of the following chapters, there are quite a few attempts to reach God through arguments describing our created world. However, this approach is rarely called natural theology, although today we can define it in that way.

The relation between natural theology and the supernatural is also to be noted. We should not forget that Christian theology emphasizes the supernaturalism of God. He stands above the laws of nature, above our understanding, above our sense experience. God is a mystery in some aspects - for example, when understood as the Holy Trinity. The Incarnation of Christ in a human body is also a mystery, as well as His resurrection. These are entities that are not comprehensible to our human intellect. They are supersensible, supernatural. If nature consists of laws and regularities, then we cannot say the same about God. God by himself cannot be subject to any law.

God is supernatural because He Himself created the world. As we have already seen, this takes place in a reasonable way, through the Logos (or seminal Logos, as Philo asserts). But God in Himself cannot be understood, as Dionysius Pseudo Aeropagite, for example, insists. According to this Greek theologian of the late patristic era, we can reach God in a symbolic way, through symbols and analogies.

And now we may ask: Does natural theology not contradict all this? How do we get to a supernatural God, starting from nature, from the natural? How will we describe God if we start from His creation? What should our theology look like- natural or supernatural?

Here is an example. People are both good and bad. We witness both good and evil deeds. If we proceed from this knowledge and experience, we shall conclude that God must be both good and evil at once; or that there are two Gods- an idea similar to Mithraism and Zoroastrianism.

Or another example. People get sick and die. If we proceed from this knowledge, which is absolutely certain and indubitable, we shall conclude that God is also mortal and finite. Is this conclusion rational?

These two simple examples show that things are not simple at all. The structure and content of the world cannot be taken as a pure reflection of the divine structure, of His attributes. Rather, we can describe Him negatively (saying what God IS NOT) instead of describing Him positively (saying what God IS). Since man is a creation, we should accept the axiom that God is essentially different from man. And since man is finite and mortal, we should suppose that God is not finite and not mortal. This approach is more appropriate when we talk about the relationship between the creator and the creation.

Natural theology, as understood by the French Renaissance philosopher Raymond Sebonde (14th -15th century), combines our knowledge of the world with theology. As McGrath notes, "Sebonde does not argue the case for Christianity on the basis of first principles which are independent of Scripture and Church tradition, but rather anticipates ... basic Christian ideas, which are then shown to be consonant with the natural world" (McGrath 15). After him, other philosophers would try to distinguish the two spheres - of theology and of science - starting entirely from "natural" premises. Thus appears the so-called natural philosophy, or what we now call science. Therefore, McGrath claims that "Its relationship to both kindred and rival intellectual enterprises - such as 'natural philosophy' - is frustratingly difficult to define" (McGrath 17).

Natural philosophy examines the world in itself, without concern for whether there is a God or not. Its approach is different – it does not deal with metaphysical situations. Metaphysical is that which transcends our sensory and earthly experience. Natural theology, however, necessarily includes some metaphysical postulates. It begins with the axiom that there is more to the world than we see and experience. It deals, for example, with the question of why the world exists in the way it does. Science, or natural philosophy, does not ask such questions - it deals only with the world as something already given.

According to McGrath, there are six different approaches to natural theology. Here we will analyze two of them. He quotes George Joyce who describes this type of theology as "a branch of philosophy which investigates what human reason unaided by revelation can tell us concerning God" (George Joyce, quoted by McGrath 18). McGrath explains that "It is here understood as an attempt to demonstrate the existence or determine the characteristics of God without recourse to divine revelation" (McGrath 18). In short, there is no need to refer to the Bible here; our reason is sufficient to reach God.

The other interesting approach to this type of theology concerns the evidence for the reality of God. This understanding can be named physico-theology. As McGrath puts it, "Natural theology is a demonstration or affirmation of the existence of God on the basis of the regularity and complexity of the natural world. This specific formulation of natural theology appears to have emerged in Protestant contexts during the early modern period" (McGrath 19). An interesting example of this approach is William Paley's work of the same name from 1802. This philosopher attempts to carry out an analogy between the world as a mechanism and a clock. The world is so perfect, filled with various regularities, that we cannot help but think about the existence of Watchmaker. Such a complex mechanism could not have appeared on its own. It is the complexity and regularities in the world that show that someone created this world.

This conception, McGrath points out, "worked so well partly because it resonated with the cultural assumptions and biases of his day; today, it is generally regarded as discredited" (McGrath 30). Some theologians later opposed this concept of the Watchmaker insofar as it completely excluded the need for Revelation: "John Henry Newman argued that our epistemic situation was such that we had to approach the natural world in the light of an informing 'mental map' derived from revelation, rather than trying to derive a mental map from an amorphous and ambiguous natural world" (McGrath 33).

Both points of view have their right. According to Newman, we must start from the Bible. According to Paley, it is enough to look at our world to become certain that there is a God. But the concept of the Watchmaker does not tell us enough about God himself. It only points to Him; it looks for His traces here, around us. Hence, it can be said that both Paley and Cardinal Newman have their point: Revelation is necessary to know God; natural theology is needed to ascertain His reality. Surely, however, the concept of the Watchmaker cannot be completely disavowed by Christianity because the world does appear to be a complex mechanism that could not have appeared by itself.

Another interesting example of natural theology, according to McGrath, is Dante. As he commented, "In a brief discussion of Dante's Divine Comedy, C. S. Lewis noted its powerful imaginative vision of a unified cosmic and world order. For Lewis, works such as the Divine Comedy reflected a 'unity of the highest order' " (McGrath 36). Indisputably, in Dante we find an interest in our world, which is seen as strongly related to divine reality. It is true that Dante's main purpose is rather to express his own philosophy of virtues, values, knowledge, but he also always takes into account the presence of the divine in our world. That is why his work is called "divine."

McGrath's conclusion is that a natural theology is inevitably connected to the question of the divine. As he writes, "A Christian theological framework ... thus enables us to account for the existence of the natural human activity of seeking to find God within or through the world of nature" (McGrath 39). Of course, this search is not at all easy; we must say that the example of the Watchmaker is too simplistic to show us all the complexity of the world and the essence of the Creator (the Watchmaker). It is also true that we cannot reach God without His revelation. That is why we should not completely replace theology with science. By itself, science cannot lead us to the divine, as we shall see later in this work.

Natural theology is present in St. Thomas Aquinas, but not thoroughly. On the one hand, Thomas takes it as an approach to God; on the other hand, he puts more stress on Revelation. As Clemens Webb remarks, "Being rational, the means by which God orders them is not natural instinct but law. Such divine laws will include injunctions to hold the truth concerning God, for the love and desire towards him which they aim at promoting presuppose a correct conception of their object" (Webb 280). Then, it turns out that we live to love God and follow His commandments. Natural law is "written" within us so that we can listen to it without question. We constantly have "access" to this law.

However, natural law is closely related to Revelation. The former leads to the latter: "Thomas condemns the view that it makes no difference to a man's salvation with what religious belief he serves God. Thus Natural Theology itself proves, according to Thomas, the need of a positive Revelation, the contents of which lie beyond its scope" (Webb 280). Revelation is necessary for our salvation; we cannot rely entirely on natural law.

Nonetheless, natural law is not the only kind of law that exists. St. Thomas talks about several types of laws. As Webb comments, "he distinguishes the lex divina from the lex naturalis, and the lex naturalis from the lex aeterna. This last is the law by which God governs all his creatures, irrational as well as rational" (Webb 281). But the three laws are connected: "The lex naturalis is 'nothing else than participation in the law eternal of a nature ordained to an end which is above nature'. This divine law is discriminated into the 'old law', and the 'new', adapted respectively to different stages in the development of the race" (Webb 281). Thus, the eternal law governs the whole world; natural law helps us adhere to it, and the Divine Law is what we see in the Bible.

St. Thomas eventually arrives at the idea that Revelation stands above natural law: "Thus he arrives at the fourth book, where he abandons altogether the ground of Natural Theology for that of Revelation. Man's natural ways of attaining to the knowledge of God being insufficient they must be supplemented" (Webb 282). This is a good example of the attitude of medieval thinkers to natural theology: it does not actually exist autonomously, but only within the framework of the Revelation. True natural theology, at least in the context of Christianity, appeared later - in the Renaissance and the modern era. Prior to this, Christian theologians almost exclusively focused on Revelation (with few exceptions, such as the Five Proofs of St. Thomas, for example).

Mentioning natural philosophy, it will be good to look at a philosopher who clearly distinguishes the "two ways" - that of science and that of Revelation. This is the English thinker Francis Bacon, who lived in the late 16th and early 17th centuries. Bacon is very important to historians of philosophy. His theory of knowledge is associated with the beginning of the modern age. Accordingly, Bacon marks the end of the Renaissance era, which was characterized by a slight detachment from the religious and a greater focus on the human.

Bacon is interested in how we can achieve full and perfect knowledge of the world. He is known for rejecting the so-called four idols (logical fallacies that hinder scientific research) as well as with his theory of induction. Bacon completely breaks away from medieval metaphysics and focuses on the concrete and the sensible. In his theory, natural theology is eliminated from the knowledge of the world. With Bacon, in fact, began the English-language tradition of holding as non-scientific of everything that cannot be reached by the senses or through our experience.

As the Turkish researcher Ünsal Çimen shows, Bacon was perhaps the first philosopher to try to separate the knowledge of nature from metaphysics. The English thinker wished to transform science into a system of pure experiential knowledge subjected to control by reason. As Çimen notes, "Bacon tried to remove these obstacles for the development of natural philosophy by reinterpreting the religious texts and removing the search for final causes from natural inquiries" (Çimen 108). In effect, this means that Aristotle's (and later St. Thomas') objective reason was removed from science. Thus, the question of why the world was created and what it is moving toward remains unanswered, or rather simply removed from natural philosophy.

Bacon expresses his stand against attempting to know God through the world. The result of such an act would be a serious error: "If someone tries to understand the 'will of God' (i.e., the Scriptures) through natural philosophy, the result of this inquiry produces 'broken knowledge' or 'vain philosophy'." As Çimen adds, "the true way to learn the 'will of God' is the Scriptures, and God's creatures express only his power" (Çimen 112). This is the beginning of his attack on metaphysics, without declaring it explicitly.

We would later see such an attack in other British philosophers such as John Locke and David Hume. We must say that the rejection of metaphysics does not automatically lead to atheism - for example, Locke is not an atheist. But it is a fact that the British empiricists emphasized the importance of sense experience in our knowledge. From empiricist standpoint it follows that everything outside of this experience must be rejected or thought of as doubtful. Thus, the empiricist definition of nature is formulated: the collection of entities and things of which we have experience. No nature exists beyond our sense data and perceptions!

Francis Bacon does not deserve to be accused of trying to eliminate theology or religion. Of course, we cannot say the opposite - that he argues in defense of theology. His task is rather to make an essential distinction so that philosophers can do their work and theologians can do theirs. Two centuries later, with David Hume, we already see the elimination not only of metaphysics but also of religion. Hume sneers at various religious concepts, which he says are "made up" or are the product of certain intellectual errors. We cannot equate the concepts of Francis Bacon and Hume - these are different approaches to natural philosophy, as well as different philosophical tasks. Bacon is looking for a way to a scientific system that adequately describes and knows the world.

In connection with all this, as Çimen notes, Bacon clearly shows that in order to know God, we must turn to the Bible: "To prevent natural philosophical inquiries from intermingling with religion, Bacon accepts the Scriptures as something that shows us the 'will of God', and he accepts nature, that is, the 'works of God', as something that shows us the power of God" (Çimen 114).

In this way, Francis Bacon clearly separates the realms of religion and science. This, according to him, is necessary so that science can go its own way without interfering in religious matters. Later, this division would become even sharper, and the sphere of religion would be greatly reduced. With the advent of evolutionary theory, the realm of religion was narrowed, and various important theological principles were repudiated. But this has been a long-term effect of the division that began with Bacon.

Francis Bacon was far from the aim of eradicating metaphysics entirely. For him, metaphysics is a very important part of our knowledge. It is necessary to make sense of such problems as the beginning of the world, the First Cause, the Final Goal, etc. Çimen comments that "By taking the scopes of physics and metaphysics into consideration, Bacon assigns material and efficient causes for physics, and formal and final causes for metaphysics" (Çimen 116). The final cause is what the world is moving toward; this cause is defined (probably) by the First Cause, or Creator. We should not confuse the two types of causes: "Bacon believes that not only Plato, but Aristotle, Galen and many others made the same mistake, which is mixing final causes with physical causes" (Çimen 118).

All this shows that not everyone who analyzes the world and describes it wants to continue his path even further, toward God. Some minds just stop there. Then, people like Francis Bacon turned their minds outward, to the outside world. But besides this world, there is also our microcosm or our inner world. These are our feelings, thoughts, perceptions, memories, values. Our microcosm is also related to natural law; what is more, we can safely claim that this law is most powerfully present in ourselves. How does this occur and how can this fact lead us to God?

2.3 Natural law as reflected in morality

Summary:

The natural law contains the foundations for morality. The moral law is universal and objective. However, it is not absolutely immutable because some definitions can be modified over time. As we will see with references to the Catechism and Cardinal Daly's works, the New Law replaces the Old Law, but it does not erase it altogether.

One of the arguments in favor of the truth of Christianity has always been defined as morality. Where did morality come from? Why do we all have an understanding of goodness? Why do all people know that killing is bad, and helping and loving is good? There must be some law that was pre-established before our existence. By looking within ourselves, we will discover the moral law.

Here we cannot help but recall the moral concept of the great Immanuel Kant, according to whom the moral law in us is something similar to natural laws. In his major work *Groundwork of the Metaphysics of Morals*, he exposes his view on the universal moral law.

And just as we explore the world around us, we must also explore the depths of our soul. Kant introduced the idea of a universal moral law that we must follow. He calls it an imperative because every free will of a rational being can formulate only one imperative: "The universal imperative of duty can also go as follows: act as if the maxim of your action were to become by your will a universal law of nature" (Kant 4:421). It means this: do only what you think all rational beings should do. If you think something is not right for any person, then do not act like it.

The more specific formulation, or the practical maxim of this categorical imperative looks like this: "So act that you use humanity, whether in your own person or in the person of any other, always at the same time as an end, never merely as a means" (Kant 4:429). According to Kant, this is the only correct maxim that derives from the categorical imperative. It is a maxim that exists in our reason; it does not come from outside. We do not need to learn it from anyone else. The idea of treating the other as an end in itself means to respect her/him; and the love for them is implied although not explicitly formulated.

It is very important to realize the fact that this principle is a priori, it does not depend on our experience or external influence: "This principle of humanity, and in general of every rational nature, as an end in itself ... is not borrowed from experience" (Kant 4:431). With this thought of his, the German thinker wishes to show that the moral law is something that stands before us; it is not something abstract. The law of goodness is within ourselves, it is not pure metaphysics (in the sense of something beyond experiential). Therefore, if we want to know ourselves, we must begin with the moral law.

Based on this concept, we can confidently assert that the moral law is eternal. This means that in its form, it does not change. The categories of good and evil do not change, they have always existed. The content of the moral law may change slightly, but this is rather the result of the movement toward truth. Over time, we move away from Original sin and move closer to the Judgment Day when the whole truth about the world and about ourselves will be revealed.

As we shall see from our brief discussion of the moral law as part of the natural law, change is entirely possible in this realm. But this must be a change that is consistent with Revelation and God's will.

According to the Catechism of the Catholic Church, *the moral law is contained in the natural law itself.* As we read there, "The natural law expresses the original moral sense which enables man to discern by reason the good and the evil, the truth and the lie" (Catechism 1954). This means that we have access to this fundamental knowledge. It is inborn in us, and we do not need to learn it from some external agency. Of course, in the process of upbringing and socialization, we learn many new views and ideas, therefore we are not born with this ready knowledge. A small child, for example, as we have already said, does not know that it should not hurt animals. But it learns this fact over time. This child's problem is that animals do not talk, so it has no way of knowing that they are in pain when it hits them.

We must make a significant distinction here. The idea of moral law as part of natural law is not called naturalism. Moral naturalism holds that morality is a natural process that arises at a particular time and develops over time. Naturalism does not take into account the existence of a supernatural source of morality. Thus, moral naturalists are not concerned with the divine at all. For them, morality exists objectively, but only within the framework of the human.

Moreover, we must also consider the evolutionists' attempt to develop their form of moral naturalism. Evolutionists believe that all human activities - ethics, religion, science, politics, art - develop over time, but they have their foundations in evolution itself, i.e., they appear due to some "evolutionary pressure." For example, our morality can be explained by certain biological and evolutionary needs: love arises from the need to protect other members of our species; all this because a community is stronger than a few isolated individuals. Love also exists in animals, evolutionists say, because it protects the future generation. Thus, it turns out that *love and altruism are simply tools to aid the survival instinct.*

Richard Dawkins, one of the champions of the evolutionist worldview, admits the following in his work *The Selfish Gene*: "The argument of this book is that we, and all other animals, are machines created by our genes. I shall argue that a predominant quality to be expected in a successful gene is ruthless selfishness. This gene selfishness will usually give rise to selfishness in individual behavior" (Dawkins 3). At the same time, altruism is not excluded from such a conception: "There are special circumstances in which a gene can achieve its own selfish goals best by fostering a limited form of altruism."

For evolutionists, nature is evolution itself. They put evolution on a pedestal - it is the explanation of all social processes. Art appears as an attempt to imitate reality. But what is its evolutionary function? Here evolutionists do not explain why there is art, but according to them, it developed along with the change of our nervous system. Neanderthals have one nervous system and brain, and we have a different nervous system. That is why our art is superior to theirs. Science also evolves with our brains. If we had not evolved so much, evolutionists say, we would not have been doing science.

Evolutionism itself is a metaphysical theory that transcends the limits of experience. It departs from the idea that life has evolved and that all our activities are related to evolution, i.e., they serve for our survival or adaptation. But the problem here is the narrow interpretation of the word "nature." Nature, it is simply our biology, our physiological needs and processes. Man is interpreted in the context of his corporeality, not spirituality. Thoughts, feelings, memory - all this is simply a secondary manifestation of the primary (bodily, physiological).

This is a crude attempt to eliminate morality from our lives. It is not at all surprising that Sigmund Freud's theory of human instincts and the subconscious appeared shortly after the publication of the works of Thomas Huxley, Ernst Haeckel, and other evolutionists. Freud adopted exactly this approach - to consider morality as a secondary manifestation of the biological in man. For him, the most important thing in our psyche is the subconscious - these are our instincts, the strongest of which is the sexual instinct (libido, Eros). Our psyche has developed as a complex conflict between instincts and morality (which arose as a result of the emergence of society). With the development of civilization, this conflict deepens and thus neuroses appear. To be calmer and free from neuroses, Freud suggested, we must reduce the pressure on the sexual instinct, whatever that means.

This is called a naturalistic conception of morality, but in fact its proper name is a biological conception of morality. Everything is put into the context of biology and explained through that lens. There is no spirituality, there are no spiritual needs - evolutionists replace the word "spirit" with "psyche" and thus declare that nothing of man survives after death - the psyche ceases to exist together with the body!

We can see the consequences of this attitude nowadays- we live a life full of consumption, shopping, gaining material things. Our life is deprived of meaning. We are not certain of why we live at all. The notions of good and bad became relativistic. Since our instincts are held to be the basis of morality, then our egoism becomes natural and even recommended. Even though Freud differs from Darwinism in some respects, his psycho-ethical theory leads to one result: moral decay and loss of our belief in the Good.

It is in this context that we must understand the Christian concept of morality today. We must admit that the Christian understanding is vigorously attacked by different camps – evolutionism, existentialism, and relativism. On the one hand, evolutionists argue that morality changes in response to "evolutionary needs" (whatever that means); on the other hand, according to relativists, morality is entirely subjective, and there is no objective system of values. These criticisms must be answered in some way, and we will do it in what follows now.

Christian theology considers natural law to be created by God. Hence, the moral law is of supernatural origin. Why, then, do we not call this understanding "supernaturalistic"? To some extent, this is supernaturalism because morality is believed not to be man-made. But, as we have already shown, the natural law can be seen, realized, and understood by every person. If the moral law was entirely supernatural, then only the prophets would understand it in conversation with God. But the moral law has existed since the beginning of the human race, so we emphasize its naturalness, that it is universal to all men.

As we read in the Catechism, "the natural law states the first and essential precepts which govern the moral life. It hinges upon the desire for God and submission to him, who is the source and judge of all that is good, as well as upon the sense that the other is one's equal" (Catechism 1955). The best manifestation of this law is the Decalogue, or the Ten Commandments of the Lord. They are formulated in Exodus 20, where we see that these Commandments come from God, i.e., they are of divine origin. They are repeated in Deuteronomy 5, where we read the following:

> These are the commandments the
> Lord proclaimed in a loud voice to your
> whole assembly there on the mountain
> from out of the fire, the cloud and the
> deep darkness; and he added nothing
> more. Then he wrote them on two stone
> tablets and gave them to me. (Deut. 5:22).

The unique fact here is that this law was written down and did not remain only in oral form. It was preserved for future generations. The Decalogue is the foundation of the Covenant between God and His people: If Israel obeys God, it will prosper. In this passage, God expresses His trust in Israel.

The symbolism expressed with fire and darkness is also interesting. This is a curious contrast that shows how unattainable God is. Therefore, He spoke directly to Moses and not to the common people who were afraid of God's glory which could kill them. God gives His commandments to Israel because the Israelites do not know about them. They are not yet familiar with basic moral principles.

Now, someone may object: is not the killing of Abel a proof of the existence of these Ten Commandments from the very beginning of the human race? What did the Israelites think about morality before God gave them these Commandments?

Such an objection has its grounds: moral commandments are "written" in the hearts of people - for example, about murder, theft, adultery. These are rules that God himself "wrote" in their souls and minds. But this is the first attempt to systematize them into an integrated whole. The Ten Commandments effectively formed the basis of the future Israelite laws, which are well recorded in Deuteronomy. Also, this passage clearly shows God's disapproval of those who break the laws in question. These are people who do not just break the law; they break the Covenant itself.

> Moses then wrote down everything the
> Lord had said. He got up early the next
> morning and built an altar at the foot of
> the mountain and set up twelve stone

pillars representing the twelve tribes of

Israel (…)

Then he took the Book of the Covenant

and read it to the people. They

responded, "We will do everything the

Lord has said; we will obey" (Exod. 24:4-7).

The Israelites accept their covenant with God, being obliged to keep His commandments. In this way, God encourages the use of their conscience - this is the internal control that will help them follow the rules. The Covenant is more than a promise. It is a sign of friendship between God and man. After the Fall, man lost his hope. Suffering became unbearable. But with the Covenant, the Lord showed His benevolence, His trust in man. The Covenant is the divine law sent to us; at the same time, it is the basis of our freedom as friends of God.

What is striking here is the presence of the First Commandment, which concerns faith in God and that the Israelites shall not have other gods, i.e., idols. Perhaps this is the new thing entering into the moral life of the ancient Israelites, for up to this time they had been hesitant about idols. It is clear that concepts such as murder and theft exist quite naturally in our minds. But what about this First Commandment - is it part of the natural, universal law? And if so, why then should God emphasize it? Why did the ancient Israelites allow themselves to deviate from this commandment?

As we shall see later in this chapter, morality moves forward, to some extent. For example, the Old Law is replaced by the New Law. The ancient Israelites had no clear concept of the One God in whom they should believe. They were incapable of understanding this idea. They stood closer to the polytheistic understanding of the gods. Moses' task was to teach them that God is only one and there are no other gods; all other gods are just idols. Therefore, the Decalogue represents a combination of already known moral rules with as yet unconscious (or misunderstood) ones. The Decalogue was a unique set of laws at that time; but today, for us, it seems completely natural. We do not even need to discuss it at length- all these principles look normal and universally accepted.

In his initial state, man was naive and does not see reality well. He was unable to transcend his sense experience, so he believed that the natural elements and celestial bodies are gods. God left man alone to realize the idea of the One God who created the world. Yes, God could have given the Decalogue to Adam, but He did not. What is the reason for this? The reason probably is that it takes time for man to come to the idea of One God on his own. This is a very abstract idea, and it cannot be easily understood. On the other hand, killing and stealing are actions whose effects are easily realized as they take place before our eyes. That is why even the ancient Israelites before Moses were aware of what murder is, but not what idolatry is.

Why was this commandment, which came from God himself and was given through Moses, not followed later? There are various reasons for this, but the most important is human freedom. We must not forget that we are endowed with free will; it means that we have the right to choose evil as well as to do evil. Of course, we will then be responsible for these actions. But God cannot just program us like we do with computers. The acts of idolatry enrage Moses, but they are, to some extent, necessary: they open the eyes of all the Israelites that God will punish them severely.

Hence, natural law is eternal but at the same time it allows for certain societal changes. There is development in society and this exists within the framework of history - i.e., the movement from Original sin to the Day of Judgment. It is usual for people to have no clear idea of morality at the beginning of mankind's history. But the natural law does not change significantly, as we see in the Catechism: "The natural law is immutable and permanent throughout the variations of history; it subsists under the flux of ideas and customs and supports their progress. The rules that express it remain substantially valid" (Catechism 1958). This means that changes in human morality are only small and gradual. A "moral revolution" is a fact not only inadmissible, but also impossible.

One relevant example of this is the attitude toward slavery. Many centuries ago, slavery was considered acceptable, even though God's Ten Commandments clearly state that one cannot kill or steal. Many slave owners mistreated their slaves, breaking God's commandments. Gradually, these public relations were reduced and finally abolished. But this is done with a better definition of man (slaves were not considered human) and with a clearer awareness of caring for the other person. It is a fact that, with Christianity, the phenomenon of slavery greatly decreased, but Christianity alone could not eliminate a social and economic phenomenon such as slavery.

Christ adds many important elements to what people at first thought of as morality. Here the Catechism speaks of a New Law: "The New Law is called a law of love because it makes us act out of the love infused by the Holy Spirit, rather than from fear; a law of grace, because it confers the strength of grace to act, by means of faith and the sacraments." Here the Catechism calls it also "a law of freedom, because it sets us free from the ritual and juridical observances of the Old Law" (Catechism 1972).

But does this mean that the ancient Israelites were living in delusion? Or did Jehovah himself mislead them? Why didn't He give them the New Law back then?

This cannot be answered with certainty. What God's plans are, we cannot know for sure. Perhaps God could have given them the New Law earlier; perhaps God felt that the Israelites were not yet ready for this law. Moreover, the very person of Christ is a fundamental model for people to follow. Without Christ, people would not have believed the

New Law. That is why there is no particular point in sending the message of love if there is no one to embody it. The Law of love must be demonstrated in practice.

Still, does the New Law mean that the Old Law is not needed? Should we simply abandon the Old Law, and the Old Testament with it?

Revelation comes gradually, not suddenly. People have to wait a long time to have access to all of Revelation. Therefore, the Old Law is only one part of the natural law. It should not be rejected because it is the foundation of the New Law. Of course, there are some elements in the Old Law that can be criticized from the point of view of the New Law - for example, the cruel actions of Moses against the idolaters (Exod. 32). But these actions seem justified from the point of view of the Old Law; they were inevitable, because otherwise the belief in the One God (perhaps) would not have survived.

That is why we say that the very understanding of natural law is changing. There is progress in this understanding. After the coming of Christ, we now have a clearer idea of this law. As the Catechism says, "The precepts of natural law are not perceived by everyone clearly and immediately. In the present situation sinful man needs grace and revelation" (Catechism 1960). Then, with our reason alone we are incapable of reaching the essence of natural law. We need God's help. We must pray that He will illuminate us with His light, pray for Him to enlighten our minds.

We will now turn to a 1965 lecture on morality by Cardinal Cahal Daly. He developed his lecture in response to some criticisms against the concept of natural law, which some theologians considered too "outdated." As Daly states, sometimes it is claimed that "natural law morality is somehow 'reactionary' and opposed to the great Johannine movement of renewal in the contemporary Church. But this is to forget that Pope John's great encyclicals... were based explicitly on an appeal to natural law" (Daly par. 3).

Here comes another problem - what should be our attitude, for example, to contraception from the point of view of this law. The Cardinal comments the following: "Clearly natural law is central to Pope John's thinking about freedom, equality and brotherhood among men; and so far from being oppressive and restrictive, he sees it as a force for liberation and progress." It is from this point of view that Pope John declares himself against the Pill: "It is in virtue of the very same natural law that Pope John, in Mater et Magistra, condemns contraception as a means of population control" (Daly par. 4).

What is the logic behind this denial of the Pill? Natural law means not to interfere in the affairs of God, i.e., in what happens in nature. It is not our business to create life or to take it away; it is not our job to prevent conception. In this way we usurp the functions of God. The Church's long struggle against contraceptives is based on the idea that nature decides what the population of the earth will be - we cannot (in a moral sense) control the population. But the Church is completely consistent in its policy, as today it declares itself against certain technologies such as in vitro fertilization, artificial conception, surrogate motherhood and the like, which are considered dangerous for man and society.

The charges against the natural law theory are based on one assumption: that morality changes, as do social and economic relations. This theory is seen by its critics as too conservative, insensitive to change and modification. Cardinal Daly explains that "Natural law by no means implies a static or 'closed' view of morality. On the contrary, its insistence on immutable moral principles is the very condition of moral progress." As he goes on, "Moral progress takes place within... standards which are themselves fixed and unchanging" (Daly par. 9). We have already said that one such standard is murder - it has been considered prohibited by all societies in human history. At the same time, there has been a major shift in the definition of what constitutes murder. In ancient societies, not all people were considered citizens; not all people had rights. Accordingly, killing a slave, for example, was not real murder. Over time, people began to realize that all people have equal rights and they all have the right to live. Then, here we see a particular example of a moral law that changes over time, but not significantly - the definition of the crime itself changes.

Over time, we begin to see other people as our neighbors, as our friends. Here the cardinal explains that "Growing moral insight leads us to see more and more of our fellow-inhabitants of the planet as fellow-humans, as persons, as neighbors, rather than, e.g., as booty, slaves, 'hands' 'lower orders,' 'natives,' 'coloured' peoples" (Daly par. 11). The moral law is also changing in this direction - some ancient prejudices are falling away. We are moving toward a community of equal people who love and help each other. Therefore, the natural law fully accepts the idea of equality between people, but does not accept contraception - one is useful for humanity, and the other is not.

The moral law in its eternal form can be taken as a principle of respect and love for people within our common nature - we are created by God, who is the Good itself. Respect for each other's personality is essential. Kant's categorical imperative, which focuses on respect for the other person, "is an excellent statement of the central principle of natural law; and it is at the same time the justification for Kant's view of morality as unending progress towards an Ideal of Perfection not wholly of this world" (Daly par. 12).

The categorical imperative is derived from human nature itself. It is contained in our mind. Any reasonable being would logically arrive at its formulation. The idea of respecting and loving others is quite natural; and vice versa - the idea that others are our enemies or simply tools to achieve given goals is unnatural! The very fact that a person is a person means that we have a duty to treat that person with respect. And this idea does not stand far from Christianity: "Kant's ethics is a philosophical reflection on the great Christian moral concepts of absolute love of our fellow man, absolute duty to strive for perfection, unconditional law and perfect liberty" (Daly par. 12).

This moral ideal represents our nature - to use Aristotle's terminology, the Categorical Imperative is our final cause (goal). We must always start from it and we must always strive toward it. It is no coincidence that the cardinal also refers to St. Thomas and his interpretation of the moral ideal: "'Nature' in Aquinas, as already in Aristotle, is a principle of purposive action, of self-perfecting progress, rather than something fixist and inert. Above all, human nature in Aquinas is not something static and closed" (Daly par. 14).

From these reflections, which we find in the Catechism and in Cardinal Daly's lecture, we understand quite clearly that *the moral law does not remain static*. Reasonably, the Decalogue was later modified in form and (to some extent) in content. As we have shown, definitions of what constitutes murder change over time. Also, the word "slave" is mentioned in the Decalogue - for the ancient Israelites, slavery was a normal phenomenon and it was not explicitly condemned in these Commandments. People needed some time to come to the simple truth that no man should be a slave.

That is why we must explicitly emphasize that for Christianity morality is not something frozen and petrified. We cannot take the Decalogue literally as it was formulated 4000 years ago. There are elements in its wording that need reworking (the mention of slaves is not clear enough). But the foundations of Christian morality (and natural law in general) are seen in these Commandments.

However, today some liberals in the Christian camp are asking the question: can we not proceed with the modifications of the Decalogue? Can we not supplement it with new Commandments, or reformulate the old ones? This is possible, but we should not deviate from the very framework of the Commandments. These limits have already been set. We may change some elements that today seem outdated - but we must explicitly say that this is only one modification, and the original version should be preserved for comparison. This includes the problem of whether we can call God by a feminine name or pronoun - She instead of He, or He-and-She. Such a change would deny many basic ideas and principles of Christianity - God is always used as a male pronoun, regardless of the fact that God actually transcends this gender division. Such is the tradition and we must preserve it. Perhaps, to avoid such misunderstandings, it is best to use the word God, without pronouns.

Undoubtedly, the law of the ancient Israelites was, at times, strict and even cruel (for example, adultery was punishable by death). There are many examples of this in the Torah. We should not conceive of all these precepts and commandments as absolutely valid at all times. That is why we can formulate the moral norms, which are universally valid, in the following way:

1. Absolute respect for human life. Prohibition of killing, except in a moment of necessary self-defense. Respect also includes banning abortion, because unborn children also have certain rights.

2. Absolute respect for personal property. Ownership is a natural thing; it must not be taken away or destroyed without the consent of its owner.

3. To treat the other man as a person. This rule automatically prohibits adultery (which effectively means looking at the other person as an instrument of pleasure) and envy.

4. Always to be aware that we are created beings and that we have a Creator. Let us be grateful to our Creator. To be aware of the spiritual side of our personality and not to neglect it.

All other commandments derive from these moral norms. The latter should not contradict the former. Of course, positive law often goes beyond these norms - we must keep in mind the difference between morality and legislation. But our thesis here is that a universal morality exists, even if some of its elements are subject to redefinition over time. It is not true that morality is purely subjective, nor that morality performs "evolutionary functions."

2.4 Conclusion

In the present chapter, we have shown that there is a division between nature and convention, but it is not very clear. Our discussion of Aristotle, Plato and Democritus showed some important meanings of the terms *nomos* and *physis*. Nature and convention should not be seen as opposites. We can interpret morality as a combination of the two because nature is not something absolutely unchanging. At the same time, human convention is based on nature. Thus, many of our moral norms and laws actually derive from nature.

It is vital to realize that nature is not something that constantly restricts us and pulls us back. Nature can also be a moral ideal, something we aspire to. It is our nature to be individuals and to treat others as individuals. It means love and respect for them, their feelings and emotions, and their property. It is a respect and love that comes from our character as created by God, as equal beings before and with God.

We believe that morality is a manifestation of natural law, not the other way around. Natural law is first in its essence. From it, other forms of human activity arise - morality, science, religion. They all point to its reality. This demonstrates that morality is not subjective and does not depend only on my desires. I cannot change morality, although I may have a different idea of what is good. My idea will be wrong if I depart from the natural idea of the good. That is why some people are good and others become bad - their ideas of the latter are wrong.

The Decalogue is the best example of natural law; and at the same time, it is of divine origin. These two meanings do not contradict each other - God is the creator of this law, so the latter is both natural and divine. The Decalogue contains the most important eternal truths. They are variable only in part, and particularly in regard to their language. The truth contained in them does not change. It is another matter that we gradually come to know the Truth of the Decalogue and slightly approach the state of absolute familiarity with the truth of God.

Chapter III: The Logos as incarnated in Liturgy

Up to now, we have been introduced to the concept of natural law. As we have already seen, the Logos governs the world in a reasonable, yet at the same time, way that transcends human reason. The Christian concept transforms the Stoic understanding of the Logos into the understanding of our Savior as the Logos, as well as into the notion of the participation of the Logos in Creation.

There is another interesting form of the Logos that we often ignore. The church service, or liturgy, is an experience, an emotion, a mystical experience. We often think of the liturgy in the context of going back to Christ's earthly life. The liturgy also unites us as a Christian community - because it is actually the beginning of this community. Without the liturgy, there is no church. But what exactly is the liturgy and what is its relation to the Logos? Here we will show that the liturgy is a symbol that points to God, and it also contains a part of God - this is the Logos, which can appear and incarnate itself on earth.

3.1 St. Maximus: Liturgy as the world and the world as liturgy

Summary:

There are various functions of liturgy, and thus we cannot reduce it only to one of them. Liturgy has intellectual, emotional, social, mystical sides. However, it does not simply make us remember the death and Resurrection of Christ, but it also helps us relive again this moment. We will also turn to St. Maximus' account of the relation between liturgy and the world, thereby showing that we find the world order in liturgy.

As we all know, every religion has its well elaborated rituals. Religious rituals have been known for thousands of years. The first rituals described are in the Hindu holy books, the Vedas. The Christian liturgy has its connection with the liturgy of Judaism, in the same way that Christian churches resembled synagogues at the beginning.

Before we begin our analysis, we must say that rituals perform various functions:

1. They express a relation to the divine: in themselves, they effect such a relation. A priest is always present in the liturgy.

2. They have social functions: they unite the religious community.

3. They maintain the memory of past events - in the case of Christianity, these are the events described in the Old and New Testaments, and especially the lives of the prophets, Christ, and the Mother of God (but we should not miss the lives of the saints).

4. Maintain faith and hope in the salvation of the soul, depending on the particular religion (for example, in Buddhism salvation is understood much differently than in Christianity).

5. They also perform a cultural function - the text and music of the ritual are an important part of every ritual.

In this chapter, the liturgy and the Eucharist will be considered as the same act, although, theoretically, they are not the same. The Eucharist is an important element of every liturgy, but the latter also includes other moments.

Now we could assert that religious rituals are nothing novel. Christianity, however, presents its liturgy in a new way. It is not merely a connection with the divine, but an embodiment of the divine. This takes place through the Eucharist, where the Body and Blood of Christ are very real. In Ancient Greece, for example, the gods were not present in their temples directly - it was believed that they might inhabit them sometimes, but were not constantly present in them.

It should be noted that many people believe that the function of the church service is simply to recall past events. In short, it is a kind of history textbook in which events are described in an archaic language. It is crucial to realize that every ministry exists in a timeline that leads from Original sin to Judgment Day. Every single service is thus a part of human, earthly history. It cannot be a mere repetition, but is a progress towards future salvation.

Today, not a few people perceive the service as something unnecessary or, at best, something that believers have the right to avoid. They justify themselves by saying that they are busy (due to the new lifestyle where people work flexibly, including on Sundays). Some are even convinced that it is an old-fashioned tradition that is beautiful in itself, but gives us nothing but knowledge of past centuries. This opinion was noted by the French theologian Gaspar Lefebvre, according to whom the liturgy "stands in most minds for something purely accessory in Christian life and is placed in the same category as Gothic ornament, long ceremonies and Gregorian chant. To such as these liturgy is merely a revival of ancient art, with which archeology is chiefly concerned" (Lefebvre xiii).

Thus, it appears that Christians must place emphasis on faith and knowledge of theological principles. They should have more "freedom," to choose whether to go to church or not, etc. Liturgy should not be seen as fundamentally important - this individualistic approach appeals to people today, and that is precisely why it must be criticized. As we can see, this attitude existed already at the beginning of the 20th century, when this French theologian noted the following: "Others again, without going so far, are content to look upon the liturgy as simply the organization of exterior and public worship paid by the Church to God—the carrying out in extenso of her rubrics and ceremonies, intended only for priests" (Lefebvre xiii).

Now, the liturgy cannot be considered only "decoration." It is not just a series of rituals and speeches that the priest delivers. It also has an inner meaning that cannot be grasped so quickly by people who are not familiar with Christianity or do not go to church often. That is precisely why Lefebvre states: "This is indeed the body, the visible part of the liturgy. But we must bear in mind that the liturgy also has a soul, which is invisible and for that reason, alas, too often ignored. This soul is the power of glorifying God" (Lefebvre xiv).

As we will show here, the inner and outer meanings of the liturgy coexist in harmony. Both aspects symbolize the divine reality, and at the same time embody it. It is not right to differentiate them sharply. If we take church music as an example, can we say that it is entirely immaterial? To some extent it is, but the tools that produce it are material! Thus, we see how the external is related to the internal, the material and visible is related to the immaterial and invisible.

Hence, it is a huge mistake to think that the liturgy is just an "obsolete thing," that we today can reduce our attendance at church; that we can calmly live our lives away from the church. This is the result of the new "fashion" of religious syncretism that allows one to accept ideas from different religions and live as one likes. But Christian liturgy exists on a different level than Buddhist or Islamic rituals; this liturgy signifies not only the divine, but the cosmos itself, which was created and ordered by God. In the liturgy, we see the whole order of the world, as well as the forces that govern it.

Andrew Louth, who we already referred to earlier, reports that "The church building is then said to be an image of the cosmos, for as the church is divided into sanctuary and nave, so the cosmos is divided into the invisible and the visible" (Louth 72). In the church building we see the meeting of the mystical with the sensible, of the ineffable with the sensible. But just as the church building is an indivisible whole, so the mystical and the rational, the invisible and the visible exist in unity: "This division is not a separation: it is a division within a unity. Nave and sanctuary are separated by being related" (Louth 72).

We see the same division in the church service itself. The sacrament of the altar cannot be fully understood by intellectual means; it is not just a work of art, nor a chronicle of historical events. The altar is a symbol and at the same time the abode of the divine. That is why believers treat it with respect and reverence - without an altar, every church would be just a common building.

The divine presence is a view characteristic of Christian theology and its relation to the liturgy. *Church service is both a relationship with God and an embodiment of God.* It is immediately present, sensibly as well as insensibly. If believers open their hearts to Him, they will feel Him immediately - in the same way that every believer entering a church feels the divine presence in the images, sculptures and the altar itself. It is a presence that is felt by the senses, but in a strange way - it cannot be explained because nothing in our earthly experience can compare to it. That is why we talk about mystery - because it is another level of sensibility, where other, unknown senses seem to open up.

One possible theoretical explanation for this strange, unfamiliar sensation is the idea that we are merging with the divine. But we merge not in the way Hindus or Buddhists describe it; we rather share God's being, not becoming a part of Him (this is possible only beyond earthly existence). The Fathers of the Church call this participation. As Andrew Louth writes, for Maximus "By holy communion of the spotless and life-giving mysteries we are given fellowship and identity with him by participation in likeness, by which man is deemed worthy from man to become God" (Louth 73).

Of course, the last words do not mean that we become really gods or divine; it is only about the opportunity to co-participate in God's being, to touch Him, thereby removing our earthly limitations. God's grace is absolutely and unconditionally necessary for us to participate in God's being. We cannot do this on our own accord. In this case, we are dependent on God's will and mercy. And yet, as Louth notes, "We believe that in this present life we already have a share in these gifts of the Holy Spirit through the love that is in faith" (Louth 73).

Thus, it turns out that the liturgy is neither a pure symbol nor a necessary ritual that strengthens our faith. During the liturgy, we actually become one with God's being. Here we turn to the observations of the Swiss theologian Hans Ur von Balthasar, who comments as follows: "The liturgy is, for Maximus, more than a mere symbol; it is, in modern terms, an opus operatum, an effective transformation of the world into transfigured, divinized existence" (von Balthasar 322). We cannot simply say that God comes down to us during Masses; the truth is that the world itself becomes God's being. That is why, as the Swiss theologian notes, "the liturgy is ultimately always 'cosmic liturgy': a way of drawing the entire world into the hypostatic union" (von Balthasar 322).

Yes, the world itself can be seen as one magnificent liturgy: the world sings to God, its creator. This is precisely what is described at the beginning of the book of Genesis: the world is not only created, but also it understands (through man) the splendor of its Creator! The world is a "cosmic liturgy" in the sense that we can reach God even during our earthly existence, despite the fact that God is by definition transcendent to us. But also, *the liturgy is the world itself* - it is the highest dimension of our earthly existence. The liturgy is another reality that elevates us and brings us closer to God. This is our meeting with God - unique, unrepeatable and inexpressible entirely through words or intellectual means.

As von Balthasar points out, according to Maximus, there are many moments in the liturgy that symbolize the history of humanity and God's interventions in this history: " 'The entrance rite of the holy liturgy' recalls the first coming of the Savior; the ascent of the bishop to the altar and to his throne recalls his Ascension; the entry of the people, the gathering of the pagans in the Church, or of sinners in grace" (von Balthasar 323).

The symbolism of all these moments refers us to a certain point in time that has a specific meaning; but at the same time, we empathize with these moments; we become part of them - our individual existence is part of that of the entire human race. The history of Ancient Israel is also my personal history; the story of the conversion of the Gentiles is also my own biography. History is not what happened, but a progress, a movement toward the ultimate end- salvation. It is not finished, and we have only a partial understanding of it - which will become complete at the time of the Second Coming of Christ, our Savior.

Nonetheless, *the fact that the liturgy is a symbol does not mean that it is just a decoration*, a tradition that we follow and that is deprived of any spiritual value: the Eucharist is a symbol, but not in a Calvinist sense, rather in an Alexandrian sense (von Balthasar 325). It is both the signifier and the signified, if we can put it that way in semiotic terms. It points to another reality, but it is also another reality itself. As we will see a little later in this chapter, for the ideologues of the Reformation, the liturgy is a symbol rather in the sense of a "trace" that reminds us of some historical moments; there is no other reality in it, no God energy or being.

Why can we not say the world itself is one huge liturgy? It is not without reason that the Swiss theologian states that "If the Church is a 'world,' the world is also a cosmic Church, whose 'nave' is sensible creation and whose 'choir' is the world of intelligible realities" (von Balthasar 327). As mentioned, the world itself is a kind of praise to the Creator; it is true that only man can realize this fact – animals are not able to. But they are also a kind of praise in so far as they point to their Creator.

Yes, the world is like a cosmic church service. The world itself is like a church if we look at it in a different way. Everything created by God is holy and everything is good;

everything is filled with love. Even the most trivial things then become a mystery to us. We are accustomed to take the world as a given, as intelligible in itself; and the truth is the opposite - the world is a miracle, life is a miracle, being itself is a miracle!

Here we can refer to an important definition formulated by Mircea Eliade in his work *The Sacred & the Profane*. According to him, the church is a sacred space, i.e., this is not the ordinary (profane) space we are used to. It is not just a construction or an object of admiration. When we enter the church, time and space seem different. We come into contact with the divine, and the place of this contact is sacred. Eliade states the following: "Every sacred space implies a hierophany, an irruption of the sacred that results in detaching a territory from the surrounding cosmic milieu and making it qualitatively different" (Eliade 26).

The same can be said about time. Sacred time helps us to relive the earthly life of Christ: "The service celebrated inside it marks a break in profane temporal duration. It is no longer today's historical time that is present... but the time in which the historical existence of Jesus Christ occurred, the time sanctified by his preaching" (Eliade 72). This act is not exactly like going back, but rather turning to Christ and His time on earth - because Christ is with us at every liturgy!

On the other hand, in Christianity, the idea of historical time appears, of the idea of progress that starts from one starting point (Adam and Eve) and ends with another point (the Second Coming of Christ). That is why Eliade claims the following: "Christianity radically changed the experience and the concept of liturgical time, and this is due to the fact that Christianity affirms the historicity of the person of Christ" (Eliade 72). Therefore, we can safely say that there is a higher reality in our world, which sometimes appears to us precisely during the liturgy and through the liturgy.

To some extent, the created world itself is a liturgy; but we must bear in mind that the world cannot be entirely sacred because that would negate the very definition of the sacred. *The sacred is the place and time of the manifestation of the divine*; if the divine appeared everywhere and at all times, then the world itself would be divine. Transcendence is what makes the sacred exactly what it is. Therefore, we can agree with von Balthasar's comment that the world is a liturgy; but we must also be careful with this statement since it is rather metaphorical - the world can be seen as a liturgy in a certain sense, but it is not entirely sacred. Otherwise, we would enter the mindset of occultists or modern New Age culture, according to which "divine energy" is everywhere and mostly within us.

In a metaphorical sense, it can be said that there are two liturgies – "small" (in the church) and "big" (outside the church). As the Swiss thinker notes, "The two kinds of worship - worship in the Church and worship in the world - are united, without being transformed into each other, in a total service that is the goal of both sacrament and wisdom: the worship that is realized in love" (von Balthasar 328). Then, love is the unifying force that can transform everything profane into sacred.

Speaking of love and of the Logos in the liturgy, we cannot miss the question of the real presence of Christ during the Eucharist. Is He really present and what exactly does that mean?

3.2 Christ's presence in the Holy Mass

Summary:

We discuss in what sense Christ is present during the Eucharist. Is this just a "remembrance" or "memory" of Christ, or is He present in reality? We will also turn to the initial Protestant rejection of the Eucharist and the emphasis on its symbolic meaning.

During the Last Supper, Christ shares a very important secret with His apostles-

something to be foundation stone of what we call Eucharist:

> After taking the cup, he gave thanks
>
> and said, "Take this and divide it among
>
> you.
>
> For I tell you I will not drink again of
>
> the fruit of the vine until the kingdom of
>
> God comes."
>
> And he took bread, gave thanks and
>
> broke it, and gave it to them, saying,
>
> "This is my body given for you; do this in
>
> remembrance of me." (Luke 22:17-19)

From this moment on, Christians begin to perform this act, which we call the Eucharist (from Greek, "Thanksgiving"). These words confirm that Christ is really with us during the Eucharist. But the last words we quoted lead to some controversy. Is the Eucharist just a commemoration? Why do we perform this act?

The word "remembrance" indicates that we are remembering Christ, going back in time to Him. But is that really the case?

Another of His words, about His Body and Blood, point to the opposite - He is with us constantly. And this is quite logical - we can commemorate a person who has died and is not with us now. But isn't the Son of God with us always and everywhere? It is no coincidence that in the Catechism of the Catholic Church we read the following: "Christ is always present in his Church, especially in her liturgical celebrations. He is present in the Sacrifice of the Mass not only in the person of his minister" (Catechism 1088). It is not some token or half-hearted, partial presence; Christ is present completely, though not in material form.

Therefore, the word remembrance must be interpreted in the following sense: let us remember the day when Christ was betrayed and began His journey to Calvary. This is a memory not of the Son of God, but of this terrible day, which at the same time is connected with the salvation of the entire human race. Without Calvary, there would have been no Salvation. We must remember how the human race betrayed its Saviour; we must know that we must follow Him whatever they promise us, whatever they offer us.

Therefore, during the liturgy, the whole Christ is present in reality (not symbolically). He is not present in the sense of the earthly, historical Christ, but rather *substantially*. We do not see Him, but He is here and we can feel that presence. That is why we talk about *transubstantiation* - because one substance turns into another. The wine and the bread become Christ; Christ appears in them. And this is not a symbolic act!

Additionally, during the liturgy we can also come into contact with the Holy Ghost. Through Him, we reach the divine, if only for a brief moment. We ascend to God in a mystical and rationally unknowable way. Thus we share in the true Life, because only in God there is life. The liturgy is in no way a cognitive act, insofar as the intellect is related to knowledge. It is mystical, secret; it is an act of veiling, of an even more mystical experience of the divine. After liturgy, we are not more rational, on the contrary- which does not mean that we should reject reason altogether.

We will now turn to the Catechism of the Catholic Church to see how it describes the liturgy and the Eucharist. There we read that "In the Church's liturgy the divine blessing is fully revealed and communicated. The Father is acknowledged and adored as the source and the end of all the blessings of creation and salvation" (Catechism 1082). But every liturgy has its purpose - to ask the Father to bring us His grace and mercy: "Until the consummation of God's plan, the Church never ceases to present to the Father the offering of his own gifts and to beg him to send the Holy Spirit upon that offering, upon herself, upon the faithful, and upon the whole world" (Catechism 1083). Thus, God the Father is also the object of our veneration.

The Holy Ghost is vital to our faith and to our belonging to the Church. As stated in the Catechism, "In the liturgy the Holy Spirit is teacher of the faith of the People of God and artisan of God's masterpieces, 'the sacraments of the New Covenant' " (Catechism 1091). Thanks to the Holy Spirit, the transcendence of God turns into immanence - it turns out that God is with each of us and we can find Him inside ourselves. If God had had only two persons - the Father and the Son - we would have been forced to rely solely on the Son to bridge the gap between the divine and the human. Through the Holy Spirit, this problem is solved - but it does not happen in the way described by the pantheists.

For pantheism, the world itself is divine in itself, and there is no need to seek God outside of it. This is not true - there is no way a creation can be completely identical to its Creator! This is like saying that a book is the same as its author. Therefore, the Holy Ghost plays His part, which is sometimes underestimated by believers; and in fact, we meet him very often during the Holy mass.

The Catechism gives due credit to the role played by the Jewish sacred texts. These texts are the basis not only of the Bible, of our Holy Scriptures, but also of the liturgy. As already mentioned, the first Christian churches resembled Jewish synagogues. That is why the Catechism says the following: "For both Jews and Christians Sacred Scripture is an essential part of their respective liturgies: in the proclamation of the Word of God, the response to this word, prayer of praise and intercession for the living and the dead, invocation of God's mercy." The logical conclusion follows: "In its characteristic structure the Liturgy of the Word originates in Jewish prayer" (Catechism 1096).

The liturgy does not express only the past. In fact, this misunderstanding comes from our misunderstanding of the concept of sacred time. Sacred time is another dimension. All important events for a given religion take place in it. Thus, we can say that the life of the prophets, Christ, the saints, the Fathers of the Church is measured by sacred time. That time never remains in the past. That is why we should not turn back either; in fact, we are moving forward, toward the end of history, which is not the end of sacred time!

Yes, to some extent we need to look historically at certain events. Christ is also a historical figure - otherwise, we would have to claim that He exists only immaterially or invisibly to us. But sacred time exists in another way; it is measured differently; it does not feel that time is passing, but rather that an idea, a plan is being realized. That is why we read in the Catechism that "Christian liturgy not only recalls the events that saved us but actualizes them, makes them present. The Paschal mystery of Christ is celebrated, not repeated" (Catechism 1104).

The Eucharist is the center of the liturgy. As we have already seen, it is based on the Last Supper, on the words of Christ to His apostles. That is why we should not miss it or underestimate its importance: "The whole liturgical life of the Church revolves around the Eucharistic sacrifice and the sacraments" (Catechism 1103). However, the Reformation led to a new interpretation of the Eucharist that no Christian would have considered earlier. What was behind this attack and why do we see its effects even to this day?

The Reformation began as a criticism of the role of the Pope and some practices of the Catholic Church. Undoubtedly, its beginning was political - the Reformation was based on the struggle for independence of some German states from the power of Rome. The German states were many and spread over a vast territory. They were distant from Rome not only socially and culturally but also geographically.

The Reformation subjected to a violent attack the basic ideas of Christian theology - the leading role of the Pope; the role of the Church as a single community that should not break up into local branches; the function of the priest as a link with God; the role of Holy Tradition, i.e., of the works and deeds of the great Fathers of the Church, saints and popes; the hermit and monastic tradition and the abstinence from hedonistic practices. We cannot say for sure if Martin Luther had political ambitions nailing his Theses to Wittenberg Cathedral. His role was rather to overthrow the doctrine of the Church; while other of his compatriots from the German states took up the idea of political independence.

As the Reformation scholar Mark Greengrass notes, "Luther's central critique of the Roman Church was that it was weighed down with human traditions that popes, cardinals and ecclesiastical authorities claimed as 'holy', confusing the divine with the human" (Greengrass 104). It is a criticism of the very idea that the Pope can be God's vicar on earth, and that the Church has the right to contribute to the Christian teaching spread by the apostles.

And as soon as the role of the Pope as God's vicar is denied, it logically follows that the role of the Church as a unified leader of the flock must be rejected. Henceforth, the burden must be shifted to the individual: belief becomes an individual matter, and the role of knowledge and education in theological principles is neglected (though not entirely denied). Theology must be based entirely on the Bible, Luther argued, and anything that appears to be "added" later must be "deleted" from the theology.

The attack on the authority of the Church means that a new approach to the liturgy and the other sacraments must be adopted. If the priest is just a "preacher" and not a mediator between God and man, then the liturgy must acquire a "more human" side. Some of the Catholic mass elements should be removed - so thought the first reformers.

Here Greengrass refers to one of the political leaders of the German Swiss Reformation, Huldrych Zwingli. The latter attempted to remove some Catholic practices, and at some point he even got to extremes, particularly regarding the Holy Mass. As Greengrass remarks, "Zwingli banned instrumental and choral music from the liturgy in Zurich in 1525 on the scriptural grounds of Matthew 6:6 and Ephesians 5:19. He regarded church choirs as ostentatious and distracting" (Greengrass 108).

However, in Ephesians we do not see anything prohibiting church music:

> Speak to one another with psalms,
>
> hymns and spiritual songs. Sing and
>
> make music in your heart to the Lord,
>
> always giving thanks to God the
>
> Father for everything, in the name of our
>
> Lord Jesus Christ. (Ephes. 5:19-20)

There is nothing here that can be taken as a basis for denying traditional music. Church music cannot be called "nonspiritual." But early reformers felt that the church had become a place of entertainment instead of a place for minds and hearts to be directed upward. They wanted believers to turn primarily to the Bible, without needing an intermediary for this. The music distracts the flock, they thought, and the priest has such rights to which he is not entitled (at least as interpreted by the reformers).

It would be a mistake, however, to think that this criticism by Zwingli expresses the opinion of all the early reformers. At the beginning of the Reformation, there was unity only on the question of the Pope as God's vicar on earth - the reformers denied the authority of the Pope and his right to control the Catholic Church. Gradually, many ideas appeared, and with different reformers, they took different forms. Therefore, Greengrass notes that "The practical implementation of these changes varied across Reformed Europe - Basel, for example, never banished hymnody as happened in Zurich until 1598" (Greengrass 108).

Nonetheless, the attack on the traditional form of the Catholic mass is common to most reformers. There is some presence of God in the Mass, but its main purpose is to praise God and strengthen our faith. There is no real presence of Christ in the Eucharist, both Zwingli and Luther stated: "He readily followed Luther in agreeing that the mass was not a sacrifice and that transubstantiation was absurd. Why not, therefore, abandon any notion of Christ's physical presence in the bread and wine of the eucharist?" (Greengrass 109).

Here the reformers draw on the aforementioned quote from the Gospel of Luke, where we supposedly see the view of the Eucharist as a "remembrance" of Christ. It is a ritual that they believe has a purely symbolic value. The only practical meaning of the Eucharist is that it maintains the unity of the Christian community (all Christians together participate in this ritual). We must look upon transubstantiation as something symbolic, in which there is no transformation of the bread and wine.

But what would such a view change? Someone would say that this does not matter - the faithful will still receive their communion, regardless of whether the bread and wine are only symbols or whether they are the Body and Blood of Christ. Why should we dwell more deeply on this question?

In fact, whether or not we meet the real Christ during communion is an important issue. If we meet Him only symbolically, then we can even claim that the liturgy itself is a series of *symbolic* rituals. This would mean that each person can practically conduct a liturgy by himself - since everything is only symbolic, why can I not take on the role of the priest?

The reformers here would reply that we cannot be sure how much of the liturgy itself contains God's presence. They believe that at least the Holy Ghost is present during this series of rituals. Here Zwingli develops his semiotic concept of signs: "The sign is not the reality, but it stands in a corresponding relationship with reality as an 'analogy' between the visible, material sign and the invisible, spiritual reality of the sacrament, an analogy so close as to be a 'metonymy'."

This is an attitude of analogy that, to some extent, preserves the mystery in the liturgy: "The reality of the signified is so strong that it 'vivifies' us. That is why the sacrament involves the ingestion of the sacrament, rather than simply the viewing of it. God is really 'ingrafted' in us by the 'mystery' (and Calvin retained that sense of the 'sacrament') of the eucharist" (Greengrass 118).

Either way, the liturgy is seen primarily as a symbolic act. This allows the liturgy to be changed as the faithful wish. It no longer matters what the tradition is - what matters is how the individual interprets it. As a result, we have many different forms of liturgy today, all of which are considered "valid." In charismatic movements, for example, the church service has a completely different appearance than the Lutheran service. And this Reformers' interpretation, which attacks the traditional form of the mass, is to blame for this. The transformation of the priest into an ordinary preacher leads to exactly this - to the *de-sacralization of sacred space and time*.

Zwingli's conception of Holy Baptism is similar. According to him, it has more social value: "Since Zwingli was not convinced by original guilt, baptism was not a washing away of sin. It was simply the entering into a new life and community. In practical terms, baptism was thus to take place during Sunday worship" (Greengrass 110). The other sacraments were rejected by this reformer. After all, later Reformation theologians would accept only two sacraments as divine: the Eucharist and Baptism. The role of the other sacraments is denied or ignored.

As we look back in time, the criticism against the traditional form of the Catholic Mass is completely unwarranted. The result of this criticism, however, is the emergence of all sorts of strange forms of "service" that have nothing to do with Christianity! The Lutheran service, as well as some other Protestant liturgies, resemble the Christian one; but what we see in the charismatic movements has nothing to do with the liturgy! We do not here deny the fact that the Reformation has some value to the adherents of that movement. But why did Luther, Calvin, Zwingli and the other reformers have to change the liturgy in such a startling way? Should they criticize the form of the Catholic service at all? Couldn't they just criticize the Church instead of attacking the priests and the sacraments?

Of course, the fact that some people deny the real presence of Christ during the service will not change the fact that He is really present, that He is really there. To me, as a believer, what Zwingli thinks on the matter is just another person's opinion; but as we see, historically this criticism of the liturgy has had some significant consequences.

It is for this reason that we must oppose any attempt to change the liturgy as it has been for 2000 years. Today it is argued that women can become priests; that the faithful may go without the Eucharist; that prayers in the church are something superfluous and old-fashioned. There are even attempts to introduce modern music during the liturgy - these are exotic attempts that should not become the norm, something usual. Yes, culture exercises some influence - 500 years ago, all liturgies were conducted only in Latin, but today this is not the case. But the change about the language was made so that more believers could have access to the cognitive side of the liturgy, to the text that expresses the Word. Because the Word must also be understood intellectually, and when this happens in a foreign language, the understanding becomes blurred and unclear.

In this regard, Gaspar Lefebvre states the following: "It is evident that the public worship of the Church is the ordinary way—the normal and safe way—in which the Church exercises her teaching power, for there she herself, under the direction of the Holy Ghost, displays before us the riches of Scripture and Tradition" (Lefebvre 45). This is the best way to learn directly the basic principles of Christianity - both through the sermon and through the sacraments, music, images, and the very presence in the Christian community.

Thus we gradually have come to the question of the intellectual side of the liturgy, to God's wisdom, to God's plan. Let's see what this is all about.

3.3 The Liturgy as a symbol of God's economy

Summary:

God has His plan for mankind and this is expressed in liturgy. Attending Church service means access to the knowledge of this Plan. The truthfulness of the liturgy comes not from our own opinion but from objective reality, from God Who commanded His people to build a tabernacle and worship Him.

The word "economy" is associated with finance and monetary policies today. The word itself originates from Greek, meaning "care of houschold." Thus, cvcry cconomy is taking care of some household. This is the way the science of economy appeared- as a care of all houses, all households.

This word appears in St. Paul in a strange way. In 1 Timothy we read the following:

> As I urged you when I went into
>
> Macedonia, stay therc in Ephesus so
>
> that you may command certain men not
>
> to teach false doctrines any longer

nor to devote themselves to myths and

endless genealogies. These promote

controversies rather than God's work--

which is by faith. (1Tim 1:3-4)

In other translations, the word "work" is often conveyed as "economy". In the original Greek text we read "οἰκονομίαν" (*oikonomian*). What precisely should that mean?

St. Paul asks Timothy to be careful with those disciples and believers who try to spread wrong ideas. Delusions can deprive believers of salvation. Thus the word *oikonomian* is used in the sense of salvation or saving purpose. We can easily translate this word as "plan" or as "salvation plan."

This is where the concept of God's plan comes into practical use. This is not something new or unknown - already with the appearance of the first prophets, it was clear that God has a plan for the salvation of man. It is no accident that He sends various obstacles to test the Chosen People. In both prophets Amos and Isaiah we see clearly that all historical events are designed by God; hence they are not the result of His spontaneous emotion. It is evident that God has a plan for man.

With the coming of Christ, the Son of God, the plan moves to its visible realization. Salvation already exists in visible prospect for man; it is near, or at least nearer than it was before Christ's earthly incarnation. The next stage of the plan is the organization of a single Christian community, or Church, to follow the commands of its Lord. Without this community, we cannot hope for salvation, because only few individuals will be able to save themselves. And that is not what God wants - for Him, all people must have their chance for salvation and achieving immortality.

According to Tom Smith, one possible interpretation of the word "economy" here could be the following: "In ancient times, a wealthy family would have such an arrangement, carried out by a household steward. The steward's job was to make sure all the members received adequate food, clothing and other provisions" (Smith par. 6). Therefore, God is like a steward who must take care of us, to help us through His Plan.

Obviously, this is just a metaphor. Human society is like a house that God takes care of. He is the Helmsman and also sets the purpose of our movement. He is our Lord, but at the same time He serves us with His Wisdom. It is important to note that for the Apostle Paul we must not deviate from this course, from this plan. The wrong interpretation of the words of Christ can lead precisely to the falling away of many people from the community of believers, from the united Church.

God's economy contains many resources. In a sense, God distributes His resources in a certain way, and this is what we call economics: "This mysterious God has a good pleasure to distribute Himself freely. This is His purpose, His will, and ultimately His glory (Eph. 3:21; Rev. 21:10-11)" (Smith par. 10). Smith turns to the Epistle to the Ephesians where we read that we should give glory "to him who is able to do immeasurably more than all we ask or imagine, according to his power that is at work within us" (Ephes. 3:20-21).

Thus, it turns out that *God's economy deals not only with the works of God, but with our works*, with man. God gives us a hand and shows us where to go - all this on the condition that He leaves us the free will to decide whether we want to listen to Him. It is our business to decide what to do; God's work is to leave us an open door on the way to salvation!

What Christ bequeaths to us is to create a single true Church. This is what God craves for; this is His solution to the problem of how people find their salvation: "God wants all the saved ones to be built up as Christ's one Body, the church. It is this built up, corporate Body that will make God's wisdom known to the entire universe including Satan and all the angelic powers" (Smith par. 31). This is our way forward; we may deviate, but our path to reconciliation is predestined. Sooner or later, we have to go for it.

But God's plan does not mean that we do not have our share in it. We must actively accept our mission, just as the prophets in Ancient Israel did it. We should not be afraid or turn back. Backsliding will bring us nothing: "When we see God's economy, we will sense that this is our commission. We will realize that we must cooperate with God to freely distribute His riches to others. This is more than leading sinners to be saved. It is to impart to them the riches of Christ given to us" (Smith par. 34).

Therefore, we must accept the Church and the liturgy as part of God's economy, and not as some supplement that is not essential. *We cannot reach Christ without the Church*; we cannot do this all by ourselves, individually and by our faith alone. Faith is needed, works are needed, and a united Christian community is needed to listen to Christ's earthly vicar. As noted by the already quoted Lefebvre, "in the whole world there is nothing greater than the Church; in the Church there is nothing greater than the Mass; and in the Mass there is nothing greater than transubstantiation" (Lefebvre 63).

The Holy Liturgy realizes anew the self-sacrifice of Christ, a self-sacrifice that He made out of love for us. This is also the connecting link between the liturgy and God's economy, God's plan. This self-sacrifice is at the center of God's plan. Without it, even the possibility of being cleansed of sin would not have appeared. That is why the French theologian commented that "The sacrifice of the Mass, therefore, represents, recalls and applies the Sacrifice of the Cross" (Lefebvre 66). The sacrifice of Christ leads to the realization of God's plan. Without this sacrifice, we would have no chance of salvation - unless God changed His plan somehow.

Therefore, the Eucharist is very important for our salvation. We should not miss it, thinking that the other sacraments will save us by themselves. This is not true - all the rituals of the Church must be seen as a whole, as acts that exist in synchrony. That is why Lefebvre states the following: "Let us set great store by the holy sacrifice and not imagine that it is inferior to the sacraments from the fact that it does not of itself remit sin or directly increase grace as they do. Its effects differ from those of the sacraments but are not at all inferior" (Lefebvre 73). It is very dangerous for Christianity to turn to an individualistic, subjective interpretation of the Eucharist and the liturgy in general.

We can claim that this pragmatist understanding (to some extent it is due to the famous philosopher William James) does a lot of damage to faith. According to James, in religion, truth is what "works." As he puts it in his work *Pragmatism* (1907), "On pragmatistic principles, if the hypothesis of God works satisfactorily in the widest sense of the word, it is true. … Experience shows that it certainly does work" (James 299). Hence, what matters is whether something "works."[3] But so we can argue that it is the effects of our faith that matter, not its truth and validity. Thus faith is reduced to something purely individual, where the most important thing is whether I feel good while performing a certain religious act.

Contrary to James, we have to say that whether I consider a belief to be true or "useful" should have no bearing on its truth. Whether or not I believe in the Sacrifice of Christ does not change the historical fact of His tragic death and Resurrection. The Eucharist should not be seen from the perspective of whether it "works," whether it has "beneficial effects" for us. What exactly do these effects mean? Am I getting healthier, or more confident, or more optimistic, or physically stronger? This idea is very reminiscent of the New Age movement - according to it, every individual has the right to create his own religion and believe in its principles, although... it was created by the same individual!

---

[3] We should not accuse James of radical subjectivism here. He adheres to the view that the psychological dimensions of faith are most important. He introduces the so-called pragmatist argument in favor of faith: if my faith has positive effects for me, then it is a valid faith (maybe not true, but it seems as if it were true).

Therefore, the truthfulness of the Holy Mass is contained in itself, as well as in its relation with the divine. As we noted, it is not of symbolic character. Whether it is useful for me or not, the Mass remains an open door to God's plan of salvation; and the fact is that it does not guarantee that I will be saved for sure. And yet, I have to attend Holy mass since this shows my belief and hope in Christ and in the future life beyond physical death.

Now, a little more about the term "usefulness." There is something extremely important to be said here for every Christian. Our life is a tangle of happy and sad moments. Suffering exists alongside joy. It is a misconception that life should be a series of happy moments. This is the Hollywood vision of a happy ending - but life is not like that. And the fact that there is pain and suffering in this world should not be taken as an argument *against* the Creator of this world. God has a plan and suffering is part of it. There is no way to become aware of our closeness to God if we are not distant from Him, at some point. We cannot appreciate our freedom if we do not lose it. We cannot regret our immortality if we do not face death. That is why Christ's Sacrifice should not be considered something sad - it is a holiday, it is a joyful event! In the same way, we must also say that the liturgy may seem sad, or complicated, or very deep, or even too far for us - but this does not mean that there is no Truth behind it!

Yes, when entering the church, we often think about our problems or happy events. We are not always able to detach ourselves from these thoughts and emotions. This is normal - throughout the week, we are engrossed in our affairs, family issues, our job. That is why we cannot completely get rid of them. Therefore, it is possible that the liturgy does not have a special "psychological effect" (in James' sense) on us. Perhaps only certain liturgies will have such an impact. But this does not negate the importance or sacredness of the liturgy!

The liturgy cannot be fully experienced by human beings. It is given to us directly by God. These are not rituals that someone invented and decided to implement. Because God stands far above us and is unknowable in his essence, the liturgy is also so deep that we cannot fully immerse ourselves in it. Perhaps certain individuals are capable of this - the mystics, the saints; but not ordinary believers. That is why we speak of the liturgy as a system of symbols.

However, symbolic reality is not fictitious; it is not made up. Our whole world consists of symbols! The sun symbolizes kindness; flowers symbolize Beauty; the lamb symbolizes Christ; water signifies innocence and purity; and so on. If we look at each other, we will see symbols everywhere! Knowledge of these symbols is the same for all people because it is inborn in our minds. God often communicates with us through symbols. Sometimes we see them in our daily life; sometimes we do it in our dreams. That is why there are such symbols in the liturgy.

A good example of the symbolic reality of religion is the holy icon. These are religious images that denote Christ, the Virgin, the Holy Trinity, certain saints and martyrs. Can we say that an icon of Christ is Himself? Is Christ there, in this holy icon? And if He is there, does that mean He is not in the other icons? No, this question is not correct. Christ is there, but He is also elsewhere. *The holy icon is like a door that leads us to Christ*; but this door is meant to lead us, it is not the end itself.

And this is not the Protestant idea that the liturgy is just a "remembrance." What Protestant theologians fail to realize here is that the elements of the liturgy are symbolic acts of communication with God. They are not a human invention.

Certainly, the Holy Liturgy is not only a symbol of God's presence. It is the covenant left to us by God. One of the first things that God revealed to Moses had to do with the Tabernacle. As we have already said, neither the church building nor the liturgy are our invention. These are things that are strictly defined by God in His covenant meeting with Moses. God wills to have constant contact with His people, and this happens precisely in his tabernacle. This is where He lives on earth, if we can put it that way. It is the holiest place on earth.

Along with His laws, God gives us a clear description of His temple as well as the various rituals that must be performed in His name. All this is done to give thanks to our Creator. We praise Him for His work.

In the book of Exodus we see the Lord's instructions regarding His temple, the various rituals to be performed, who is to perform them, and when. After carefully describing the Tabernacle, God states the following:

> "There, above the cover between the
>
> two cherubim that are over the ark of the
>
> Testimony, I will meet with you and give
>
> you all my commands for the Israelites" (Exod. 25:22)

This is where God will meet with representatives of the Chosen People. Such a way of communication is necessary so that people can know for sure what they are obliged to do.

Here we will skip the whole description of God's temple and move on to the question of who should serve in this temple. Who is entitled to this? God delegated these rights to Aaron and his generation. From this moment on, they will serve in the temple:

> "In the Tent of Meeting, outside the
>
> curtain that is in front of the Testimony,
>
> Aaron and his sons are to keep the
>
> lamps burning before the Lord from
>
> evening till morning. This is to be a

lasting ordinance among the Israelites

for the generations to come." (Exod. 27:21)

This passage well answers the question, is it possible that any man become a priest. Clearly, this should not be the case; only a certain group of people can be mediators between God and man. In Ancient Israel, these were the descendants of Aaron. This is their mission and they cannot deviate from it. No one else can take their place.

The temple will be the place of meetings and councils. God will appear there. He will be there really and live on earth with His people:

> "There I will meet you and
>
> speak to you;
>
> there also I will meet with the Israelites,
>
> and the place will be consecrated by my
>
> glory.
>
> "So I will consecrate the Tent of
>
> Meeting and the altar and will
>
> consecrate Aaron and his sons to serve
>
> me as priests.
>
> Then I will dwell among the Israelites
>
> and be their God." (Exod. 29:32-45)

To all this, God adds the importance of the Sabbath. This day should be dedicated to God alone. Nothing else can be done; no one shall work then, because God has ordered it to be a day of rest. And this commandment of God is not without reason: it means that people should not get too involved in earthly affairs. They should not only look down at the earthly affairs. People must look to heaven, to the kingdom of God. This must occur on the Sabbath.

All these instructions form the basis of today's Christian liturgy. Of course, some details have been changed - for example, the animal sacrifices are missing, as well as the idea that certain animals are "unclean." But overall, it does not change the big picture much - God gives us instructions on how to worship Him. In this way, He helps us build a sacred time-space that stands between Him and us.

In view of what has been written so far in the present work, we can safely assert that *these commandments express the will of the universal Logos,* or the natural law. The Logos is what regulates the universe. Sacraments and religious rituals are part of this order, albeit on another level. God's will, in this case coincides with natural law; this is also why God is so specific in His instructions. Otherwise, He would have simply left it up to us to decide how to worship Him - where, when, and who worships Him. As Lefebvre states, "Like the evangelical dogmas revealed by Jesus Christ and the moral law of the decalogue given by God to Moses, the liturgical worship, flowing from and based on these, is always old yet ever new" (Lefebvre xv). In this way we experience sacred time again and again, we enter into the present with God again and again. It is a time that repeats itself and that is always unique; time sacred and time symbolic.

3.4 Conclusion

Liturgy has been an important part of the life of believers for centuries. It represents both an encounter with God and an experience of sacred time and space. It is guided by the Logos, or Wisdom and Law of God. The Logos is embodied in the liturgy as we find Him in the church building or in the church community.

It is wrong to think that we do not need the liturgy today and that everyone has the right to choose whether to attend it. It should not depend on our opinion or desire. The church community is part of God's plan, of God's economy. Separation from the liturgy also means separation from God's plan. This reduces our chances of salvation.

As we see, the liturgy is an experience that transcends the limits of reason, even though it derives from the Logos, from the Word. But can we reach God only within the limits of reason? Can we understand and know Him, departing from our human reason? We will deal with this in the next chapter.

Chapter IV: Natural theology- to know God from without

The existence of natural law in the world is evident and easily proven. So far we have shown that this law is universally available to every rational being. At the same time, our knowledge of the law changes because human history progresses.

Now, a new obstacle appears before us. If the Law is evident and accessible to all, then why does not everyone believe that it was created by God? What is the reason that there are so many different opinions about the reality of God? Is there a way to know God through nature, through natural theology?

In this chapter, we will consider three approaches to natural theology: the one proposed by St. Thomas Aquinas, the one by Alvin Plantinga, and the one elaborated by William Paley. All three of them find a way to prove the reality of God, starting from premises that are obvious to us and come through our sense experience.

4.1 The interaction of faith and knowledge

Summary:

Why should we rely on knowledge of God? Could we not reach God only through faith? Here we will discuss a few passages from the Bible and will explain why knowledge is essential for our salvation.

Before we begin our analysis of the problem of how to prove the reality of God, we must set our feet on a biblical foundation. What does the Bible say about being able to know God? Is this even possible?

We will draw attention to three passages that throw light on this matter. It turns out that knowledge of God is possible, but not completely. Let us see exactly how this process takes place.

In the book of Proverbs we find the following words: "The fear of the Lord is the beginning of knowledge, but fools despise wisdom and discipline" (Prov. 1:7). The fear of God makes us know Him. But what exactly do we know in that case? And why fear and not something else?

Fear, in this case, expresses the vast difference between God and man. God is so far away that we feel awe (perhaps not exactly fear) of Him. God is unattainable. Nevertheless, we want to know God, because there is a longing for Him in us. This urge is "built into" us and we can dull it, but not eliminate it. Thus, fear may be the beginning, but after that comes curiosity and the desire to return to our Creator.

This knowledge is not infinite and absolute because, as we have already noted, God is unattainable. Therefore, what we are most interested in should be the opportunity to prove His reality.

We must insert an important remark here. The difference between reality and the existence of God is quite significant. Although medieval theologians use the word "existence," it should be clear to us that this *existence* is not the same as ours. Our level of being is not the same as God's. We are limited and finite beings. Saying that God exists is like saying that a dog "thinks." Yes, a dog has some human-like reactions and behaviors; it remembers commands and executes them; it learns from its experience; but we cannot call these reactions "thinking." In the same way, we must use another word for the being of God, the fact that He is - and that is the reality. God is real, and here we will talk about evidence of His reality, of His Being.

The knowledge of God does not exist by itself. It is shared by faith and kindness. Knowledge of God in itself is good because God is Good. We see this in the following quote from St. Peter:

> His divine power has given us
>
> everything we need for life and
>
> godliness through our knowledge of him
>
> who called us by his own glory and
>
> goodness. (2 Pet. 1:3)

Evidently, the knowledge of God is possible because He Himself wills it. God does not want to shroud Himself in mystery and isolate Himself from us. Quite the opposite - He provides us with opportunities to know Him. But this is done not only intellectually but also through faith and our works. It turns out that knowledge is a way of life, and not just a collection of facts that we study in school. Therefore, Peter adds the following:

> For this very reason, make every effort
>
> to add to your faith goodness; and to
>
> goodness, knowledge;
>
> and to knowledge, self-control; and to
>
> self-control, perseverance; and to
>
> perseverance, godliness;
>
> and to godliness, brotherly kindness;
>
> and to brotherly kindness, love. (2 Pet. 1:5-7)

A knowledgeable person should love and be good. Without this, we cannot say of him that he is truly knowledgeable. Knowledge does not derive from our mind but from the world itself. Our knowledge is directed to the universal law, to the Logos. The coming into contact of our mind with the Logos is actually knowledge, and the result of this process we call truth.

While speaking of the Law, of the Logos, certain confusion may arise. We have already said that our knowledge of the Law changes over time because God gives us new knowledge so that the Old Law is supplemented by the New Law without the former being eliminated. That is why St. Paul explains that we must follow the Law not only because it is given to us by God, but also since we must live in such a way that we hope for salvation. And salvation will not come only by explicitly following the letter of the Law. In his letter to the Romans we read the following:

> Now we know that whatever the law
> says, it says to those who are under the
> law, so that every mouth may be
> silenced and the whole world held
> accountable to God.
> Therefore no one will be declared
> righteous in his sight by observing the
> law; rather, through the law we become
> conscious of sin.
> But now a righteousness from God,
> apart from law, has been made known,
> to which the Law and the Prophets
> testify. (Rom. 3:19-21)

St. Paul teaches that we can achieve salvation only through the New Law that was sent to us - or that is the Logos, Christ. Apart from Him, we cannot be saved! By following the Law (in its old form) we become aware of our sinfulness and change. But this knowledge alone is not enough. Therefore, for St. Paul, it is important that knowledge is combined with faith.

Now, we come to a serious problem about which theologians have never stopped arguing. Can we rely entirely on our faith to save us? Do we even need to know God? From some passages of St. Paul we can come to the idea that we are saved by faith alone.

Faith is of paramount importance to our salvation. This is because God has made the world difficult to know. Not everything is given to us ready-made. God could give us all the truth at once; but He decided that it should not be so. We must reach Him ourselves - of course, with the help of His grace and mercy. But God neither appears to us directly nor does He "stuff" all the truth into our heads. Therefore, we need to believe - until we know the whole truth, we will need faith; i.e., only at the end of our history will we have fully arrived at the truth and will not need faith - but in the same sense, we will not need reason either. But this is already another theological problem - what will exist after the end of history?

It is easy to say that faith and knowledge complement each other - it is an obvious fact. That is why we are rational beings. If God had decided that we only needed faith, He would not have given us reason! But reason is necessary to exercise our free will. Through our reason we can make choices, and this is where our freedom is expressed.

No theologian has ever claimed that we do not need our reason or knowledge. Even Tertullian, who declares, "I believe because it is absurd," does not intend to say that our faith must contradict reason. He shows us that faith goes beyond reason and thus complements it. Today, however, there are so many branches of Christianity that one can get confused.

Protestant branches in particular lean toward this idea - that we should ignore our reason because we are saved by faith alone. But this understanding is wrong - if it were so, then Christ would simply perform miracles on earth, and that would be enough for us to believe Him. But instead, Christ tells us parables!

Here, a proponent of the "by faith alone" conception would object like this: knowledge often leads us away from God; when thinking we know a lot, we become proud. Those who built the Tower of Babel believed they knew everything. And as Ecclesiastes says: "The more knowledge, the more grief" (Eccl. 1:18). The development of science proves this statement: with all scientific discoveries, we are moving further and further away from God. People are becoming less and less religious. Secularism dominates today precisely because of scientific discoveries.

As we will see here and in the next chapter, the last statement is not quite correct. *Secularism and scientific development are not necessarily causally related.* Not a few scientists were believers and set their religious worldview apart. Scientific discoveries and theories do not directly reject the reality of God or the fact of Creation. Yes, evolutionism denies that God created man directly and immediately, but evolutionism also has many shortcomings and is not a fully proven theory. Science is not identical with evolutionism! It is entirely possible for a society to be technologically advanced and full of believers - America is a great example of this; and vice versa - a society can be atheist without having well-developed technologies and without serious scientific progress (for example, Soviet society).

Secularism does not arise directly from scientific progress. Rather, it is the result of the idea that man can satisfy his own needs. This is a hedonistic and consumerist worldview, in which the most important thing is to possess material goods and resources. A religious worldview would only hinder the accumulation of these goods.

Yes, we know from personal experience that the more we know about a problem, the harder it seems to solve. The deeper and deeper we go into a realm, the more mysterious it seems to us. Today we have a lot of knowledge about the world, but we still feel like we know little about it and about ourselves. Why do we need knowledge if it only provokes anxiety or causes stress?

We can add more evidence to this position. Our personal experience also shows that people who know less are generally happier. They live and experience more than sitting in a study over their books. Happy people are active people; but they also think less about the serious things in life. If we think about these difficulties, will we really be happy?

But, for good or bad, we are gifted with reason. We cannot escape this fact - we are rational creatures. Whether knowledgeable people are happy or not, we should strive for knowledge. This is our nature.

Therefore, *knowledge and faith must go hand in hand* - along with good works and hope. We must know what we believe, otherwise we risk being influenced and manipulated. The idea of trusting in blind faith led to the emergence of charismatic churches as well as cults. Cults tell us that we have to "trust" them, and that everything we know about God is untrue or distorted. But they do not offer new knowledge- they only distort what we already know. Cults change principles and dogmas, introduce new ideas and even "re-translate" the Bible.

Any person who claims to be a Christian must be well-versed in the basic principles of Christian doctrine. We are not talking about having read all the Fathers of the Church. But a Christian must know the basic principles - metaphysical, theological, ethical principles. Without them, the believer can come under the wrong influence.

A huge role in counteracting the principle of "blind faith" is played by St. Thomas Aquinas with his understanding of the Five Ways to God. Through them, he shows that we reach God also with our intellect and not only with our faith.

4.2 St. Thomas Aquinas: The Five Ways to God

Summary:

The most renowned medieval theologian, St. Thomas Aquinas, offers his conception of the Five Ways to prove the reality of God. These proofs will be discussed here. We will see if they are valid logically and how we should perceive the general approach of St. Thomas. Is it too rationalistic? Is it near to helping us understand God?

We already mentioned the teaching of St. Thomas when we were speaking of natural law earlier. As we know, St. Thomas deals very seriously with the question of how to reach God in an intellectual way. Thomas believes that we can start from nature, from the sensory world, and reach God. This is not theology in the full sense, because theology always starts with God and ends with creation. We can claim that the teaching of the Five Ways (or Five Paths) is philosophical, and more specifically, metaphysical.

Contrary to those who stand against philosophy and philosophers, Thomas believes that theology and philosophy can be combined. Theology deals with the salvation of the soul; philosophy is a natural science of things. It starts from creation and reaches God; and theology does the opposite. Likewise, he is eager to proceed from intellect to faith, not the other way around.

It should be noted that faith and knowledge have the same source; hence, they match. Both resist delusion. Thomas believes that what is contrary to natural principles is also contrary to God Who created them. Hence, we can reach God through nature, faith not hindering us in any way; but for the Five Ways, he prefers to use the intellect and sensory experience.

Aquinas chooses to ignore the evidence that comes from looking into our mental world. His wish is to depart from the external world because he relies on the senses as the basis of knowledge. These evidences start from sensibility and imply a hierarchy in the world.

The five proofs are described in Part One of his *Summa Theologiae*, Question 2. This question deals with the existence of God. According to Aquinas, the very existence of God is self-evident because the concept of God includes being in itself: "Therefore I say that this proposition, 'God exists,' of itself is self-evident, for the predicate is the same as the subject, because God is His own existence as will be hereafter shown" (Summa I, Q2, A1). At the same time, we cannot directly know God's essence, and we can only do so in terms of his effects. In short, God is real and this is easily proven, but things are more difficult with His qualities and accidents.

Even if it turns out that the reality of God is not so obvious, we can still arrive at it by proceeding from the effects, i.e., from what we see in the created world. According to Aquinas, "because since every effect depends upon its cause, if the effect exists, the cause must pre-exist. Hence the existence of God, in so far as it is not self-evident to us, can be demonstrated from those of His effects which are known to us" (Summa I, Q2, A2). This is also the main axiom (or a position that does not need to be proved) of his teaching: *we can start from the effects*, from the "traces" left by God in the world.

We will now look at these Five Paths one by one. We will lay out each of these pieces of evidence and subject them to critical analysis.

1. The First Way- or the evidence of the First Mover. According to Aquinas, we see that there is motion in the world; but everything that moves is moved by another thing. Thus we arrive at infinity unless we assume the existence of a First Mover. This is what he says: "Whatever is in motion must be put in motion by another. If that by which it is put in motion be itself put in motion, then this also must be put in motion by another, and that by another again" (Summa I, Q2, A3).

This proof comes from Aristotle's book *Physics*. Although Aristotle does not specifically state that the First Mover is God, this is still a possible conclusion.

It is difficult to find a critical view of this evidence. The fact that everything exists in motion is obvious. From the laws of physics, we know that every physical body is either at rest or in motion. And since we see that there is movement in the world rather than rest, we must think about where all this comes from.

An alternative solution to this problem would be this: the movement somehow came about and only got stronger without us knowing who set it all in motion. Evolutionism tells us something similar - life appeared by chance and then life forms also developed by chance. Hence, an alternative explanation is possible, but it is not a reasonable one - and Aquinas is looking for exactly the reasonable explanation here.

2. The Second Way - proof of the First Cause. When we look at the sensory world, we see a whole series of operative causes. But we see nothing that is the cause of itself. Thus we can go to infinity unless we accept the existence of a First Cause. Aquinas writes the following: "Now in efficient causes it is not possible to go on to infinity, because in all efficient causes following in order, the first is the cause of the intermediate cause, and the intermediate is the cause of the ultimate cause, whether the intermediate cause be several, or only one" (Summa I, Q. 2, A 3).

Causality in the world makes us always look for a reason for everything. Everything is caused by something else. Going back and forth, we must arrive at a First Cause that is independent of anything else. It must exist, no matter what we call it. But self-cause is a quality of God – that is why we can assume that it is God.

Aquinas can be criticized for not seeing the possibility of an infinite series of causes. And why is it impossible for there not to be a cause that stood at the beginning of the world? First, because medieval philosophers did not recognize a concept such as infinity (it appeared at the beginning of the Renaissance). And secondly, Thomas sees a progression, an order of causes from the higher to the lower ones. It is not simply a matter of a series of causes - we see that *simpler things are caused by more complex ones*. That is why we must admit the reality of a Most Complex cause that stands at the beginning.

3. The Third Way - proof of the Necessary existing being. We see in the world many things that are possible, potential existences. But if there had been only such things in the whole world, the world would not have existed. Full potentiality leads only to potential existence, not to necessary existence. Hence, there is something that exists necessarily. Necessary things either have a cause in themselves or in something else. But we cannot go to infinity. Hence, there is something that exists necessarily and that stands at the beginning of this line. As expressed by St. Thomas, "if at one time nothing was in existence, it would have been impossible for anything to have begun to exist; and thus even now nothing would be in existence...Therefore, not all beings are merely possible, but there must exist something the existence of which is necessary" (Summa I, Q2, A3).

Here it might seem that Thomas is playing with words, juggling with them. We see two concepts: possibility (potentiality) and reality. These concepts come from Aristotle, who called potentiality "matter" and possibility "form." Both need each other, according to

Aristotle. Thus Thomas' thinking is this: if we assume that there is nothing in the world that exists necessarily; and all things exist as potential (i.e., they could not exist), then it seems bizarre that the world and we exist at all. So there must be something that must have come into being (i.e., there is a necessary being). This, according to Aquinas, is God - and necessary being is one of His attributes.

4. The Fourth Way- proof of the Degrees of Being. We see how in all things there are degrees. Heat has different degrees, with heat being its maximum. There is something that is the truest, the best. So, we can say that this is God - He is the perfection of all things. As Aquinas puts it, "But 'more' and 'less' are predicated of different things, according as they resemble in their different ways something which is the maximum, as a thing is said to be hotter according as it more nearly resembles that which is hottest." Therefore, we can assert that "there is something which is truest, something best, something noblest and, consequently, something which is uttermost being" (Summa I, Q2, A3).

One possible criticism here is this: all degrees of quality are relative. They depend on our sensations and perceptions. For example, we perceive the tea before us as very hot, and the water in which we bathe as warm. But is it so in an objective sense? Water itself has a certain temperature - it is neither hot nor cold in itself. The only objective fact is that the temperature of a given water is, for example, 100 degrees. Now our perception says that this water is hot; but to some other person, it might even be not very warm!

However, this can be answered as follows: if all these qualities were completely subjective, then we would not be able to understand what is what at all. What are concepts like "truth," "good," "beauty"? If each of us had our own understanding of them, there would be no scientists, no saints, no masterpieces. These qualities are objective; and they all have some degrees, some gradation. Even if we do not agree exactly what is hot and what is warm, there are still degrees in the world. Having degrees means that there is a highest degree of something. In short, the maximum of all things - this is God!

5. The Fifth Way- proof of the Supreme Designer of the world, or the argument for design. We see that everything operates with a view to some end; the goal is reached deliberately. It does not matter if something is living or non-living - all things have some kind of drive in themselves. For example, the fall of a stone (an example given by Aristotle) shows that this stone is going somewhere. But this stone has no mind. How is it that it moves toward some goal? We must admit that which has no knowledge moves forward only because of the Knower - that is God. Aquinas explains the following: "Therefore some intelligent being exists by whom all natural things are directed to their end; and this being we call God" (Summa I, Q2, A3).

This evidence is very familiar to us from the theory of Intelligent Design, which today rivals evolutionism. Still, there are some differences. Aquinas does not address the problem of the origin of life or Creation. Rather, he reflects on the fact that we all strive for a goal - minerals, and animals, and people, and heavenly bodies. This view is related to the proof of the First Mover; because everything must have been moved and "thrown" toward some goal. But here it is also about a plan, a deliberateness. Someone has planned how we all move, where we move to. Who is this someone? According to Aquinas, this is God - He is the Supreme Helmsman, He steers our "ship."

This evidence is very important for morality and law because it clearly shows that the good is actually a movement toward a common goal. Morality and law guide us to the Common Good, and that is our common purpose as a society. We can understand and realize this purpose through our reason - it is available to all rational beings. In fact, the law (lex) derives from reason; it aims at the common good. Participation in divine law is called *lex naturalis*. We are bound to follow the natural law. But this law, as we have seen from the Fifth Way, is planned and designed. It is not the result of human fiction, nor is it something inexplicable that God sent us because it "happened to Him."

The five proofs are not easy to analyze because they require a better knowledge of Aristotle and medieval metaphysics in general. They also give rise to a lot of criticism - can we rely so much on our reason? Why do we put faith aside? Now, we must answer this: Aquinas does not ignore faith, but wants to present evidence that proves the reality of God in a way that does not derive directly from the Bible.

As we can clearly see, Revelation has no role here. It can only serve to build up our axiom laid down at the beginning - namely, that God exists and that we can prove it. Reason should be our starting point, but along with our senses and perceptions. For St. Thomas, reason alone cannot reach all this knowledge - here he closely follows Aristotle, according to whom our knowledge comes from the senses. This is a position that is sharply opposed to Plato, for whom the sense world is rather a distorted reality, or a reflection of reality, i.e., of the World of Ideas. While Plato openly states his doubt in the reality of our world, then his student, Aristotle, enters the stream of empiricism and states that we cannot know anything if our senses are not involved in this process.

Many criticisms can be leveled at these proofs of Aquinas from today's perspective. Because of the development of physics, we can deny most of them. And yet, we must bear in mind that these proofs do not depart from physics. They are metaphysical because they consider a First Cause or a First Mover that exists beyond the physical world. St. Thomas starts with the sensory world because these are facts difficult for a sane mentally person to deny. But this does not mean that these five ways are physical or part of the science of physics.

Many philosophers today would say that these proofs are "metaphysical delusions" and that there is no solid foundation in them. Today, metaphysics is not revered; philosophers focus only on the concrete and the individual, not on the big picture of being. But anyone who reads this evidence carefully will see that there is common sense in it. For example, the idea of the First Cause is difficult to disprove through physics because this view goes beyond the scope of science. Science deals only with operative causes, not with the First Cause. But it is clear that there must be one; likewise with the First Mover - all this motion must have started from something self-moving, not from chance.

All of these Five Ways represent a system of statements that exist in coherence. This coherent system helps us see the big picture - of a world in which God is the First Cause, the First Mover, the Maximum, the Supreme Designer, and the Necessary Being. Each statement must be considered in this context, not in isolation. For example, the principle of the first two proofs is the same - we start from a phenomenon we observe today and go back all the way to the first being that caused this phenomenon. Because the First Cause and the First Mover are practically the same thing. The Mover is the Cause and the Cause is the Mover!

What is the relationship of these Five Ways to the Logos? The Logos is the Law that determined all these principles. For example, thanks to the Logos (as Philo understands it) there is causality today; or principle of motion; or else gradation in all things. There is constancy and regularity here. The laws of nature are contained in the Logos. The very idea that there should be natural laws comes from the Logos, from Wisdom, from the Universal Law.

Contrary to all of the above, today's dominant "scientific" worldview holds that the world and life arose by chance, and that the universe came into existence after some sort of Big Bang. But what was there before this Big Bang, and why does science not attempt to explain it? How did life appear by chance - is this possible with such a beautiful and remarkable phenomenon? We are not talking about the appearance of stones or even chemical elements, but of life, which is a very complex phenomenon. Causality is excluded from this worldview, which is concerned only with what we see now, but is not interested in the First Cause.

We will deal specifically with chaos theory a little later in this book to show that modern science not only fails to rationally explain the phenomena in our world, but also tends to cling to the irrational. This is exactly what some scientists, and especially evolutionists, accuse Christianity of! According to them, Christianity, and monotheistic religions in general, deny the rational and rely only on the mystical. For these scientists and philosophers, behind science is reason, while behind religion are only emotions and beliefs that have no particular relation to reality.

The truth is that the basis of modern rationality, of the belief in the complete superiority of science, is medieval scholasticism. Without this scholasticism, the idea of knowledge as power (Francis Bacon) and then of science as the only sphere of human activity that has access to universal truth (Descartes) would not have appeared. Scholastic rationalism is an approach by which the world and nature are examined, with a view to any regularities and principles that are present in them. But the modern age takes this approach to an extreme, completely excluding Revelation and faith, and thus arrives at the state of a "naked and blind" rationalism, which does not need the idea of God.

To some extent, the blame for this also lies with René Descartes, who tried to separate the evidence for the existence of God from science. For Descartes, the existence of God and the soul is certain, but he places them outside the realm of experience, thereby actually isolating these concepts. Thus it turns out that science deals with everything else but not with the problem of God or the soul.

We cannot accuse Aquinas of unnecessary rationalism or of trying to explain God entirely rationally. Thomas is not trying to describe God, but to find His traces in our world. A complete description and definition of God cannot be rationally realized! We can define His attributes only partially. However, some concepts remain incompletely defined - how is God the First Cause, or the First Mover? How does He exist before time (because there is no time outside the world)? How does God come down to earth to save us? How is it that God exists in three Hypostases that are connected and separate? All these points are a mystery - we cannot fully penetrate them through our reason, through our language. We don't have the right terminology for them. What is it like to be out of time? What is it like to create an entire world? These are questions we will never be able to answer.

Therefore, the correct attitude toward the Five Proofs of Aquinas is to accept them as pointing to the traces left by God in our world. These are traces that lead to our Creator, to the First Cause; but they are still only traces, not part of Him. God also exists in the world, as we have already shown in our study of the liturgy. But this presence and existence does not mean that the world is God! Looking at the mountains, the oceans, the forests, we cannot claim that they are God. God created them and left his mark on them. But we cannot say: Behold, I see God in this forest over there! Therefore, we cannot accuse St. Thomas of pantheism, or the doctrine according to which the world itself is divine.

Likewise, we must see the proof formulated by St. Anselm as pointing to God but not identifying our world with God. However, Anselm offers us a different proof. Let us see what it is and how the famous philosopher Alvin Plantinga interprets it.

4.3 The Ontological proof of St. Anselm

Summary:

The Ontological argument of St. Anselm is discussed in the interpretation of Alvin Plantinga. We will pay attention to the core of this proof and will answer some misunderstandings. Anselm's argument follows the line of the necessity of the Greatest possible being, and it is not based on Berkley's type of solipsism.

About 200 years before St. Thomas Aquinas, another theologian attempted to prove the reality of God. This was the Italian theologian Anselm, who lived in the territories of today's Italy and France. After the conquest of England by the Normans, he was sent there. Anselm's argument is so remarkable that it is hotly debated even today.

We know about the theology of St. Anselm from his two main works: *Monologue* and *Proslogion* (translated as *Discourse*). In his earlier work, the *Monologue*, he tries to reach God through reason alone. He offers two proofs: for the Supreme Good (someone must have created the good things) and for the Supreme Being (everything exists through something other; but one thing exists through itself).

In his other major work, the *Proslogion*, he offers a new proof. Here Anselm combines faith and reason. According to him, we must start from our faith. It teaches us that there can be nothing greater than God. This is something we believe in; it is not provable by our experience (we cannot have experience of the greatest thing in the world, for it transcends both our senses and reason).

And so according to Anselm this great thing cannot be in the mind alone, but outside it. We think of this thing as existing in reality. We think of it because that thing existed before our thinking.

It is important to say that Anselm begins his argument with the question of whether there is a God. All the while he is actually arguing with a fictitious atheist. How can we prove the reality of God to this atheist? Here is how that argument goes:

In our mind we have the knowledge of existence of different degrees. There are small things, medium things, big things. But in our mind we find the concept of something maximally large - i.e., one beyond which no other can exist. And even the atheist must admit that such a concept exists: "For when he hears of this [being], he understands [what he hears], and whatever is understood is in the understanding. But surely that than which a greater cannot be thought cannot be only in the understanding" (Anselm 93).

The last sentence can be interpreted in different ways. If we can intellectually grasp the maximum of all things (or the Highest Being), then that Being must (of necessity) be real. It cannot be only in our mind.

Here some critics of Anselm wrongly accuse him of solipsism. Solipsism is the doctrine that "only I exist." A good example of a solipsistic philosophy is that of George Berkeley (17th-18th century), according to whom only what is in my senses (perceptions) is real. Hence, critics argue that according to Anselm, anything we think about is real. In this way, they easily refute his argument in defense of the reality of God. They reduce his claim to absurdity, then repudiate it. For it is absurd to say that what is in my mind (or consciousness, to medieval theologians the two things are the same) is real. We think about many things; we have many images in our minds. We cannot claim that they are all real. Therefore, Anselm is on the wrong track!

But Anselm does not say this. The argument does not state that what is in our mind is real. We must pay attention to the term "that than which nothing greater can be thought." What is that thing? As we have said, it is the Maximum, or Being, which surpasses all others. But this Being cannot be in the state of non-existence, because then it would not be the greatest, it would not be the Maximum! The non-existent cannot surpass the existent. Lies and untruths cannot stand above the truth. Illusion cannot surpass reality. That is why Anselm writes the following: "Hence, something than which a greater cannot be thought exists so truly that it cannot even be thought not to exist" (Anselm 94). Because existence is part of the definition of this Supreme Being.

A little further on, Anselm turns to God, describing him thus: "What indeed are You except that which—as highest of all things, alone existing through Himself—made all other things from nothing? For whatever is not this is less great than can be thought. But this [less greatness] cannot be thought of You" (Anselm 95). The Supreme Being cannot be deprived of existence, as he goes on: "What good is lacking to the Supreme Good, through whom every good exists? Consequently, You are just, truthful, blessed, and whatever it is better to be than not to be. For it is better to be just than not-just, blessed than not-blessed" (Anselm 95). These are real attributes of God; we cannot think of Him as devoid of any of these attributes, qualities.

Let us try to disprove this claim. Can we think of the Supreme Being as unreal? There is one way to say this: by saying that God is not, in fact, absolutely perfect. We can always find some weakness in Him as described in the Bible. For example, in the Old Testament we can find passages that say that God is influenced by his emotions and sometimes acts spontaneously. If God is not so perfect, then perhaps He is deprived of some important attribute.

Another possible refutation might be the following: Anselm speaks all the time of the Highest Being, of the Maximum. But he must prove that this Maximum is indeed God! However, God is not impersonal; He is not just a Being closed in Himself. He is not Kant's *Ding-an-Sich*; He is not Sartre's *being-for-itself*. God has constant contact with us; therefore, He is not a closed Being. Why should we not be able to say that this Maximum is different from God?

This way of reasoning may seem absurd to any believer - after all, God is the maximum of all things; He is the ideal, the perfection. But such an ideal would be absolutely isolated from us. His very opening to us can be a sign of weakness.

Therefore, there is no way to prove that the Maximum and God coincide, that they are exactly the same Being. It is a matter of faith; here we must rely on the description of God in the Bible. We cannot reach God in any other way. Our reason takes us in another direction - where the Supreme Being is devoid of human qualities. This is the result of over-rationalization, but we should not blame Anselm for such. He has a specific task - to show that in our minds we have a clear idea about God, and at that about an existing, real God. It is a matter of faith to identify the Maximum with the God Who is described in the Bible.

Alvin Plantinga believes that this argument for the reality of God is extremely solid and logically conducted. In his book *God, Freedom and Evil*, this philosopher deals with the problem of the reality of God. As he mentions, "According to Immanuel Kant, there are essentially three different kinds of argument for the existence of God: the cosmological argument, the teleological argument, and the ontological argument" (Plantinga 75). Kant criticizes all three, and Plantinga thinks the first two are not logically sound.

An example of a cosmological argument is the Third Way of St. Thomas Aquinas. This is the proof of the necessary existing being - there must be at least one thing in the world that exists necessarily, because not everything can exist only potentially. The problem here, as Plantinga points out, is the notion of "necessity." This notion is not entirely clear, and it is even more unclear in what sense one thing owes its existence to something else (for, Thomas thinks we owe our existence to God). But the final shortcoming of the Third Way is this: we have no way of knowing that at any given moment, no potentially existing thing exists. Because something never was, does not automatically mean that there was a time when nothing was at all. That is, the fact that centaurs never existed (so they existed only potentially) does not lead to the conclusion that nothing existed at some point of time! That is why Plantinga notes the following: "Suppose it's true that for each thing there is a time at which it does not exist; we can't properly infer that there is some one time such that everything fails to exist at that time" (Plantinga 80).

Paley is one example of the Teleological argument. But there are some weaknesses here too. What exactly is Paley trying to prove? According to Plantinga, there are six basic propositions that theists adhere to:

(1) The universe was designed;

(2) Designed by one person;

 (3) The universe was created ex nihilo;

 (4) It was created by the person who designed it;

(5) The creator of the universe is omniscient, omnipotent, and perfectly Good;

 (6) The creator of the universe is an eternal spirit (Plantinga 83-4).

Those claims, Plantinga says, are controversial. Of these, only statement 1 can be asserted with certainty. All the others do not prove the existence of One God: "We know of many large, complicated things that have been designed by one person; but just as often something of this sort is the product of a joint effort" (Plantinga 84). In a word, Paley's conception, which we shall analyze a little further on, does not prove the reality of the One God; it only proves that the world was created, but not by whom exactly.

The ontological argument, this philosopher thinks, is much more solid than the other two. According to him, this argument has been wrongly accepted by many philosophers, as mentioned by Kant. Kant criticizes it from the point of view of the idea that the thinkable is the same as the real. That is why Plantinga states the following: "At first sight Anselm's argument is remarkably unconvincing if not downright irritating; it looks too much like a parlor puzzle or word magic" (Plantinga 85).

There is a lot of logic behind Anselm's argument. The only thing we have to take on faith is actually the identity between the Maximum (the greatest thing) and God.

Hence, according to Plantinga, Anselm's argument runs along these lines:

1. Let's take it for granted that God exists in our mind, not in reality.

(premise) 2. However, existence in reality is greater than existence in our mind alone.

(premise) 3. We can conceive of God's reality.

4. A real God would be the greatest of all Beings (existences).

5. Still, we can conceive of a being greater than God.

6. However, this Being would be the greatest of all beings, therefore it would be even greater than God. (Plantinga 87-88)

Here Plantinga states that the latter claim "is absurd and self-contradictory; how could we conceive of a being greater than the being than which none greater can be conceived?" (Plantinga 88). This Being should be called God, and it is nothing than God. Therefore, "It is false that God exists in the understanding but not in reality" (Plantinga 88).

In short, Anselm does not claim that if we have the idea of God, then He is real. Anselm rather states that the reality of a thing is its most important property, so that we cannot grasp the reality of the Greatest Being if that Being does not exist!

As Alvin Plantinga describes the situation, for Immanuel Kant this argument is also not valid, like the previous two that we have already mentioned. For Kant, this is an existential proposition, i.e., it deals with the question whether a certain entity exists or not. Our propositions cannot deal with this question but only with what a given thing is (which is

confirmed by experience). As Plantinga describes this criticism: "No existential proposition…
is necessarily true" (Plantinga 92-3).

This criticism of Kant derives from his view that our reason is limited in certain ways;
these limitations fit into an interesting combination between the intellect and the senses.
Without sensory experience, we cannot reach truth. But Kant does not go as far as, for
example, Aristotle (nor the British empiricists). He tries to find a middle way between the two
camps of rationalism and empiricism. Therefore, he is also very careful about any attempt to
derive the reality of a thing only from our mind and not from sensory experience.

Moreover, Kant does not claim that we cannot prove the existence of a Being in a
purely intellectual way. According to him, even if we grasp the existence of some entity, we
have no way to prove its *necessary* existence. This existence remains potential!

Plantinga points out a serious problem with Anselm's argument. How exactly are we
to understand the phrase "potential existence"? How do we prove that there are things that
exist potentially? Plantinga asks the following: "But are there any possible beings- that is,
merely possible beings, beings that don't in fact exist? If so, what sorts of things are they? Do
they have properties? How are we to think of them? What is their status?" (Plantinga 102).
Anselm fails to derive the necessary existence of God from the idea of the Greatest Being
(Maximum). That is why Plantinga explains: "All we are really told, in being told that God is
a possible being, is this: among the possible beings there is one that in some world or other
has a degree of greatness that is nowhere excelled" (Plantinga 103). Thus, there is no way to
prove that God is necessarily existent.

It is not without reason that Anselm formulates his argument again, and yet he fails to
convince his opponents. That is why Alvin Plantinga offers his version, according to which
we should rather talk about the *property* of a thing being the greatest, instead of talking about
degrees of existence. This is how Plantinga formulates his statement in a negative way: "

'There is no omnipotent, omniscient, and morally perfect being' is an impossible proposition" (Plantinga 111). In a word, the Fool cannot deny the reality of the Greatest Being; we may not know the other qualities of this Being, but we know for sure that it exists, it is real.

Anselm's argument remains one of the most influential in the history of theology. The fact that it has provoked so much criticism means that there is something solid and compelling about it. A weak argument would have been ignored by atheist philosophers.

We now proceed with another similar argument, which, although it arose much later, has not ceased to exercise its influence. This is the argument of the Watchmaker.

4.4 God as the Watchmaker

Summary:

William Paley elaborated the conception of the Watchmaker, or a premature Theory of Intelligent Design. We will discuss some aspects of this theory, its historical context, and will look at its shortcomings.

Natural theology entered its culminating phase in the 19th century. The age of modernity is accompanied with the rise of rationality and trust in science. Gradually, the Christian worldview shifted and was replaced by mechanicism, i.e., the doctrine according to which the world is a giant mechanism. When we better understand how this mechanism moves, we would be able to control it.

At that time, belief in Creation had not yet disappeared. The view that the universe resembles a mechanism does not change the fact that it was created by God. The two things do not contradict each other - God and universe-mechanism are compatible ideas.

At the beginning of the 19th century, however, the materialistic worldview and physiological reductionism developed. Ideas began to emerge that the body actually existed and the soul was only a "function" of it; that the spiritual dimensions of the universe are man-made; that man himself is a machine. These ideas gained popularity in France a little before and during the Revolution, which was a stage of powerful opposition to Christianity and the Christian worldview in general. These ideas permeated Britain and Germany. People tend to believe that a Creator is unnecessary. Contrary to the evidence of St. Thomas Aquinas, the view appears that there is no First Mover! The universe moved itself without any external cause or Prime Mover.

At this point, interest in biology began to overtake that of physics. Physics has been a well-developed science since ancient times because of the ability to observe physical phenomena directly. But not so with biology, oddly enough. Hence, in the late 18th and early 19th centuries, scientists turned to the origin of life. Why is there such animal diversity? Why does human organism look so much like some animals? Why does man look exactly the way he does today?

The researchers zoologists Comte de Buffon and Jean-Baptiste Lamarck presented their ideas, according to which life developed gradually under the influence of external factors. These ideas coincide with the theory of the geologist Cuvier that once long ago there lived animal species that today have disappeared due to environmental factors. Gradually there emerged the tendency to ignore the idea of the Creator.

All this must be responded to with appropriate logical arguments. The theories of the geologists Cuvier and Lyell, as well as Lamarck's (and later Darwin's) evolutionism went too far - they claimed to give us reliable data about events in the distant past. Assuming that certain animal species once lived that are now extinct, these scientists arrived at the illogical conclusion that these changes are due not to anything else but to the adaptation of the species.

Moreover, life itself arose by chance and developed chaotically, without being subject to specific regularities. This does not appear to be science at all!

Here appeared a British philosopher who devoted his work to the question of the structure of the human body. The *Natural Theology* by William Paley appeared in 1802. This was a serious objection to the ideas of Lamarck and other scientists who attempted to eliminate God altogether from the picture of the world.

Let us imagine, Paley tells us, that we find a device (a watch) on the ground that we see for the first time. We do not know what this watch is, nor what it is for. What will we think when we see it? Shall we regard it as something natural, or as something created by a skilled craftsman?

We might first think that it is a stone that has a more odd shape. But if we look at it carefully, we will find many differences compared to the stone: "When we come to inspect the watch, we perceive... that its several parts are framed and put together for a purpose, e.g. that they are so formed and adjusted as to produce motion, and that motion, so regulated as to point out the hour of the day" (Paley 2). Of course, we will draw this conclusion after long observations, but we will still find that this device is related to measuring time.

When we realize that it is a watch (or a device we can call a watch), we will inevitably come to the assumption that it was created by someone. This mechanism must have been created by an external agency. It is more logical to assume that it was made by a craftsman than that it appeared out of nowhere, completely by chance.

And now one may object: but if I have never seen anyone make a watch, how can I perceive this device as having been made by someone? This does not matter at all, claims Paley: "Nor would it, I apprehend, weaken the conclusion, that we had never seen a watch made; that we had never known an artist capable of making one; that we were altogether incapable of executing such a piece of workmanship ourselves" (Paley 4).

Here one can clearly see a counter-thesis to the argument for the existence of a Designer of the universe: we cannot know how the world was created, and whether anyone is even capable of it. No one has seen the Act of Creation - so there is no way to prove it.

Paley rejects this objection thus: we can well recognize a device, a mechanism. It is so made that we cannot think that it appeared by chance. It does not matter if we have seen anything like it – it is clear that someone created it. We see clearly that behind this mechanism stands one idea, one plan, one goal.

No man, continues Paley, would believe, "by being told that it was one out of possible combinations of material forms; that whatever he had found in the place where he found the watch, must have contained some internal configuration or other" (Paley 6). This cannot be a random configuration; nor can we say that part of this mechanism was contained in the soil. This is not only illogical but also untrue.

But the course of our reasoning does not stop there. We have already realized that this thing in front of us is a watch. But what if we find other watches? Here is what Paley states: "SUPPOSE, in the next place, that the person, who found the watch, should, after some time, discover, that... it possessed the unexpected property of producing, in the course of its movement, another watch like itself" (Paley 9). This would already be a huge sensation: right, only living things reproduce? We cannot help but think that all these watches were made by the same person, or at least by the same group of people.

After all, "Our observer would further also reflect, that the maker of the watch before him, was, in truth and reality, the maker of every watch produced from it" (Paley 17). This statement can be objected to as we have already seen earlier in this book: it cannot be certain that the world was created by a Creator. The traces of the Act of Creation are visible and traceable, but it is not clear whether the Creator is only one. Therefore, Paley is making a huge logical leap here. Not every watch we see in the store is made by the same watchmaker.

Once a man has learned his trade, he can now make watches himself. Potentially we could all be watchmakers. How then can we prove that the Creator is one?

It is probably more important for Paley to prove the creation of the world than who exactly created it. At the same time, however, his main work also contains some ideas about the attributes of the Creator. It is logical to assume that Paley goes too far here; but still, that is natural theology - it has to get to God at some point, sooner or later. We can also assume that the belief in the One Creator is based on Scripture, not so much on the visible facts.

In one place, Paley argues his concept of the One God as follows: "OF the 'unity of the Deity' the proof is, the uniformity of plan observable in the universe. The universe itself is a system; each part either depending upon other parts, or being connected with other parts by some common law of motion" (Paley 482). The very fact that the universe is one whole proves that it was created by one Intelligence. Many intelligences would create different universes or else bring more chaos into this universe, into this one system. This argument is well founded, but still it does not fully satisfy us. We have no way of knowing what the universe looks like in its far reaches and whether the uniformity of natural laws is preserved there.

At one point, Paley even gets to the question of what atheism is. According to him, we have atheism when we replace God with nature. No matter how complex a given thing is, the atheist will claim that nature created it because it is complex in itself: "THIS is atheism: for every indication of contrivance, every manifestation of design, which existed in the watch, exists in the works of nature; with the difference, on the side of nature, of being greater and more, and that in a degree which exceeds all computation" (Paley 19). Evolutionism, which was not yet well formulated at the time, claimed just that: nature tended to create increasingly complex organisms on its own. The design we see with our eyes is therefore not the work of a

Creator, of Intelligence; it is the work of nature itself, which is something of a "creator," but not quite.

Here Paley turns to the structure of the eye and its function. How come all people have eyes? Why do mammals have vision? How did this amazing device come about? The eye is like a mechanism - it helps us see the world through a tiny part. We can say that the eye is similar to a small observation glass - the principle on which they are built is the same. What wonder is it that we can form a picture of the world in this way? How could nature herself have created this organ of sight?

There is no denying that the eye appeared for a purpose. This purpose is clearly seen in the device. And the same can be claimed about our other sense organs. We are used to owning and using them, we take them for granted. We do not ask how they appeared and why. But our sight is a real miracle! All this appears as a perfect mechanism. It is true that with age, this mechanism wears out and weakens, it begins to work less. And yet, it exists! Surrounded by miracles, we do not pay attention to them. Aren't all these mechanisms in our body worthy of admiration? That is why Paley states the following: "Sturmius held, that the examination of the eye was a cure for atheism" (Paley 35). An atheist could not explain the perfection of the human body by purely natural action. What we call nature came into existence at one point. Nature is not a creator; we do not see her creating anything, as evolutionists claim. Yes, it is a wonderful thing, but that is precisely because the handwriting, the imprint of the Creator is clearly visible in it!

At one point in this text, Paley explains the logic of natural theology. We can reach God most easily by experiencing His presence. When we study His tracks, we will know more about Him. The Great Watchmaker, the Great Artisan wished to leave few traces; our task is to analyze them. Here Paley claims that "It is only by the display of contrivance, that the existence, the agency, the wisdom of the Deity, could be testified to his rational creatures.

This is the scale by which we ascend to all the knowledge of our Creator which we possess, so far as it depends upon the phenomenon" (Paley 42).

Today, this argument is found frequently in various apologetic Christian texts. We can find it in many books for children and for people recently converted into Christianity. What criticism can we make of Paley?

We have already mentioned that, according to Cardinal Newman, Paley is being too rational here. He does not leave enough room for faith. We should not seek God only in a rational way. It is very important to be able to rise above our reason; and at the same time, reason aids our faith and explains the nature of God well.

 But here our criticism of Paley will focus on another of his weaknesses. This is the British empiricism that is clearly visible in this work. Empiricism claims that we know the world only through the senses. Reason only serves to categorize and summarize our knowledge that we have derived from the senses. Now, through reason, we can communicate what we know. Then, Paley begins his natural theology from empirical knowledge. We reach God through our senses and perceptions.

Someone would say: well, right - St. Thomas Aquinas also departs from the senses! After all, our world is sensory, of material essence. How could we start from reason, from purely intellectual concepts?

However, that is not exactly the case. St. Thomas does not exactly start with the senses. He talks about phenomena that we perceive and understand with our reason - the idea of a final purpose (cause) in the world; the idea of the Prime Mover; The Prime Cause. All of this begins in our mind, and subsequently the senses support these concepts.

Paley offers a picture of a rational explanation for the strange object we find on the street. But in this picture, too great a place is taken by our experience. All the while he talks about what our personal experience contains. Do we have experience with such bizarre objects? Have we ever seen a watchmaker make watches? Have we even seen how mechanisms are made?

Paley's great mistake is that he fails to appreciate that the concepts of God and soul are built into our intellect. These are not experience-dependent concepts. Therefore, finding in our mind the idea of God, we will always be able to recognize Him, regardless of whether we have ever entered a church, whether we have read the Bible and whether we have had a mystical experience connected with Him.

That is why the argument for the Watchmaker is wonderful, but it veers in the direction of excessive empiricism. We cannot prove the reality of God entirely through experience, and certainly not through human experience alone.

The watch we found on the street was instantly recognized by us. Even if we have never seen a watch, we will recognize it because the concept of it is in our mind! Yes, with a real watch this will not happen, but with the idea of God it will. Nothing material can and should not compare to this idea!

Still, we can find many good sides to the Watchmaker's argument. As we have seen, this argument is a modern version of one of the proofs of St. Thomas. While in Thomas we see more elements of rationalism, in Paley we notice a more serious emphasis on personal experience. Our personal experience can help us reach God, but without the idea of God embedded in our mind, this may not happen.

No matter how much he is criticized, Paley deserves a good word for his successful opposition to nascent evolutionism. He quickly countered the attempt to replace God with nature. In addition, in Paley we can also find the beginnings of the theory of Intelligent Design; therefore, his work is of some theological value, even though it was not written by a professional theologian.

4.5 Conclusion

Christianity seeks to understand the nature of God. It offers a way to reach Him not only by faith, but also by reason. Although God is unknowable in His essence, yet we can approach Him and describe His attributes.

It is not easy to understand the unity of our faith and reason. Man is prone to putting emphasis on either of them, but not on all two at once. Faith is needed to grasp the essence of God which is hidden from us- for example, the nature of the Holy Trinity is a mystery. Whatever we do in this respect, we will be unable to reach a state of ultimate knowledge about the Trinity. Faith cannot be ignored in such a matter.

But reason is also needed to grasp some important attributes of God. His existence, for example, is susceptible to our intellectual analysis. There is a variety of ways to prove the reality of God. Thomas Aqunias, Anselm, and other theologians propose their own solutions. Evidently, their proofs seriously differ from each other, but this does not mean that all of them do not lead to the same God. On the contrary- we can attain to God in various ways.

The Bible is the foundation of our faith and knowledge of God. However, medieval theologians also turned to other ways to prove that God is real. St. Thomas does not stay entirely within the realm of faith, but instead tries to depart from nature and reach God. The Watchmaker Argument developed by William Paley is similar. With the theological conception of St. Anselm, things are a little different – in him, we do not find a natural theology but rather an argument for the reality of God, which is derived from our own reason. Anselm shows that we have an innate idea of God, even if we do not call Him that. On the other hand, St. Thomas eliminates the notion of an innate idea, in order to prove the reality of God a posteriori, i.e., from experience, from the outside world.

All this clearly shows that it is wrong to understand Christianity as rejecting reason and offering to reach God only by "blind faith." But along with this, there is another misunderstanding - namely, that religion and science are in a state of total opposition, of real "war." In the next chapter, we will clearly demonstrate that science can also prove the reality of God, or at best, it does not deny His reality at all.

Chapter V: Scientific proofs for the reality of God

By now, we have dealt with natural theology. As we defined it, it seeks evidence of the reality of God by making its way from the earthly world and then ascending to God. Very often, however, this approach is accused of a lack of logic and illogical leaps. The dominant attitude today is that of science, i.e., the modern worldview is based on the belief that science alone can give us *all* knowledge about the world.

With the progress of evolutionism (as a worldview, not just as a scientific theory), the belief in God as the Creator of the world began to be marginalized and pushed into a corner. In school, children are taught that man descended from something like an ape, and that life appeared out of nowhere by chance. Worse, however, is that unproven claims are presented as absolute facts and our children are manipulated into believing it all! This is the effect of the "scientific worldview," which represents only one worldview, not the truth itself.

From all this, a believer might think that science always stands against faith and religion. Can we scientifically prove that God exists? Do we not come to Him by faith alone?

In the Bible, as well as in the works of theologians, we will find many proofs that science should help us on the way to God. The approach according to which science is the "adversary" of religion, and more specifically of Christianity, is not correct. This is an approach that rejects reason and the work of the intellect in theology. All theologians, through Augustine, St. Thomas, and Etienne Gilson, would be outraged by such a claim.

In this chapter, we will prove that (1) scientists also believe in God as the Creator of the world, (2) science can provide evidence for the reality of God, and (3) reason should not be ignored on our way to God. As a consequence of these three statements, we will refute the recently popular chaos theory, which aims to present the world as devoid of rationality and patterns. It is a theory that largely aims to deny God's intervention in the world and to show that we are actually "abandoned" or "thrown away" in this world.

5.1 The scientist is not an atheist

Summary:

This chapter is focused on the relation between religion and science. Are they adversaries? Can we reconcile them with each other? As we will show, it is not obligatory for a scientist to be an atheist. Furthermore, some great minds in the history of science were religious. Our thesis to be demonstrated here is as follows: the spheres of religion and science should stay apart, and they should not intervene in the proper sphere of the other.

When we talk about science today, we cannot avoid the topic of what kind of person a scientist is. What is his character? What does he believe in? What is his attitude toward religion? Is there a way for a scientist to work and at the same time believe in God?

In fact, history shows quite clearly that these are two spheres that are compatible. Scholars are generally also believers. Some of the greatest scientists in human history were believers.

Let us first begin with what the task of science is. Science aims to describe the world objectively, going beyond our sensory limitations. It divides the world into parts so that it can be explored more easily - this is how the sciences of physics, biology, chemistry, and others appear. But it is also aimed at the human spirit and psyche - this is how sciences such as history, psychology, ethics appear. They are no less important than the other, "objective" sciences, because they also affect our lives.

The most important thing about science is that it abstracts itself from the human point of view. Science must rise above the human, move away from it. A true scientific theory must be "non-human," or at least it must not represent the human perspective! It does not matter how it will affect our thinking or our lives.

Therefore, a scientist should try to analyze everything from this "non-human" perspective. The scientist conducts research, experiments, observations. They are recorded in a database and compared with the research of other scientists. When some regularity and repeatability are demonstrated, then a hypothesis is considered to become a scientific fact.

But where is faith left here? Does all this interfere with faith?

Here we can formulate three types of relationships between religion and science:

1. Science completely displaces religion and requires religion to prove its claims scientifically.

2. Religion completely rejects science and denies scientific theories.

3. Religion and science separate into their own spheres and "agree" not to interfere in each other's spheres.

The truth is that these are only ideal models of the relationship between religion and science. There is no way that only one of these models exists. Things are much more complicated than this description. The important thing is to demonstrate that the third approach is the best way to maintain the relationship between these two spheres. These are precisely spheres of human activity, of human pursuits.

The problem with the first approach is that it requires only scientific facts. Everything must be proven, there must be testimony or evidence for everything. If something is not repeatable or testable, it is not scientific. But this approach has one serious shortcoming: it completely ignores morality, because there can be no "scientific facts" for our moral categories! Good is simply good, and we understand it intuitively, through a particular moral intuition, and we do not try to prove it scientifically. Ethics cannot work with axioms and theorems, as Benedict Spinoza once tried to do. Here is an area that cannot be dominated by science, but must be left alone.

Now, the first approach has another weakness. Within science itself, not everything can be fully proven scientifically. We will not go deep into this matter here, but we will just say that quantum physics has greatly changed the human understanding of the universe. It turned out that not all scientific statements can be proven at any time and by every person. Quantum physics presents us with a different universe that is not strictly deterministic and governed by regularities. Therefore, even in science itself, not everything can be proven exactly by the scientific method!

The second approach is incorrect because science is an important part of our lives. Science has helped mankind overcome many diseases and prolong human life. Thanks to science, today most people live without hunger, serious disease and war. The role of science is very important and it is wrong to deny it just because it sometimes conflicts with religion.

A great example is the theory of evolution. At the very beginning, the reaction of the Church and the believers was strong and emotional - a reaction of disbelief and complete denial. The mistake of these believers was that they did not try to prove the creationist worldview scientifically; they only referred to the Bible. Over time, this weakness has been overcome and it can now be said that there is pretty good *scientific* evidence against the Darwinian approach to evolution; as it is evident that thanks to creationism as a branch of the natural sciences, today we know much more about the earth's past and have exposed some glaring errors of Darwinism. For example, evolutionists themselves today admit that perhaps evolution was realized by leaps and bounds rather than gradually; and also that our ancestors were not apes, but some creatures that disappeared completely and could not be called apes in any case.

The Catholic Church often points out that reason should not come into conflict with faith. Total denial of science would be fanaticism, as would total denial of religion. Since St. Augustine, theologians have emphasized the problem of intellect and faith and proved that we should not rely on blind faith. Here we have already analyzed St. Thomas Aquinas and his Five Ways of proving the reality of God. That is why we must continue on this path: reason should not be abandoned.

Then it seems that the most correct approach is that of "autonomy" - the two spheres stay far from each other and do not interfere with each other. But how does this take place? What are their own spheres?

Intuitively, we can define the realm of religion as the belief in God as the One and Powerful Creator of the world; belief in Creation; the belief in the potential immortality of the soul; belief that matter is secondary to spirit. Thus, any attempt by science to step in here and deny any of these claims must be considered an improper intervention.

There is one more thing to note before we continue with our account of scientists believers: attempts are being made today to "scientize" religion. There is an idea of religion becoming a system of scientific statements about the spirit, our mental world. There are attempts to build something like "physics of God," i.e., creating the concept of a material God Who exists only in our material universe. All this limits the powers of religion and corners it so that it loses its autonomy.

Here we should not forget the attempt of some scientists at the beginning of the 20th century to take up a new science - parapsychology, or an attempt to study religious phenomena in a scientific, experimental way. Ultimately, they concluded that these phenomena could neither be replicated nor empirically proven. But this should serve as a lesson to us that science should not enter so proudly into the realm of religion.

The theory of the co-existence of religion and science as two autonomous spheres can be supplemented with the assumption that analogies and common ideas can be found between them. This assumption can be formulated as the 4th approach, and it can also be taken as part of the 3rd approach. Here we will turn to one researcher of the relationship between religion and science- Anthony Walsh.

In his book *God, Science and Society. The Origin of the Universe, Intelligent Life, and Free Societies*, this philosopher analyzes the problem of whether science should really be hostile to religion. He provides some evidence that not few scientists in human history were believers, and that some scientific theories point to the existence of a Creator and Creation.

Walsh introduces the main problem of his book with a reference to a society known as the New Atheists. As he remarks, "Despite the ever-increasing evidence for the Creator... the Christian foundations of American faith, morality, and freedom have become increasingly under attack by a loose confederation of public intellectuals dubbed the 'New Atheists' " (Walsh 1). It is not a coincidence that the percentage of atheists in America is increasing.

The philosopher of religion adds that our adherence to science does not automatically lead to a denial of God and the Creator: "Affirming science does not imply disclaiming God, as countless first-rate scientists attest. However, there are scientists who refuse to let God into their world at all and place all their faith in materialism/naturalism" (Walsh 14). According to him, an example of such a scientist is the geneticist Richard Lewontin, who considers science not a system of theories, but rather a worldview: "Lewontin admits that it is not the demands of the scientific method that compel scientists to accept only materialist explanations, but rather it is their faith in materialism that forces them... Atheists push the notion that they believe only in science and reason" (Walsh 15).

In this way, a false dichotomy is achieved: atheists against believers, rationality against irrationality, science against non-science, moderacy against fanaticism. However, this is not a real dichotomy or controversy- neither are atheists rational all the time, nor are believers living on blind faith or being fanatics. Of course, there are rational atheists as well as radical believers - but this cannot apply to all atheists and all believers.

A scientist's job is to deal with a specific problem in his field of study. A geneticist will deal with genetics. He should not be concerned with the question of whether there is a God or not. Furthermore, this geneticist should not present his personal beliefs as the result of scientific research. No scientist can say the following: "I am an atheist because my research proves my atheism." The reality of God cannot be fully proven or disproved by science because God transcends our reason and our system of concepts. His existence is both natural (which is what natural theology deals with) and supernatural (which is what Revelation theology deals with).

As Walsh points out, the clash here is not between science and religion, but between materialism and religion. Not a few scientists adhere to materialism as a worldview. This is the view that matter has a primary ontological function; that spirit is only a secondary thing, something produced by matter. In a word, matter is eternal, and spirit is temporary. That is why Walsh states the following: "There is no conflict between science and theism, but there is conflict between theism and materialism/naturalism... viewing everything that exists as either due to random processes or necessity; that is, the combination of chance and the laws of physics" (Walsh 19).

Here we can slightly correct this researcher of religion and define Lewontin's worldview as *scientism*. This is the attitude or approach to science that considers it to be the absolute authority on all matters - moral, economic, political, etc. Materialism is something much more general - it can be interpreted both ontologically and ethically (for example, as a desire to accumulate material goods). Scientism is the more appropriate description of this phenomenon that we see in many scientists and educated people today - the belief that science should dominate and guide us.

The implication of these words of Anthony Walsh is that the atheism of scientists is their personal belief and not the result of their scientific activity; nor is a man required to be an atheist to become a scientist. The two things are not related in any way. On the other hand, looking back in history, we will see that the roots of modern science are Christian roots; just as the roots of Western civilization are mostly Christian, not Greco-Roman (as atheists often point out). Here Walsh gives the following examples: "Friar Roger Bacon is the father of the scientific method; Jesuit priest and mathematician, Roger Boscovich, produced the precursor of atomic theory; Gregor Mendel, a monk, founded the science of genetics; Nicolas Steno, the father of geology was a priest" (Walsh 17). The same group includes Jean-Baptiste Carnoy and Georges Lemaitre, also affiliated with the Catholic Church.

And all this is far from illogical: since the time of scholasticism, the Church has encouraged believers to be interested in the world around them and to look for regularities in it: "The great contribution of Christian theology to science lies in its conviction that there are laws of nature front- loaded by God at the beginning of time awaiting discovery" (Walsh 18). Here he points to the concept of Albert Magnus (a great theologian of the 13th century, teacher of St. Thomas Aquinas), according to which we should seek the causes of things and not just adhere to what we are taught.

We have already spoken about the difference in the interpretation of the Logos by the ancient Greeks and by theologians. The Logos in the Stoics is (relatively) irrational - it decides something without justifying its decision. But the Logos of Christians is a combination of the mystical (Christ) and the rational (the Word, the Law). Therefore, it is not illogical that the foundations of modern science were formed in the 13ᵗʰ century, when scholasticism was also at its peak.

Science can accept materialism only on a relative level. All this logically leads to the following words of Walsh: "I have no problem with materialistic/naturalistic science as a working assumption; we call this methodological materialism/naturalism. As a regulative principle for science, it has been enormously successful in our understanding, prediction, and control of natural phenomena" (Walsh 20). Science should go its own way without imposing a particular worldview on us. It is as if science imposes certain moral values on us, defining them as "scientific." The fact that we are not materialists does not mean that we stand against science: "Arguing against ontological materialism and naturalism is not arguing against science" (Walsh 21).

As we shall see a little further on, there is ample reason to draw an analogy between some Christian ideas and some scientific theories. Science has not yet fully disproved Christian creationism, as well as the idea of the superiority of spiritual (or immaterial) reality over material reality. It can be assumed that this is due to only one thing - that these two ideas are actually true, so there is no way for science to disprove them.

Then, with the theory of evolution, atheists thought they had already disproved the concept of Creation. But what was their shock when physics arrived at the idea of the Big Bang! The latter idea implies that something extraordinary happened then, something that cannot be regulated by the laws of nature. That is why physicists did not welcome the hypothesis of the Big Bang at the beginning: "There is little doubt that much of the opposition to the Big Bang was motivated by the idea that a beginning implied a Creator. However, an increasing number of scientists soon accepted it" (Walsh 38).

Why does the Big Bang look weird? Because before it, there was nothing - exactly as described in the Bible. How did all these subatomic particles appear, from which the first matter was formed? What processes did take place? Why were there no regularities or laws of nature at that "moment"? Why was there only a singularity? How does the Big Bang disprove the existence of a Creator?

In fact, a stable system that does not change is a much better assumption for atheists. The static universe has neither beginning nor end (both in time and space) - therefore, there is no need to speak of a Creator at all. Therefore, the Big Bang is the theory that blows atheism to dust despite all the attempts of Stephen Hawking to prove that the beginning of the universe had no connection with any intelligence, and that everything developed completely by chance.

With the proof that the universe had a particular beginning in time, and that it could not be caused by chaos or chance, atheistic physicists fell into serious contemplation. A universe created by a Creator with clearly existing natural laws can no longer be part of scientific theory. That is why these physicists are starting to create science fiction hypotheses - such as the one about the *multiverse*. This is the idea of the existence of an infinite number of universes at the same time, in each of which absolutely anything can happen. What does this mean?

There are specific laws of nature in our universe. There is strong gravity on the earth. If we drop our cup, it will fall. But why not suppose that in another world, our cup will not fall, but will go up? Why not anti-gravity? And why not just have a world that consists entirely of a vacuum?

And something more. Why not imagine that in each different world, something different happens to us - in universe A we get married, in universe B we remain single, in universe C we become president of the USA, and in universe D we become a famous artist? Then, we can say that everything we imagine is already happening in some other reality, another universe!

As Anthony Walsh notes, this theory is not only a from of science fiction but also the apotheosis of the irrational. What is the logic of introducing an infinite number of worlds? What do we prove by this? What does this change in our lives here in this world? If we use Occam's razor, we would say this: why multiply the number of things (universes) unnecessarily? That is why Walsh states the following: "The multiverse hypothesis allows the design argument to be rejected because, given an infinite number of universes and an infinite amount of time, we could insert an infinite number of probabilities into our equations and the impossible becomes probable" (Walsh 99). Therefore, if the multiverse theory is true, there is no need to appeal to any Creator!

Nonetheless, the onslaught on the idea of the existence of only one universe with its natural regularities does not end there. According to some physicists and biologists, there is no such thing as Design or Intelligence behind this Design. This Design finds its basis in nature itself and material reality, not outside of it. Everything is the result of chance: "In their book The Grand Design, Hawking and Mlodinow argue that while our universe is exquisitely fine-tuned, it is simply blind luck, and we are the lucky winner in the ultimate Powerball lottery" (Walsh 102).

Another similar example of a scientist who prefers to believe in chance rather than Design is Christian de Duve. According to him, as quoted by Walsh, "If you equate the probability of the birth of a bacterial cell to that of the chance assembly of its component atoms, even eternity will not suffice to produce one for you." As Walsh remarks, however, "de Duve believed that life is a lucky accident somehow forged by chance and necessity" (Walsh 131). What is the reason for such adherence to blind faith? Why assign such a serious role to chance? This is not a scientific methodology at all - science must always seek to explain what it encounters.

Scientists have no choice - they have to turn to the concept of God and the Creation as one that can solve some of their difficulties. It is not true that God is an "unnecessary hypothesis," as the 19th-century French scientist Laplace claimed, according to Walsh's quote. Both biology and physics lead us to the idea of Intelligence, which is the First Cause and Prime Mover: "They have observed the incredible fine-tuning of the laws of nature, the vast information content of DNA, and the intricate nanotechnology of the living cell and have ventured beyond science in their efforts to understand it all" (Walsh 178). It is a matter of conscience and responsibility for scientists to turn in the right direction instead of turning a blind eye.

Biology today is not based exclusively on evolutionary theory, as the media and some scientists and politicians try to make us believe. The theory of evolution has gone through many phases of development, and today it is subject to serious criticism. Huge breakthroughs in this theory lead to the emergence of new explanations, such as the theory of "jumps" (rather than a slow transition from one species to another). The same applies to Intelligent Design - this theory is not shared only by believing scientists, nor only by "religious fanatics." The problem of coding DNA, which is one of the greatest wonders of the world, logically leads us to the idea of an Intelligent Designer. That is why Walsh comments the following: "We have noted that prominent atheist scientists have also argued for the intelligent design of the origin life given the immense improbability of a naturalistic origin, but locate this intelligence in areas other than the creative work of a personal God." Thus new ideas appear, only to deny the concept of Intelligent Design: "They invoke panspermia, intelligent aliens, or perhaps a sentient universe manifested in its forces and laws; a doctrine known as pantheism" (Walsh 178). In short, such atheistic scholars are ready even to defend pantheism, although it is itself a kind of religion; and all this in order to keep God out of their theory! This is really absurd.

Moreover, supporters of the Intelligent Design theory do not completely deny evolution. They allow for its realization, but in a different way than Darwin, Huxley and Dawkins tell us. It is entirely possible that evolution exists on a micro level: "ID recognizes that microevolution is the only reasonable explanation for the life forms we see around us, and that no one denies it. In fact, ID uses the same principle that Darwin adopted to explain historical events" (Walsh 181). Small changes are possible and even observable; but these changes certainly do not prove that evolution occurs on a macro level (such as a transition from one species to another). There is no way to even prove that micro-evolutionary changes lead to better adaptability of the individual, i.e., to better chances of survival. If we look at the human species, where is this evolution - can we say that we change BIOLOGICALLY in a certain direction, with a certain purpose?

Yes, the human race today is different - more peaceful, calmer, with greater well-being. But what does this have to do with biology? Are our skulls bigger than those of the Greeks of Plato's time? Are our intellectual skills better developed? This is highly doubtful, considering that the ancient Greeks had to know the entire *Iliad* by heart! How many people today can recite even one of Robert Burns' larger poems? Then, Intelligent Design allows for the possibility of micro mutations, but that does not mean at all that we should accept the theory of evolution, let alone declare it the *only* scientific theory on the origin of man!

And yet, Intelligent Design is not necessarily related to religion. In the works on this subject we find no references to the Bible, so these researchers cannot be accused of "fanaticism." Moreover, even atheists can support this theory. The biologist Nagel, in his book *Mind and Cosmos: Why the Materialist Neo-Darwinian Conception of Nature Is Almost Certainly False* claims, as Walsh commented, "that ID should be taken seriously and deserves our gratitude for challenging a scientific worldview that he considers entirely ideological" (Walsh 181). That is why we must be careful when we claim that only rational people believe in evolution, and that only "blind Christian fanatics" believe in Intelligent Design. This is simply not true - and science itself today opens its doors to the idea of Creation.

This work of Walsh's is worth noting because it is full of facts about scientists who support religion, as well as about the good relationship between science and religion. To them, we can easily mention other scientists who contributed a lot to science, but were believers - Copernicus (who was a canon in the Catholic Church), Arthur Eddington, who was a famous astronomer, Isaac Newton, who compared the universe to a huge machine, created by God, and others.

After our discussion of Walsh's book, we will now turn to Eddington, who is a very interesting example of a scientist who did not stop maintaining his religious faith. At the same time, Eddington is a supporter of the 3rd approach we described earlier - that of autonomy. Religion should not get too deep into the sphere of science, and vice versa. In his Gifford lectures of 1927, Eddington spoke about the nature of the physical world in which we live. He described the most important aspects of Einstein's theory as well as of quantum physics. This book does not focus too much on the science-religion problem, but we can still find some interesting statements in it.

The first interesting claim of this astronomer is that the universe is mind-stuff by nature. But how can we explain this- as spirit, as consciousness? Eddington means rather our perceptions - everything that exists is capable of being perceived by consciousness: "As is often the way with crude statements, I shall have to explain that by 'mind' I do not here exactly mean mind and by 'stuff' I don't at all mean stuff. The mind-stuff of the world is, of course, something more general than our individual conscious minds" (Eddington 276). However, he admits that all this has something to do with our consciousness.

We can interpret this statement in two ways: first, as *panpsychism*; and second, as solipsism. The first is the theory that the entire universe is "woven" out of consciousness, that there is only consciousness within it. And the second concept says that something exists only if we perceive it. Here Eddington stands closer to panpsychism, with the idea that the spiritual still dominates the material. Of course, he does not directly attack materialism - but that is not the subject of his lectures either. However, in another place he specifies what he wants to say as follows: "That which the man himself knows as a succession of feelings is the reality which when probed by the appliances of an outside investigator affects their readings in such a way that it is identified as a configuration of brain-matter" (Eddington 278).

Elsewhere he addresses the problem of whether there are other intelligent beings in the universe. He is very careful, admitting the possibility that there are other planets with intelligent beings - but the evidence so far refutes this: "In the long run we cannot deem ourselves the only race that has been or will be gifted with the mystery of consciousness. But I feel inclined to claim that at the present time our race is supreme" (Eddington 178). This statement in itself should already lead to the question of why there is life only on earth and how it came to be - but Eddington does not want to take up this topic because it goes beyond the limits of physics.

A little further on, this astronomer draws attention to another important fact, which was noted before him by philosophers such as Kierkegaard, Unamuno, William James, Wilhelm Dilthey, and others. However much science advances, it cannot tell us what the meaning of life is; why we live; why are we here- that is not its job. Science should describe the world, not seek meaning in it. That is why Eddington states the following: "Life would be stunted and narrow if we could feel no significance in the world around us beyond that which can be weighed and measured with the tools of the physicist or described by the metrical symbols of the mathematician" (Eddington 317).

How would we live with only pure physics or pure mathematics? Yes, a robot or a machine might exist normally; but we are not machines and for us there must always be meaning in life and in the world around us.

Eddington's understanding of separating the two spheres - that of nature and that of meaning - which in German philosophy are called the Sciences of Nature and the Sciences of the Spirit, is clearly visible here. The two types of science should not interfere; there should be no intervention of one in the other. Likewise, religion and morality must stay away from science's attempts to prove facts through experiments. Certainly, we will gain nothing if we try to turn morality and religion into sciences.

A science-only world would be beautiful and precise, but there would be no life there. As Eddington describes one such situation, "In fact the scientific world of pointer readings would be an impossible sort of place to inhabit. It is a symbolic world and the only thing that could live comfortably in it would be a symbol" (Eddington 324). In fact, the world of scientific facts means nothing by itself; it is neither good, nor beautiful, nor meaningful. We cannot live in it, nor can we feel good in it.

Here Eddington turns to the problem of the origin of life. Can science explain this origin well? Eddington asserts that "It is the aim of physical science... to lay bare the fundamental structure underlying the world; but science also has to explain if it can... the fact that from this world have arisen minds capable of transmuting the bare structure into the richness of our experience" (Eddington 335). How did spirit arise from matter? How did thought and language come about? Can evolution explain all this? Certainly this problem remains unsolved by science, as noted by the British astronomer.

Against criticism from materialists, Eddington defends himself by arguing that the world does not look as they imagine it. According to some of his critics, he is a "supernaturalist." But should this be taken as a negative label? This is what the astronomer answers during his Gifford lectures: "In so far as supernaturalism is associated with the denial of strict causality I can only answer that that is what the modern scientific development of the quantum theory brings us to" (Eddington 347). It is now clear that the world is not completely governed by strict laws, and that it is not absolutely deterministic in its character (not everything in it is initially determined). It is clear that we cannot explain the world entirely with our reason; thus it turns out that there may be some truth in mysticism as well. Supernaturalism does not require a complete denial of natural laws; it only clarifies that in some cases these laws are not valid for one reason or another - in the case of religion due to the intervention of God.

In the end, Eddington again repeats his main statement: the two spheres should stand apart and not interfere with each other: "Science and theology can make what mistakes they please provided that they make them in their own territory; they cannot quarrel if they keep to their own realms" (Eddington 351).

This British scientist clearly demonstrates that there is no need for science to be hostile to religion. In no way will such hostility make us better scientists! And here we must add something else – Eddington's observations, the beauty of the universe and the idea of the Beginning certainly lead him to understand that some Intelligence must have intervened here. We can read this between the lines - namely, that the world could not have appeared completely by chance, nor that life on earth appeared just like that. On the other hand, Eddington is reluctant to go too far and bring God into his scientific theory. Surely, however, God is not an "unnecessary hypothesis" here.

Now we turn to the thoughts of another great scientist, one of the greatest in the history of mankind. Albert Einstein was also a supporter of separating science and religion into two spheres. However, we need to carefully analyze his ideas about religion and its relationship with science, because there are some misunderstandings here.

Einstein was the physicist who made a huge breakthrough in science at the beginning of the 20th century. His theory changed the Newtonian vision of a static world in which absolute coordinates exist. The theory of relativity assumes that time and space are connected in a continuum, therefore we cannot think of something distant in time if it is not distant in space. Einstein also helps us understand why we cannot observe the physical frontiers of the universe - it is the distorted space, because of which we see a limited number of stars, and not all the stars in the universe.

After all, relativity has important consequences for our understanding of large objects and the relationships between them. It has no particular practical consequences for our life on earth. But if we want to know more about the Milky Way or the universe itself, then we must apply the theory of relativity.

Hence, there are two types of misunderstandings about Einstein: the first type is that he was a sincere believer; and the second type is that he was a staunch atheist. The truth here is in the middle between these two statements - Einstein stands on the side of a tolerant attitude toward religion, without choosing a specific form of religion - whether Judaism or Christianity.

Here we will turn to a work by Max Jammer (1999), who analyzes subtly the religious views of Einstein. According to Jammer, Einstein was brought up in the religious teachings of Judaism and specifically in the Talmud. When he turned 13, however, he refused to participate in the *bar mitzvah* ritual. This act of Einstein represented something of a rebellion against authority. Einstein's religious views changed gradually, which may have been a result of the liberal interpretation of religion in the late 19th century. According to this interpretation, Christ is more a symbol of Goodness and Wisdom, and religion aims to maintain moral order, not so much to bring us closer to God.

And yet, in time, Einstein returned to the idea that a Creator created the world. As Jammer notes about one of his biographers, "Moszkowski claimed that the beauty and splendor of nature opened the gate of the 'religious paradise,' as Einstein once called this phase of his youth. Moszkowski pointed out that yet another factor played an important role in Albert's religious feeling, and that was music" (Jammer 17-18). In music, Einstein saw a way to touch the divine without going to church. Of course, this sounds absurd, but we must keep in mind that Einstein did not attend religious services often. This was noted by the author: "Einstein never attended religious service and never prayed in a synagogue or at any other place of worship. He visited such places only to participate in social events" (Jammer 27).

That is why we can claim that Einstein is neither exactly a Christian/Judaist, nor exactly an atheist. He stands in an intermediate position somewhere between these two positions. Very often, however, he is given as an example of a scientist not believing in God and skeptical of religion. And is this so?

According to some biographers of Einstein, he owes his discoveries to his anti-religious sentiments, the attempt to distance himself from religion. They claim he intended to show that religion does not correctly describe the world: "Some biographers see in his religious skepticism the source of his freedom of thought and intellectual independence in scientific reasoning and even regard it as a necessary condition for his discovery of the theory of relativity" (Jammer 29). But how is it possible for a physicist to discover such an important theory just because he puts some efforts to become independent of religion, to "run away" from it? Is there any connection between the religious worldview and the Theory of relativity? The latter refers to the space-time continuum and gravity, and these are phenomena that are not denied by Christianity. What does the idea of a space-time continuum or the constant speed of light have to do with Creation? That is why we must confirm that Einstein's atheistic biographers are wrong in emphasizing his unfavorable attitude toward religious dogmas. This bad attitude is only his personal belief and it has nothing to do with his great discoveries.

That is why Jammer recalls that for Einstein, science and religion were not enemies: "But Einstein never conceived of the relationship between science and religion as an antithesis. On the contrary, he regarded science and religion as complementary to each other or rather as mutually dependent on each other" (Jammer 32). Both spheres are necessary for our life - one sphere describes the material world, and the other deals with the meaning of our existence.

Einstein approached the religious worldview more from a philosophical point of view. Undoubtedly, there are philosophers who have a positive attitude toward theistic religion, even if they frame it in a philosophical framework. An example of such a thinker is Benedict Spinoza, a 17th-century Dutch Jew who developed a vast metaphysical system. The most important part of it is ethics, which is based on some Aristotelian principles (for example, that we all strive for happiness). Spinoza believed that the entire universe is strictly deterministic, i.e., governed strictly by natural laws established by the Creator. As Jammer notes, "Einstein was most influenced by Spinoza's thesis of an unrestricted determinism and the belief in the existence of a superior intelligence that reveals itself in the harmony and beauty of nature" (Jammer 47). Thus, Einstein never denied the possibility that a Creator created the world, instead of the concept that the world and life appeared by chance. This God is not exactly the same one described in the Bible or the Torah: "Like Spinoza, Einstein denied the existence of a personal God, modeled after the ideal of a superman as we would say today" (Jammer 47). Therefore, for him, God is rather a Supreme Intelligence which is present in the whole universe. We can call these beliefs "spiritual pantheism."

Einstein did not want to deal with strictly Christian or Judaic principles. He does not discuss such matters as the Incarnation of the Son of God; His miracles; The Resurrection; the nature of the Holy Trinity. What is important to him is that there is something true in religion, and that is the religious feeling. Through this feeling, we feel ourselves connected to the whole world, to everything living and also to everything that exists. Jammer writes, "In 1930, Einstein was invited by the New York Times to contribute an essay on his conception of the relationship between science and religion. In this article, entitled 'Religion and Science,' Einstein used, apparently for the first time, the term 'cosmic religious feeling' " (Jammer 52).

This view is very reminiscent of some philosophers of religion, who at the beginning of the 20th century focused more on the psychological dimensions of belief. To these belongs the American philosopher and psychologist William James, who places a strong emphasis on personal religious experiences, which, according to him, are the most important for any researcher of religion. Our faith in God is useful and practical, so it is valuable.

This spiritualistic trend in our society is also related to the religious syncretism that appeared in the first decades of the 20th century. Then the interest in the East, and in particular in Buddhism and Hinduism, increased. Attention is paid to the idea of the unity of the world, and that the individual soul is rather an illusion. This philosophy is convenient for many people today because it does not obligate us to go to church regularly, nor to confess or repent of our sins. It is a philosophy according to which every single mistake can be corrected, and true sin does not exist. We will always be part of the universal unity, of the harmony, and nothing can break it.

Thus, we can argue that most 20th-century scientists did not explicitly express their religious beliefs, nor did they adhere to a particular belief system. Neither Eddington, nor Einstein, nor the physicist Roger Penrose stated clearly and categorically that they were practicing Christians. But this does not mean that they deny religion, and in particular, Christianity!

A recent story with Penrose is very indicative of what we are saying above. Penrose himself considered himself an atheist, but during a discussion about it, he was forced to admit that his famous colleague Hawking was wrong. The world is not at all easy to explain rationally, as Penrose puts it; there are some mysteries in it. In October 2019, in the video series *The Big Conversation*, Penrose expresses his perspective on the complexity of the world. According to him, there are three mysteries that are difficult to solve for now without turning to religious ideas: "Mystery number one is the fact that this world of physics is so extraordinarily precisely guided by mathematical equations. The precision is extraordinary... Mystery number two is how conscious experience can arise when these circumstances seem to be right." The first is the problem of the beginning of the natural laws - who created them? How did they form themselves? The second mystery is the question of evolution - how did consciousness emerge from matter? And the third mystery concerns how we are able to work with abstract things: "Mystery number three is our ability to use our conscious understanding to comprehend mathematics and these very extraordinary self-consistent but deep ideas, which are very far from my experiences" (Premier Christian News).

This does not lead to the conclusion that Penrose expressed a belief in a Creator or Creation. But we can assume that he looks more critically at some of his old statements, which show an atheistic bias. Therefore, the wild atheism of scientists such as Thomas Huxley, Ernst Haeckel or Richard Dawkins no longer seems quite modern, not to mention that it is not logical at all.

As we can clearly see from these analyses, the universe appears beautifully ordered and harmonious, with precisely working natural laws. However, this harmony of regularities is balanced by the absence of strict laws at the micro level (the subatomic particles). So neither of these is true: (1) that there are only natural laws in the world, and (2) that the world is governed only by miracle or chance, not by natural laws. We must combine natural theology with supernatural theology, and we cannot emphasize only one of them. The very existence of the world, its creation, the fact that we are here and now, is a miracle. But the way the world moves after Creation is already a matter of natural laws, i.e., this is already a subject of study by natural theology.

Recently, however, another trend has been developing in science. We cannot tell if this is intentional - if this trend is created by atheists trying to eliminate natural theology. Surely, however, this tendency is dangerous for rational thought, for the Logos, for all of us who want to understand the world and ourselves. This is the Chaos Theory, and we now turn to its analysis.

5.2 The Chaos Theory: The last refuge of atheism

Summary:

The Chaos theory is remarkable with its emphasis on the instability and spontaneity of closed systems. It introduces the notion of chaos as a state that cannot be predicted or explained well. We will refer here to two specialists in this theory- Edward Lorenz and Leonard Smith. Both of them assert that chaotic systems are not chaotic in their nature but they are only seemingly so.

The Chaos theory is very popular in mathematics as well as science fiction. However, not many people are familiar even with its basic principles. People who have read Michael Crichton's book *Jurassic Park* know better that such a theory exists. However, we must clarify that this book does not provide a proper description of the Chaos theory, but rather a personal understanding of the author.

To understand this theory, we have to say that the Chaos theory is part of systems theory. It is a theory that does not concern individual elements or entities. It deals only with collections of things called systems.

Systems are part of our world and our lives. The Earth itself is a system. In it, everything is connected and works together. Serious human interference with the Earth can lead to visible changes and eventually destroy the system. Every system is more than its constituent elements; its properties as a system are different from the properties of the individual elements taken individually.

A society is also a system. It has specific characteristics. We cannot describe society by describing only individuals. Hence, for decades, systems have been thought to be regulated and managed. A society, for example, is regulated by various agencies - government, institutions, schools, businesses, etc.

And now we come to the most important question. In the 19th century, a very important law of thermodynamics appeared in physics. This is the Second Law, or also the Law of Entropy. According to it, the entropy (or lack of regulation) in a closed system increases with time. In short, any closed system moves toward less regulation over time. Entropy explains, for example, the wear and tear of machines - as we know, they break down after a while. In this way, physicists (but not biologists) also explain death - at some point, the organism (taken as a system) reaches a state of equilibrium precisely through entropy (as equilibrium in this case is the end of life, no matter how strange this may seem).

Then, entropy itself argues against the assumption that we can control nature. In fact, no closed system will allow itself to be controlled from the outside for long. Every system tends to increase entropy - which is something like increasing chaos.

Here we must also add the discoveries in quantum physics, according to which subatomic particles are not completely regulated by natural laws, but sometimes fall into a state of indeterminacy (there is no way to know the charge and location of a particle at the same time) - this is the Heisenberg principle formulated in 1927. Now we can see how 20th-century science is beginning to move from the idea of universal regularity (all phenomena in the material world are governed by natural laws that are strict and precise) to the assumption that regularities in the world sometimes diminish and they even disappear.

The Chaos theory first appeared in meteorology and then in mathematics. Edward Lorenz, a specialist in the field of meteorology, came to the idea that the inexplicable phenomena in this science are actually due to the very variable nature of these phenomena. The fact that we cannot make an accurate forecast for the weather seven days ahead is not because we do not have the necessary information, but because rather the weather itself is changeable and unstable. Here, even the smallest influences matter, and therefore we can only talk about probabilities, not absolute certainty. For example, if we throw an object, we know that it will surely fall (unless it is in a vacuum or the object is moved by an engine). This is a strict natural law - gravity is universal and absolute, it cannot be escaped. But how do we predict the weather with such accuracy?

Hence, in the 1960s, Lorenz conducted an experiment with weather forecasting. As he notes in his book, published in the 1990s, "I had come across a phenomenon that later came to be called 'chaos'—seemingly random and unpredictable behavior that nevertheless proceeds according to precise and often easily expressed rules" (Lorenz 5).

It is very important to pay attention to the last words - this theory is not actually based on the idea of absolute chaos, of absolute irregularity; rather, Lorentz pays heed to phenomena that appear chaotic only for our perception. He himself clearly believes that there is a hidden regularity there, but for certain reasons we cannot recognize it. At first, the Chaos theory appears to be just that - a concept of existing regularities that remain hidden beneath the surface. Later, this concept was modified and reached the version in which it explains "chaoticness" with the subtle influences that can lead to great changes (The Butterfly Effect).

And yet, this scientist must accept the idea that there is some chaos in weather forecasts: "My experiment was doomed to failure unless I could construct a system of equations whose solutions behaved chaotically... in the ensuing years I found myself turning more and more towards chaos as a phenomenon worthy of study for its own sake" (Lorenz 5). According to him, there was no way to proceed without introducing some notion of irregularity or chaos.

Why this particular word was chosen is not clear. Lorentz could explain this type of phenomenon as "lack of regularity" or something else. The very word "chaos" speaks of a complete lack of order. For the ancient Greeks, chaos stands at the beginning of everything, after which somehow it was brought into an order, and thus our world appeared. But the truth is that there is no real, "pure" chaos in Chaos theory. That is why Lorenz states the following: "Real-world processes that appear to be behaving randomly —perhaps the falling leaf or the flapping flag—should be allowed to qualify as chaos, as long as they would continue to appear random even if any true randomness could somehow be eliminated" (Lorenz 11).

Therefore, this chaos should not be taken as such in the literal sense. Rather, we are talking about a lack of determinism; a system that is not deterministic. In the chaotic system, we do not know exactly what will happen with absolute precision, but we can only guess: "A deterministic sequence is one in which only one thing can happen next; that is, its evolution is governed by precise laws. Randomness in the broader sense is therefore identical to the absence of determinism" (Lorenz 13). If we go back to our gravity example, we will see this: in a deterministic system (the Earth's atmosphere), the object we throw will fall to the ground. Nothing else can happen if we leave this subject to itself, without outside intervention. But in the "chaotic" system, it is not clear whether the object will fall or continue its flight. It is not clear how exactly it will fall to the ground - what curve it will make, where it will fall and with what force. The reason is there are many factors that can slightly change the object's fall parabola. In a deterministic system, these factors are few and it is easy to predict exactly what will happen shortly. In general, we can predict what will occur step by step. In a chaotic system, we can predict the first few steps, and then the role of "chaos" increases.

That is why Lorenz does not resort to extremes in his description of "chaotic" systems. In fact, they simply have a lesser degree of determinism, or control by regularities: "We may describe it as behavior that is deterministic, or is nearly so if it occurs in a tangible system that possesses a slight amount of randomness, but does not look deterministic." In short, by its nature such a system is not completely chaotic, but only appears so: "This means that the present state completely or almost completely determines the future, but does not appear to do so" (Lorenz 14). We do not have enough data and information about what exactly determines the actions of the given system.

Another property of "chaotic" systems is non-linearity. As Lorenz defines linearity, "A linear process is one in which, if a change in any variable at some initial time produces a change in the same or some other variable at some later time, twice as large a change at the same initial time will produce twice as large a change at the same later time" (Lorenz 166). In "chaotic" systems, it is uncertain what the change will be following a change in a given variable; here we witness a lack of reciprocity. Of course, the lack of linearity does not mean that we can turn back time or move through space by teleportation, as some science fiction imagine - Chaos theory in no way denies the laws of physics.

Chaos theory, however, developed so much and fast that some of its proponents came to the hypothesis that chaos is a property of systems and not simply a lack of information or data about them. These scientists argue that chaos is something like the quantum uncertainty principle - just as subatomic particles are not fully determined, so "chaotic" systems are not fully controlled by regularities. Thus, these scientists go to the extreme of believing that we can never plan or predict the consequences of the actions of such "chaotic" systems. In short, we will never be able to make an accurate forecast of the weather seven days from now; and the reason is that climate phenomena develop spontaneously and in a way beyond our control.

This idea has recently been applied in economics. According to the supporters of the concept of chaos, there is no complete determinism in the economy, but there is rather a certain degree of chaos. As Lorenz explains, "What some chaos-minded economists are now proposing is that, as a dynamical system, the economy is chaotic, and business cycles, at irregular intervals, are inevitable. Meddling might even suppress rather than produce the cycles" (Lorenz 154). Government intervention will not help the economy much; it may only reduce some recessions.

As we can see, today there are different definitions of what Chaos theory is. Certainly, the original intention of its founder was to explain the *visible* lack of regularity in the weather phenomena. Gradually, however, some scientists took it too literally and began to conceive of all systems as having some degree of chaos; or more precisely, all systems tend to move toward chaotic behavior - and this is not just an appearance, but the very nature of systems themselves.

We now turn to another Chaos theory expert, Leonard Smith. In his *Brief Introduction to Chaos Theory* (2007), he briefly explains the main ideas of this Theory, as well as some examples. He comments the following about the beginning of this theory: "In the three-year period between 1963 and 1965, three independent papers appeared (by Lorenz, by Moore and Spiegel, and by Hénon and Heiles), each using digital computers to introduce what would be called 'chaotic dynamics' " (Smith 73). Similar developments appeared in Japan and the USSR. We have no reason to think that any of these scholars plagiarized from the others;

rather, they arrived at similar ideas because of developments in meteorology and mathematics.

The lack of explanation of some phenomena has always caught the attention of great scientists, but they preferred to think that they had made a mistake in their calculations. This situation took place with Newton: "Newton was well aware of the difficulties nonlinearities posed for determining the ultimate stability of only three celestial bodies, and suggested that insuring the stability of the solar system was a task for God" (Smith 73). After all, after the Second World War, another approach was taken - recognizing that there is something inexplicable in certain phenomena and that it is difficult to predict them with absolute certainty.

According to Smith, Chaos theory can better explain some phenomena, and for this purpose we introduce the very concept of "chaos." But the idea of chaos is rather instrumental: "Chaos is important, in part, because it helps us to cope with unstable systems by improving our ability to describe, to understand, perhaps even to forecast them. Indeed, one of the myths of chaos we will debunk is that chaos makes forecasting a useless task" (Smith 1-2). Right from the start, he makes it clear that chaos is not an absolute property; it is not in the very nature of things, as some specialists try to point out.

After this remark, Leonard Smith explains that the theory of chaos is applied in some scientific disciplines that study systems prone to irregularity and uncertainty: "The study of chaos is common in applied sciences like astronomy, meteorology, population biology, and economics" (Smith 3). We have already addressed the problem of inaccurate weather forecasts. Here we can also add the development of various epidemics in the history of mankind. Smith himself does not refer to this fact, but we have a very recent example with the development of Covid-19. As we well remember, at the beginning, the specialists claimed that the virus would remain isolated in China and the surrounding countries and that it would be very difficult for it to spread due to the severe measures taken in the USA and Europe. We all remember the "flatten the curve" concept, which was supposed to lead to a sharp decrease in cases, and after two months to stop the development of the epidemic entirely. By staying at home and avoiding social contacts, we had to actually stop the virus from spreading and it had to be over quickly.

Even then, some experts warned that it was a virus that we are dealing with, and there was no way to control it with such measures - quarantine works only at a local level with a small population of people; moreover, this virus had a tendency to infect asymptomatically, making it even more difficult to control. Then we had to listen to those sober voices who did not underestimate the danger of the virus, but rather wanted to say that these measures would be futile because the behavior of a virus is not completely predictable. What happened in the next two years was even more bizarre- we saw the virus go through different variants, some more dangerous and some less deadly. In all these situations, we have seen how the control exercised by the institutions does not actually work. Yes, in the very beginning, there may have been such control, and it had an effect; but it was impossible to get all the people to stay at home for months, which would completely collapse our economy and immunity. It is entirely believable that even with such staying at home for months, the virus would have continued its spread.

But the end of the pandemic also came unexpectedly, if we recall this carefully. In late 2021, we were alerted that a new variant called "omicron" had appeared. Again, there were attempts to instill fear in the people and to lock them up. Shortly after, it became clear that the omicron variant was not a serious threat to us, and the measures were almost lifted. At that moment, a huge number of people got infected with this variant (thank God, without dangerous consequences for their health), and in the fall of 2022 the end of pandemic was officially announced by the WHO!

All this development of the pandemic clearly shows that the spread of viruses is difficult to plan and control. It is true that recent attempts to contain Ebola have been successful - but this is also due to the nature of the virus, which is extremely deadly, therefore spreading more slowly. Measures should be planned according to the nature of the virus; we cannot apply the same measures to both influenza and Ebola. In any case, the coronavirus has made it clear that there are still things out of our control. Yes, we can work to effectively prevent future infections; we can strengthen the health system; we can train people how to act in the event of a new pandemic. But all these measures will not be effective with absolute certainty because there are many factors and variables that we do not know; and we probably will not know - by the time we knew more about the coronavirus, the pandemic was already over.

Now we turn again to our description of Chaos theory. The great problem of all science, says Leonard Smith, is that there is too much background noise, or "noise," in the world. This data comes in and we have no way of analyzing it because we do not have the time and funds for it. It is like sitting down for a coffee in the center of a big city and trying to remember everything that happens - voices, movements, nature, music, wind, etc. That is why Smith declares the following: "Noise gives rise to observational uncertainty, chaos helps us to understand how small uncertainties can become large uncertainties, once we have a model for the noise" (Smith 4).

We have no way of knowing exactly which data to target; of course, scientists have expertise in their field and target certain data, but in doing so they run the risk of missing other data that is also significant. This is explained as follows: "When our models are chaotic then small changes in our observations can have large impacts on the quality of our foresight" (Smith 15). If we miss any small changes, then we may not be able to predict the consequences of the phenomenon we are observing. Any small difference can be decisive. But how do we find out exactly which difference is important, and which one will lead to significant consequences? This is a question that cannot be answered clearly and precisely today.

Leonard Smith arrives at a more precise definition of chaotic systems. According to his summary, they are "nonlinear, they are deterministic, and they are unstable in that they display sensitivity to initial conditions" (Smith 16). The second adjective here is a little surprising - that they are deterministic, i.e., still subject to regulation by regularities (natural laws). He subscribes to Edward Lorenz's understanding that these systems are not themselves chaotic.

All this means that there is some possibility of predicting the behavior of "chaotic" systems. That is why Smith explains the following: "One of the most pervasive myths about chaotic systems is that they are impossible to predict. To expose the fallacy of this myth, we must understand how uncertainty in a forecast grows as we predict further and further into the future" (Smith 22). Small changes will lead to larger consequences, leading to even larger deviations from the original forecast. But, according to Smith, this does not make the systems in question absolutely unpredictable!

Yet, if there is any unpredictability, it concerns the more distant future. As Leonard Smith puts it, "Chaos is defined in the long run. Uniform exponential growth of uncertainty is found only in the simplest chaotic systems. Indeed, uniform growth is rare among chaotic systems which usually display only effective-exponential growth" (Smith 93). Therefore, it is difficult to predict which change will lead to what - some changes lead to small consequences, and other changes to much more significant consequences, which is clearly visible in the weather forecast. That is why it is correct to talk about probabilities regarding the weather next week. An interesting example is New Zealand: "In New Zealand, where severe weather is rather common, the Meteorological Service regularly makes useful probabilistic statements on their website - statements like 'two chances in five.' This adds significant value to the description of a likely event" (Smith 143).

As we already know, today such type of predictions are made more often, although not by popular TV channels. Today, we can follow the forecasts of many meteorologists on social networks, and they usually issue warnings of severe weather events with a certain percentage of probability. This seems like the better option when making such predictions. The bad thing is that people are used to being told everything clearly and precisely - tomorrow it will either rain or not - there is no middle option. But it is a fact that Chaos theory deals with probabilities, not with specific properties.

It is also important to say that meteorologists deal with patterns. These models show what would happen if a given change occurred. They try to predict the future consequences of these changes. That is why today's weather forecast talks about models - according to this model, according to that model... But we must realize that the model is not reality. Reality is always different from the model precisely because we have no way of knowing all the variables in the equation. We have no way of knowing which of these variables will change exactly how. Therefore, all models regarding weather, climate, the universe, as well as epidemics should be viewed with a little more doubt. They cannot be completely exact, but that is not their purpose either. The truth is that we should be familiar with different models and thus we will have a more comprehensive view of a given phenomenon.

Another issue here is that modeling is performed by computers and therefore cannot work with chaos or lack of regularity. Computers stay away from chaos: "The computer trajectory has become digitally periodic, regardless of what the mathematical system would have done. And so it is for all digital computers. Computers cannot do chaos" (Smith 108). Even the random numbers we see sometimes are the result of programming and are not truly random numbers. This means that chaotic systems are best studied by humans rather than computers.

In mathematics, one can also speak of chaos, but this has a specific meaning. The mathematical system is not physical, i.e., it is not real (sensible). As Leonard Smith states, "The definition of mathematical chaos can only be applied to mathematical systems, so we cannot begin to prove a physical system is chaotic, or periodic for that matter" (Smith 157). That is why it is essential to distinguish the real from the mathematical, from the model.

The conclusion of Smith is not a suprirse: "Chaos has provided much new cloth for our study of the world, without providing any perfect models or ultimate solutions" (Smith 161). We should see chaos as a data deficit as well as a symbol of the limitations of our intellect. As we said, we cannot store and research data on absolutely everything; science works selectively, that is why sometimes we cannot notice the small deviations.

All this seems quite normal - both Smith and Edward Lorenz believe that the world is still governed by regularities, by natural laws. However, under the guise of this false belief are several statements that are frightening:

1. Even if there are regularities in the world, we cannot discover them all.

2. Closed systems tend toward chaos, toward disorder, lack of predictability.

3. Science can work well with mathematical models, but not with real phenomena.

Chaos seems to be everywhere; this notion appears wherever there are any breakouts. And what if evolutionists started using it too? Seeing that their "gradual evolution" hypothesis does not work, they could safely turn to chaos and say this: sometimes evolution makes leaps in an irrational way that contains elements of chaos. Nothing prevents them from coming up with such a statement - and then it will be written in the textbooks, because there will be no one to seriously oppose them! And just as until recently Americans were taught that man descended from the ape (as we have seen, this is exactly what Darwin claimed, and today it has been disproved). Likewise, in the coming decades they will be taught in school that evolution proceeds by "chaotic jumps" not easy to plan or explain.

The introduction of chaos into science means a lack of trust in the rational. But this process has another aspect - it can be well used by atheists, who already see quite a few clues leading to the One Mighty Creator of our world. Hence, instead of acknowledging the obvious - that God is real - they will simply replace it with the concept of chaos. If we do not understand something, then chaos is to blame! If something does not go as we predict it, then chaos is to blame! If evolutionism does not observe what it theorizes and hypothesizes, then chaos is to blame! There is nothing else to be - chaos is universal! And so, just as the ancient Greeks thought that the beginning of the world was laid in Water, Air or Fire, so some scientists today lay it in Chaos, in the absence of order.

Chaos theory itself does not presuppose the existence of chaos as a separate entity. The nature of things is not chaotic, at least according to Lorentz. But this theory can be abused. Can any limits be placed on its usability? Can we know under what conditions this theory will not be true, it will not work in practice?

The problem is that in reality there is no difference between "potential predictability" and "actual predictability." Today, we cannot predict anything, which is a huge problem; any explanation that this is due to minimal changes that arise from chaos does not look good. As we have already shown, we can quite easily "verify" the theory of evolution despite all its weaknesses. We will say that the failure of some predictions about evolution is due to elements of chaos, and that is it.

Of course, we cannot claim that natural laws are absolutely dominant in our world. The very presence of One Mighty Power like God already proves that the same thing cannot always happen. God can work miracles - and in the case of Christ, we see just that. But God is above the laws of nature, and in some cases He can intervene.

5.3 Conclusion

In this chapter, we aim to demonstrate that the relationship between science and religion is far from hostile. There is no "war" between these two spheres. It is naïve to say that science and religion are eternal adversaries. On the contrary, religion can provide essential ideas and explanations of the world for science to use. Religion need not oppose everything that comes from science. This can be easily understood by turning to the unity of man in body, soul and spirit. We are one and cannot be divided into mind and heart, body and soul. Similarly, it is not correct to oppose science to religion because both spheres combine reason and faith. Scientists also believe in something, but in their own way. They have their beliefs. Sometimes they are materialistic and nothing can make them change their worldview. Sometimes they change with time and realize that there is some truth in Christianity. But today, militant atheists like Richard Dawkins are fewer than before.

As we see nowadays, genetics and astronomy point to the reality of One Source of all that exists, and more specifically of life. However, atheists today are prone to ignoring these facts by emphasizing the irrationality of the world. The world itself is irrational, chaotic, full of spontaneous phenomena. Although Chaos Theory was not created with the aim of justifying some chaotic nature of things, it can still be used for this purpose - to deny the rationality of the world, and with it, the possibility of reaching God in a reasonable way. In this way, we also deny the Logos as a universal and accessible law for every reason - because where there is only irrationality, there can be no Logos! The Logos is incompatible with the irrational.

Now we will move on to a "theory" that denies not only rationality but even the very nature of the world. This is what we call de-naturalziation and it is time now to expose it from philosophical perspective.

Chapter VI: The De-naturalization of the world

Today, we often see people talking about the influence of culture on us. Humans are seen primarily as natural (biological) and cultural beings. The difference between humans and animals is that humans can create things that we call products of culture (including art and science, for example). Culture is important to us because it decisively distances us from animals and shows the gigantic difference between us and them.

The behavior of a baby is a little reminiscent of the behavior of a domestic dog - the baby crawls, licks, reacts mostly emotionally, does not express itself in words, likes to sit close to its parents (like a dog sits next to its owners). But with time, the baby develops physically and mentally and starts to speak; the baby masters different manners and becomes more independent. Here the baby already shows that it has nothing to do with animals, and when it becomes a mature individual, it can only create culture and reflect on it - something that animals are incapable of.

Nonetheless, in trying to show how different we are from higher mammals, modern social science has gone too far. It began to deny part of our biological essence, of what we call nature. This is the trend we call constructivism. However, it is actually a mixture of many different tendencies and attitudes. We will demonstrate that constructivism makes some sense as it relates to, for example, the educational process; but it cannot explain the gender differences in humans, and most importantly, it cannot eliminate them. To this current, we will oppose essentialism as the current according to which people and things have a stable, unchanging nature.

6.1 Constructivism- a simple idea that turned radical

Summary:

We will turn to the foundations of social constructivism. We will show that initially it used to have some well-elaborated concepts at is core. Later it was formulated in a more radical form that we know today- radical constructivism.

We have already mentioned the Sophists, and particularly Protagoras, who believes that human norms are primarily the work of convention, of agreement between people. Thus it turns out that categories such as good and evil, beautiful and ugly, true and false, are human constructions. Of course, today's constructivists are a long way from Protagoras, who never doubted the real existence of gender differences. But constructivism has its basis in these ideas denying the objective nature of things.

We should note that Protagoras' purpose was not so much to prove *solipsism* or some kind of subjectivism according to which "everything is as I think it is." Protagoras rather had a political purpose - to show that the current state of the classes in Athenian society was the result of convention, not a decision of the gods or pure nature. And Protagoras is right - the fact that certain citizens of Athens are more noble than others has nothing to do with nature, but with other qualities they have.

How, then, do we arrive at the present situation, where human nature is almost entirely denied? Today we see how the nature of things is rejected and social constructivism is offered as a theory to explain the world. Every single entity is a "human construct." Gender, nationality, and even race are human inventions! They do not exist objectively, according to the proponents of this process.

This is why we can assert that today the world is "de-naturalized." These thinkers are eager to make us believe nothing is natural in this world and everything can be changed according to our will and desire. We can call this phenomenon *de-naturalization*, since it does not grasp the world as an objective reality, as governed by laws of nature.

The conception of gender as a "social construct" (as expressed by the radical feminist Judith Lorber) will be analyzed in what follows. In her opinion, we are not born men or women; society itself perceives us as men or women and this is the only objective factor that makes us such. This means that nature has nothing to say here, and only the perception of others is important.

Before that, however, we will turn to the beginnings of constructivism. Where does it come from? What is its purpose? Why did it appear?

This trend in the social sciences emerged in the 1960s. Its founders were sociologists who aimed to study how society works and who creates the norms that we now call social norms and rules. At its inception, this current did not deal at all with questions such as the nature of the nation or of gender. Here we will refer to the work of Peter Berger and Thomas Luckmann, who published their work *The Social Construction of Reality*.

In general, the aim of these two sociologists is to show that we do not know reality immediately and individually. We do this within some community or society itself. For example, we live with people all the time and, therefore absorb their values. Through their view of things, we understand how to look at the world. Of course, this occurs in an individual way, since even people raised by the same parents may have different values, but the general principle is one and infallible - we learn in a community, in a group. Therefore, as Berger and Luckmann put it, "In primary socialization, then, the individual's first world is constructed" (Berger, Luckmann 155).

There is much truth in this theory - indeed, we cannot live outside of society, and in that case we will not be quite like humans (if we are isolated, we have no language, we do not learn, we do not communicate). But we must mention that the theory of Berger and Luckmann follows the traditional German science division of the world into the realm of nature and the realm of values. Humans cannot invent nature, but they create values; and values exist for people. Then, we know the physical world through science, but we learn values only through our community.

The way we absorb external reality is called *internalization*. Then the objective becomes subjective, it becomes part of our thinking and behavior. Our identity appears and is strengthened in this process: "Identity then is highly profiled in the sense of representing fully the objective reality within which it is located... In such a society identities are easily recognizable, objectively and subjectively. Everybody knows who everybody else is and who he is himself" (Berger, Luckmann 184).

Obviously, we also have a role to play in our personal development. We are not just a *tabula rasa*, or a whiteboard on which experience (in this case - others) write. We actively participate in the formation of our worldview! That is why there are different people, different characters, different value systems in the world. We cannot be the same. Realizing this, we understand that identity is not something absolute, i.e., people can be different: "A society in which discrepant worlds are generally available on a market basis entails specific constellations of subjective reality and identity. There will be an increasingly general consciousness of the relativity of all worlds, including one's own" (Berger, Luckmann 192). According to these two sociologists, this is how the idea that there is not one world but many worlds emerges. The reader should remember this idea because it is crucial to understanding constructivism.

Biology should not be denied. According to Berger and Luckmann, our biology and culture are intertwined. They introduce the notion of dialectic here as follows: "It is possible to speak of a dialectic between nature and society... Externally, it is a dialectic between the individual animal and the social world. Internally, it is a dialectic between the individual's biological substratum and his socially produced identity" (Berger, Luckmann 201). We cannot wholly escape our biology, our nature. Culture is not everything in our society. These words should be considered by anyone who is eager to know more about constructivism. What goes under the label of constructivism today is a very extreme form of this philosophical attitude.

The identity of each of us is formed through society - we understand who we are through our parents, siblings, friends, teachers. But we are also individuals, i.e., organisms. This is how we distinguish ourselves from other individuals - while we can identify with them through ethnic, national, religious affiliation, we cannot do so in a physical sense. Therefore, both sociologists say the following: "In the fully socialized individual there is a continuing internal dialectic between identity and its biological substratum. The individual continues to experience himself as an organism, apart from and sometimes set against the socially derived objectifications of himself" (Berger, Luckmann 203). That is why we should not think that constructivism is based on the idea that we ourselves create reality - the truth is that we are the ones who give meaning to reality.

However, objective reality itself is something other than us. That is why we should be careful about the following thesis: "Man is biologically predestined to construct and to inhabit a world with others. This world becomes for him the dominant and definite reality. Its limits are set by nature, but, once constructed, this world acts back upon nature" (Berger, Luckmann 204).

All this does not mean that we ourselves create nature; we are not nature itself. We are natural and cultural beings. At some point, however, we begin to control nature and dominate according to our needs and interests. At no point, however, do Berger and Luckmann state that nature is a social construct - surely they would laugh hard at anyone who says it!

Here we want to draw attention to another issue that the two authors touch on. At the very beginning of our lives, we acquire an identity through our parents and loved ones. But we do not choose anything here - this identity is formed through contact with them! This is called primary socialization. We have no influence over this process. Primary socialization is normal process because we are "social animals" (we cannot live in complete isolation). Here we do not choose anything: "In primary socialization there is no problem of identification... Society presents the candidate for socialization with a predefined set of significant others, whom he must accept as such with no possibility of opting for another arrangement" (Berger, Luckmann 154).

Secondary socialization is already the stage when we begin to develop our value system and see ourselves from afar; we distance ourselves (sometimes) from our parents and thus (to some extent) choose what we will be. But the conclusion of the two sociologists is this: we do not choose ourselves completely; our identity is the result of the influence of our family and the opportunities to acquire the identity that we see before us as we grow up. But a sudden change in identity is impossible - one retains much of what one has learned during primary socialization. Let the reader remember this conclusion well.

According to researchers Amna Saleem, Huma Kausar and Farah Deeba, social constructivism initially developed in the cognitive sphere—that is, it used to deal with matters of knowledge. According to them, "Constructivism is a theory about how people learn based on scientific observation. People create their understanding, it argues. When we learn anything new, we must reconcile it with our prior knowledge and experience" (Saleem, Kausar, Deeba 405-6). This stream is not concerned with human nature, but rather with learning.

As they explain, the Soviet scientist Lev Vygotsky introduced this concept in 1968. As they report, "Language and culture, according to Vygotsky, influence people's intellectual growth and perception of their environment. Language transmission results in learning concepts being interpreted and assimilated through experience and cultural context" (Saleem,

Kausar, Deeba 406). But all this does not mean that we "invent" the world; rather, we perceive it through our language. There are certain features of culture and language that make us see the world in one way rather than another.

This can be easily understood by comparing the ancient Greek worldview with the Christian worldview: the former sees the world as a collection of elements that are controlled by the Olympian gods. It is a world where immortality exists only in the form of the "island of the Blessed." In general, the question of the afterlife remains unsettled there, except in Plato and Pythagoras, who speak a little more about it. The heathen world is also a world of cruelty; a world where harsh behavior is considered valiant and moral.

On the other side is the Christian worldview. It sees the world as created by One God who loves all people. God is always with us and helps us. Our good deeds (to some degree) will bring us closer to the blessed life, to heaven. Moreover, love is exalted as a fundamental value. We see true manhood in the saints, not in the heroes of the *Iliad*.

Of course, philosophers like Plato and Seneca can partly be called Christians insofar as some of their ideas stand close to Christianity. And yet, they remain captive to the pagan understanding of the world. It is challenging for a person to break away from his culture, from the worldview of his civilization. That is why we say that our cultural environment strongly influences our worldview. The more Christian our environment, the more confident Christians we become; and vice versa - the more people around us deny Christianity, the more convinced atheists we become.

Constructivism can be used well in the classroom. Through it, the educational process goes more smoothly. Students can construct their lesson by themselves through different techniques, instead of just sitting and listening to their teacher: "Students, trainees, and others should develop their knowledge since their minds create new Knowledge and information.

Reasoning, accepted wisdom, and judgment are all involved. New concepts and ideas can't be grasped until they're linked to previous ones" (Saleem, Kausar, Deeba 407).

Over time, however, this academic current began to change. With the rise of liberalism and its propaganda comes the idea that each of us can do whatever we want with our lives. The logical consequence of this assumption is ethical nihilism (there is no good and evil, and everything is subjective) and the assumption that everyone chooses her/his own identity. In a word, "I am what I choose to be" - this is a position already formulated by the existentialists in France, but it is now reaching its final form (for Sartre and his partner, de Beauvoir, never have denied biological sex).

A great example of how constructivism is distorted by radical constructivists can be seen in an article by the lawyer Benjamin Gregg from 2021. He attacks the idea that there is an objective human nature by "proving" that there are no universal human rights. His position is expressed in a complete affirmation of positive law and a denial of natural law (i.e., of the Logos).

Gregg himself claims to offer a "political conception" of human rights. It is expressed as follows: "Political means to treat both human nature and human rights as social constructs... It involves multiple capacities: symbolic language, social norms (including human rights), and the science and technology that led to biotechnologies" (Gregg 315). Here we already see the concept of the social construct. Gregg does not mean at all what we have already seen with Berger. According to him, human rights are entirely based on human conventions, on "agreement" between people; there is no such thing as natural human rights. He opposes the idea that there can be anything primordial and eternal in human rights and freedom.

Here Gregg introduces the concept of "naturalistic understanding." However, this does not mean that he starts from the point of view of essentialism - quite the opposite. For him, "naturalistic" means something that relates to and explains only this world, only the phenomena we can see with our eyes here on earth. The reader would do well to remember that "naturalism" and "essentialism" are not the same thing. That is why Gregg is not on the side of essentialism. As he states, "A naturalistic understanding offers a basis for dealing productively with the abiding competition among different normative understandings and commitments that constitute the value-pluralism typical of complex modern, liberal democratic political communities" (Gregg 314-5). In short, there are different values and legal systems, so this understanding helps us understand that there is no one moral or legal system that stands above the rest.

Quite logically, this scholar of law questions the existence of a fixed, absolute human nature. According to him, our concept of human nature is constantly changing. That is why he asks the following question: "Might we humans construct the human nature to which we aspire by constructing the human rights we aspire to?" (Gregg 315). His answer is affirmative - not only can we, but we actually construct human nature ourselves!

Now, Gregg begins his attack on essentialism. He defines this metaphysical attitude as follows: "Many folk versions and religious accounts employ what I call 'human nature-essentialism.' It posits essential human traits purportedly as innate, invariant, universal, and unique" (Gregg 316). As he goes on, "human nature-essentialism identifies traits that express themselves in most individuals, traits unique to the species. Unique here refers to differences between human and non-human animals" (Gregg 317). These are qualities that only we can have - for example, a concept of good and evil, a sense of the future (we know how to plan), reflection on our actions. An animal can neither plan the future (it acts on instinct) nor think about what action is good and what action is bad.

Gregg admits that if we adhere to the essentialist understanding of human rights, then we will limit the activity of some scientific projects: "The notion of an intrinsically valuable human nature might entail that genetic engineering violates human rights—but only if one believes that engineering modifies what... should be inviolable to (almost) any technical modification" (Gregg 318). From a constructivist perspective, then, genetic engineering is acceptable since it modefiies something unfixed, and changeable. If human nature is unfixed, then we can attempt to change it, and it will still remain human nature! It is just that its content will be different.

It is hard to imagine a more absurd statement. How can we change human nature through engineering? Let us imagine an attempt to have a baby "programmed" from the mother's womb. It must be endowed with certain qualities; to have certain intellectual abilities; to be interested in given issues and avoid others; to have specific height, hair and eye color, and other physical data. Well, how can we say that we have changed human nature like this? What we have created is not nature. It is simply an artificial product, not even considering that such precise engineering is not possible (and unlikely ever to be achieved).

Moreover, if we assume that engineering can still be implemented in a perfect way, then what will this mean? Is the name "humans" proper for its products? Will they be fully human beings? The very intervention of programming means that these will not exactly be people. They will be predetermined, and will have certain qualities and data. To some extent, they will be like machines- everything that is purposefully programmed is a machine! Here we must sharply refute Gregg's statement - no, this will not change human nature at all; it will only lead to the appearance of robotic human beings, or better said, human-like beings!

The so-called political understanding of human rights is actually based on the idea of a "flexible" human nature that can be altered and changed (including through genetic engineering). In fact, if we accept such an anti-essentialist conception, we will morally (and therefore legally) justify genetic engineering! Therefore, this connection that we find in this article is not accidental. Who would think of both attacking the idea of innate human rights and defending genetic engineering? It is clear that this article was written for a purpose, and it is not difficult to guess what it is.

In support of our claim, Gregg states the following: "I develop an alternative to human nature-essentialism. It offers a general basis for the legal regulation of human genetic engineering. It works with a political notion of human nature and contains two propositions" (Gregg 318). The two propositions are anti-essentialist and pro-relativist. His first proposition reads: "Any given notion of human nature is something that is learned in particular cultures at particular times" (Gregg 318). The second proposition reads: "Political conception of human nature can guide some behavioral norming... human nature as social construct and political tool" (Gregg 319).

Here the first statement deserves more attention. Is it true that different cultures have different understandings of human nature? Let us take the simplest example - the ancient Greek understanding of man, and the modern, Western understanding. The ancient Greeks considered man a superior being who could control nature only to a certain extent. But the Greeks did not assert human nature changes, and what is human today will not be such tomorrow. It is no accident that today we can read the *Iliad* quite easily and understand what Homer wanted to tell us. The concepts of honor, glory, dignity, freedom have been the same. Yes, there is a slight difference in the way women and children are treated today. Our concept of freedom is broader than that of the Homeric Greeks, but this does not mean that the idea of man is totally different.

If we contrast the Greeks with the Christian culture, then we will see more differences. Indeed, Christianity accepts man as created and eternally related to God. This is a significant difference. And yet, the Christian understanding is better than the Greek one; we cannot say that the two are mutually interchangeable or they are equal! And this is exactly what Gregg is keen to tell us - that all views of man are equal and that none is better than others.

Moreover, *how we understand human nature has nothing to do with its objective existence*. Nature does not depend on us; we are not the ones who create it. Likewise, we can say that different understandings of the Solar System mean that there is no one Solar System. But this is not true - our knowledge has changed over the centuries.

However, this author claims the following: "Human nature so conceived is not a static essence with innate properties; it involves a dynamic relationship between biology and culture" (Gregg 320). This statement should show us that we are able to change human nature - not everything is biology, therefore it is possible for man to be changed. And why does he deny the inner, innate qualities? Isn't our intelligence something innate? Can we imagine a person without intellectual abilities? How can he prove his claim except by empty talk?

Here Gregg unexpectedly turns to evolutionism, saying the following: "Living things do not evolve to fit into pre-existing environments, but co-construct and coevolve with their environments, in the process changing the structure of ecosystems" (Gregg 320). Yes, according to Darwin, the individual develops together with his ecosystem, with the environment; but this is not absolutely the case. For Darwin, the environment is determining; it exists before the individual. Therefore, the individual must adapt to it. If the environment does not change, the individual will not change either.

Now, the mere existence of biological change (e.g., development, growth) does not mean nature itself is changing. In fact, this growth is part of our nature. Genetically speaking, we do not change significantly; our development is "programmed." That is why it is astonishing when a supporter of the "nothing lasts forever" theory relies on biology.

The idea of universal human rights, which derives from our fixed nature, gives researchers like Gregg no peace. According to him, this concept, on which the US Constitution is based, is wrong. Rights are not immutable; as our nature changes, so do our rights. He refers to the Universal Declaration of Human Rights and claims, "Most versions of human rights theory claim universal validity for themselves. As the normative foundation for human rights, some invoke one or the other notion of a universal human nature. A universal nature is an essential nature" (Gregg 321). According to him, there is no such thing as permanent human rights. Perhaps this author means that we must formulate new and new rights because "human nature changes." This view would also justify the so-called LGBT rights – since our nature is changing, it already includes LGBT people - so our legislation must reflect this change!

Here Gregg does not directly admit that this is his aim- to justify LGBT rights. Rather, he turns to genetic engineering: "A widely acceptable notion of human nature might allow political communities to characterize humans as a homogeneous group, because of evolution but also because of a cultural commitment to human rights." As he goes on, "That notion of human homogeneity offers a basis for the legal regulation of human genetic engineering along dimensions both biological and cultural" (Gregg 325).

This is the result of the view that our nature is not permanent and fixed. Therefore, it becomes easy to "prove" that LGBT people should have rights too. Thus, historical analogies are made with slaves or with women and children, who many years ago had no rights and used to have limited freedom. We can safely introduce new and new "rights" by "proving" that people today need them. LGBT rights are not even surprising anymore; more shocking is the idea of justifying genetic engineering. Why not "program" future children with the aim of "their good"? We can say that they also possess such rights - to be genetically modified and programmed!

Essentialism, as we can clearly see, is much more reasonable and closer to normality than constructivism. On the other hand, the second moves toward more and more extreme ideas - and we will now analyze these as they are described by Judith Lorber.

6.2 The anti-essentialism of Judith Lorber

Summary:

Lorber is a champion of radical feminism and the LGBT theory. She elaborates her form of radical constructivism, thereby claiming that our gender is the product of our own "self- identification." In spite of her radical ideas, Lorber at times admits that sex characteristics exist objectively. We will show some weak points of her conception and will analyze the motives standing behind Lorber's anti-essentialism.

Judith Lorber is a radical feminist who starts from Sigmund Freud and Karl Marx, like most of her colleagues. For her, gender is a "tool for enslaving" women. Radical feminists change the Marxist discourse, but its basis remains the same. For Marx, there is a class struggle in society - between the *proletariat* and the dominant class (capitalists). The latter find various ways to oppress the *proletariat* - through legislation, religion, and even through education (this is what Marx calls ideology). The workers must realize that the whole system of today must collapse in order for them to be free. Likewise, radical feminists blame all elements of our society for contributing to the "enslavement of women." For example, the family, the school, religion - they all make it so that women humbly accept their role as subordinate beings. For women to be free, they must carry out a "feminist revolution" - to overthrow all these elements, to give them up. Of course, the school should remain, but it should be subordinated to another order, to another ideology.

Freud's role in this is his emphasis on sexuality. For Freud, we must focus on this human phenomenon in order to understand people and society. Radical feminists, however, misuse this notion of Freud's. He never claimed that sexuality is a tool for submission. According to feminists, however, it turns out exactly like that - men completely dominate sexuality; for example, they "invented" marriage for their benefit, so that they have complete control over women. Hence, a free woman must reject not only marriage but also sexuality itself - at least as we have understood it so far!

Lorber is among the feminists who came to the radical idea that gender is a human invention. She gives examples of some "researchers" prior to her work who question the existence of gender. In short, for Lorber, gender is not something biological, but a purely human construct that aims to determine our place in society; and yet, the idea of gender is part of the "male agenda" to dominate women!

Admittedly, Lorber is not as extreme as some of her colleagues in the 2020s. Lorber does not dare to deny biological sex completely, nor to defend the "right of children" to "choose" their sex. This is how she introduces her thesis in her work *Paradoxes of Gender* (1994): "In this book, I offer a new paradigm of gender—gender as a social institution. Its focus is the analysis of gender as a social structure that has its origins in the development of human culture, not in biology or procreation" (Lorber 1). Thus, Lorber focuses rather on the role of gender as a "construction," as a social phenomenon that is the result of consent between people; or perhaps it is better to say, "a human invention."

According to Lorber's thesis, gender was created by men in order to dominate women, to enslave them: "In the radical feminist view, the sex-gender system of women's oppression is deliberate, not accidental, and pervades other social institutions—the family especially, and also the mass media and religion, which produce the justification for women's subordination" (Lorber 2). Here we can clearly see Marx's idea of the tools by which workers are enslaved - simply the word "workers" is replaced by "women."

Now, this feminist revolution will only take place when women realize that the concept of "gender" was invented by men. This is also the purpose of such kind of books- to educate innocent women. But as we shall see, this understanding is entirely based on constructivism taken to its extreme.

Lorber works with the concept of "deconstruction" introduced by the French postmodernists. It is a philosophical method that attempts to place the origin of any social phenomenon in the human imagination. Everything that exists in our world - even outside society - is the result of someone's invention. That is why Lorber states the following: "My politics is that of feminist deconstructionism, and my aim in this book is to challenge the validity, permanence, and necessity of gender. For that reason, I have not used the feminist 'we,' but refer to women in the third person" (Lorber 5). This deconstructionism should shed light on the origin of gender and prove that it does not exist in reality, but only in our minds. This claim sounds absurd, but we will criticize it later - let the reader just follow Lorber's train of thought for now.

Now, this radical feminist comes to her thesis, formulated in its purest form: "Gender is a human invention, like language, kinship, religion, and technology; like them, gender organizes human social life in culturally patterned ways. Gender organizes social relations in everyday life as well as in the major social structures" (Lorber 6). The first part of this statement is questionable, not to say nonsensical. However, the second part is true - gender is really important for our society. Let us see what this means.

We have already mentioned that, from birth, the baby is influenced by the surrounding people, the significant others. This is the process of socialization. The baby learns what it can do, what it cannot do, what is not good to do; but it also learns how to dress, what to play with, who to play with. The baby learns that one person is an uncle, another is a grandfather, a third is a grandmother, a fourth is a cousin, and so on. It gradually begins to distinguish relatives from family friends, and finally the concept of the "stranger who has nothing to do with my family" appears. From the very beginning, we perceive the world in a given order. For young children, this order is not as fixed as it is for us adults. The child enjoys a strong imagination and shows it often. The child frequently sees itself in a different role - for example, that of a grown man, rather than a child.

Our society is unable to function without this order. We all need to know our place in this society - its moral norms, division of labor, moral conduct, etc. Therefore, it is also true that gender plays its role - in every society men do certain things and women do other things. It does not matter whether these things are the same in all societies or not - the point is that *there is a division of tasks according to the gender* of the given individual. In most societies, men are warriors, which does not prevent women from being warriors in some smaller societies (for example, the legendary Amazons). But they are all familiar with their tasks and roles.

Here comes Lorber's most significant statement - if we play gender roles, then gender is something fictitious, made up! This is how she describes the appearance of gender in our lives: "Gender construction starts with assignment to a sex category on the basis of what the genitalia look like at birth. Then babies are dressed or adorned in a way that displays the category because parents don't want to be constantly asked whether their baby is a girl or a boy" (Lorber 14). Of course, this statement is a bit naive, because parents are often not interested in who will ask them what about their child; moreover, the sex of the baby is often known even before birth, and the parents themselves inform their relatives about it. Hence, the way the baby is dressed has nothing to do with the possible questions from other people. Rather, it is done in accordance with certain dress codes - boys should wear trousers, girls should wear dresses, etc.

As Lorber continues, "A sex category becomes a gender status through naming, dress, and the use of other gender markers. Once a child's gender is evident, others treat those in one gender differently from those in the other" (Lorber 14). The child begins to realize how important her or his gender is and how it differs from the other gender. It begins to identify itself in contrast to the opposite sex. We can say that boys often reinforce their gender identification by teasing girls who belong to the "other sex" or are "on the other side." Our gender identity is strengthened by the awareness of what we are not.

According to Lorber and other feminists, gender is a social institution, more specifically, a social status. It is something like the divide of rich-poor, educated-uneducated, native-immigrant, etc. Social status is permanent - once you have entered it, it is very difficult to get out.

It is true that gender is important in how we relate to other people and to ourselves. Gender is related to human reproduction, but not only that – it is related to love, to family. It is an essential element of our life. Even people who do not have a family feel the need to have one. We cannot imagine our society without gender division. Yes, in Plato (in the dialogue *Symposium*) we meet the idea of the androgynous man - once there were only androgynous people with the body of a man and a woman at the same time, but because of transgressions against the gods, these people were separated. That is why even today the two halves look for each other - this is the explanation of love given by Aristophanes (as described in the dialogue). However, this remains just a beautiful myth - in reality, there is no such thing as male-female (or androgynous). Whether we accept creationism or not, humans have been divided into two sexes since the beginning - and this is also accepted by evolutionism. That is right, this status is really permanent and extremely important. Gender is perhaps the most essential part of describing a person, followed by age, ethnicity or nationality. Only after that comes religion, physical data and intellectual qualities.

Here Lorber introduces the concept of gendering, i.e., the introduction of gender stereotypes from an early age. Everyone falls into these stereotypes about others and themselves, according to her. As she claims, "Western society's values legitimize gendering by claiming that it all comes from physiology—female and male procreative differences."

And now comes an interesting statement - Lorber admits that biological sex actually exists: "But gender and sex are not equivalent, and gender as a social construction does not flow automatically from genitalia and reproductive organs, the main physiological differences of females and males" (Lorber 17).

Most radical feminists today willfully ignore these words in order to go further - to deny biological sex altogether. According to these feminists, we can safely avoid giving a child gender definitions - therefore, it will be "gender neutral." Lorber herself elsewhere refers to the case of the baby John-Joan, in which case she (without realizing it) herself refutes her theory of gender. Lorber states the following: "The achievement of gender was most dramatically revealed in a case of an accidental transsexual- a baby boy whose penis was destroyed in the course of a botched circumcision when he was seven months old" (Lorber 22).

This was an experiment carried out by the sexologist John Money, according to whom it is possible for a person to construct a gender identity different from his biological sex. Baby John's parents were encouraged to call him Joan, to treat him like a girl. Thus, the child soon was given girly toys and had female friends. He dressed as a girl and accepted his gender role. But this is a hasty conclusion! Shortly after the publication of this book, baby Joan was tracked and it turned out that this is a man who rejected his female identity. A little later, it was found that this person commited suicide, and it is certainly due to this "trans trauma," as we can call it. Therefore, this example completely negates the concept of Lorber and other radical feminists that gender is solely a "social construction." The case with baby John/Joan demonstrates that gender is mainly biological.

Of course, we must bear in mind that Lorber does not deny biological sex, as we have already said; but still, we see a similar (not very daring) attempt in her. She probably would not have set this example with baby John if she had waited a little longer. This is actually the example that proves that gender reassignment does not change anything, it only confuses the human psyche and leads to immense trauma. Changing your gender is not like changing your ethnicity - a Mexican can easily feel like an American or even an Irishman if he wants to; but a man cannot feel like a woman after "gender reassignment surgery." This is a utopia and it is good that today we can prove its complete failure. It is strange that anyone could even treat gender reassignment as something real, as an operation that does not harm human health and leads to real gender reassignment.

Lorber's agenda can be seen in statements like the following: "Gender-neutrality resonates with Western concepts of achievement, in which individual talents, ambitions, strengths, and weaknesses constitute the only basis for work roles and leadership positions" (Lorber 297-8). She believes that the role of a woman is not very attractive. If a person does not present himself with his gender, if no one treats him according to his gender, then that person will have more prospects for progress. A democratic society should allow people not to identify with a particular gender, thinks this feminist.

This position is wrong for two reasons: first, gender neutrality should not be politically bound (according to Lorber, democracy requires such neutrality). And secondly, the facts show that today women can safely occupy any positions both in business and in administration. The fact that a woman is precisely a woman does not prevent her from being a businesswoman today or from becoming a soldier.

It is obvious, according to Lorber, that the differences between men and women, their status, income, education - all this is due to some scheme that exists in our mind. She does not accept the fact that differences in gender roles are due to biological differences. Men become soldiers because they are physically stronger; women become teachers and nurses because they are better at caring for people and have more empathy. Lorber and her fellow feminists are not prone to admitting this. That is why Lorber comes to an absurd proposal: "Perhaps the most drastic upset of current ways of thinking would occur if all the armed forces were half women and half men, including combat units. In many wars and revolutions, women have fought side by side with men, both openly and disguised as men" (Lorber 300).

Let us address that statement. It is true that women have always shown some fighting skills, especially during revolutions or guerrilla warfare. No one can deny that. But why are there more men than women in the military today? The reasons are several, and they are mainly biological - i.e., something that cannot be changed:

-men are physically stronger;

- men are more likely to participate in conflicts and show aggression;

-men have a stronger psyche (for example, they have no problem seeing blood);

-women rarely apply for positions in the army (this fact no longer depends on biology).

If Lorber wants the number of women in the military to be equal to men, then she should propose measures to make it so... women become men! There is no other way for women to be equal to men in the military, at least outside of wartime. Of course, during a war it is quite possible that many women will be mobilized - but this will be due to the shortage of men who died at the front.

The problem with the few women in the military is not due to discrimination but to biological factors. The same applies to other professions, such as astronautics, aviation, car racing. Women themselves have no desire to perform these professions.

Only in terms of politics is Lorber right. Yes, there should be more women in politics because they are also capable of making decisions and planning. And today this is already happening. Women in the US are increasingly active politically, and this is visible to the naked eye. Perhaps in the late 1980s it was not; perhaps it was a mistake not to have women in politics. Today, however, this mistake has been corrected and women can safely occupy positions in the government.

Can women hold the position of priests? According to Lorber, religion is a "tool to suppress" women. The Church only ordains men as priests. Thus women are "discriminated against." This feminist imagines that one day women will become priests. Here is what she states: "Suppose all the major religions allowed women to become priests, to rise in the religious hierarchy, and to interpret the Old and New Testaments, the Qur'an, the Bhaghavad Gita." Lorber dreams of something more - to change the very language of the sacred texts. The concept of God should be made "gender neutral," and religious leaders should be of both sexes: "What would happen if religions that now profess gender equality really gave women and men an equal chance to be leaders? If liturgies were completely gender-neutral? If 'God' were not 'the Lord,' 'our Father,' ... but 'the Leader,' 'our Parent,' 'Creator of the universe'?" (Lorber 301). Does Lorber have grounds for these suggestions?

Here we must separate two questions: the first is about the right of women to be priests, and the second is about the nature of God.

On the first point, we can say that the tradition is for men to stand at the higher levels of the church hierarchy. Women have the right to be nuns and to dedicate themselves to God; it is their way of approaching Him. Men, in turn, can be priests or be higher in the hierarchy. The Pope must exclusively be a man. This tradition comes from the fact that the apostles of Christ were only men. The women around Christ did not become apostles, although they also played their part. Here the Church strictly follows the tradition left to us by Christ. It also affects the role of the Pope - the first pope, as we know well from the Bible, was St. Peter. He is the stone on which the Church of Christ is built.

Can we conceive of women priests? Surely this is possible, but in a very extreme case - with a shortage of male priests. Certainly, women should have their place in the church hierarchy and their opinion should be respected. But there is no way to accept women in the role of pope or cardinals, or bishops - these roles are assigned to men according to Tradition.

The second point concerns how we describe and perceive God. Yes, it is true that God exists beyond the gender divide. God is neither male nor female in our sense of the word. Because God created us, we have no way of ascribing our qualities to Him except symbolically. Therefore, even if someone is irritated by the concept of Him when we talk about God, then that person can simply use the word "God." There is certainly no way to present God entirely in a "female form" like Her, because this understanding is quite far from Tradition and from the descriptions in the Bible. But whether we call God "He" or "She" does not change much our definition of God. Let each one call Him as he pleases, but without changing the definitions as they are recorded in the works of the great Fathers or in the Creed.

On the other hand, the idea of replacing the concept of God with "great parent" is absurd. The Creator is one thing, the parent is another. The parent does not create the child!

As we see, women have the right to their participation in religious affairs, but without going to extremes. We must adhere to the tradition, which is to give higher positions in the hierarchy only to men. That hardly changes things much. A woman today can become a theologian, can be a church superior, can help the Church, and no one can prevent her from this. But why should a woman be a priest? What would that change in her life?

The answer is that radical feminists are keen to eliminate religion from our lives. This will occur more easily when the tradition is broken. No more religious rules, no more canons of the Church- the logical consequence will be marginalization of the Church and the appearance of a "new Christianity" as a "free, individual religion." Then, less and less people will become believers, and the "moral ideal" of radical feminism will be realized- no more Christianity, no more priests to get involved in "women affairs."

So far, Lorber deals with the problem of discrimination and gendering. But she goes on to say that there are more than two genders when it comes to cultural norms in a given society. This is a third gender, which is not biological, but a purely social construction - men taking on the role of women, and vice versa. Lorber states the following: "Some societies have three genders—men, women, and berdaches or hijras or xaniths. Berdaches, hijras, and xaniths are biological males who behave, dress, work, and are treated in most respects as social women; they are therefore not men, nor are they female women" (Lorber 17). She explains what the first of these three concepts means: "The Native American berdache is an institutionalized cross-gendered role that legitimizes males doing women's work. The berdache can also be a sacred role, and if a boy's dreaming indicates a pull towards the berdache status, parents would not think of dissenting" (Lorber 90).

This is an example of a biological man - as Lorber admits - performing the social functions of a woman. But does that mean the man in question is a woman? Can this man marry another man, in that case? This is probably not the case. So, this type of person has nothing to do with either biological sex or sexual orientation.

There is no denying that such groups of people exist. Something similar in the past were the eunuchs who were the confidants of the sultan's wives in some Muslim countries, as well as in ancient Persia. But this does not automatically turn these people into persons of the other gender, or of some third gender. A third sex, at least in the biological sense, does not exist. There may be such a thing from a given point of view (for example, when we attempt to understand the role of berdache), but it is not an objective thing. Therefore, here too, we should rather talk about a third gender role, and not a third gender.

Yes, there are women who act like men and men who act like women (like behavior, speech, or attitudes toward other people). This may indicate some confusion or distortion. We will not go into the topic of transgender here, because it is very complicated. But Lorber argues that we can safely speak of a third gender; and nothing of the sort follows from her evidence.

She gives the example of women warriors who contributed to various wars in the past. As Lorber writes, "Joan of Arc said she donned armor not to pass as a man but to be beyond sexuality, beyond gender. She called herself pucelle, a maid, but socially, she was neither woman nor man. She was an 'ideal androgyne' " (Lorber 89). But what Joan of Arc thought she was has no bearing on the objective fact of her gender. She was a warrior woman; undoubtedly, as her contemporaries wrote, she was endowed with many warrior (masculine) qualities. But we cannot deny the fact that she was a woman just because she led the French army in several important battles in the 15th century. She called herself a "virgin" because she believed that God is on her side and that she actually dedicated herself to Him. If she had not been killed by the English, she might have become a nun; but who today would say that a nun is a man just because she lives in a convent? Here we cannot deny nature - the warrior woman is also a woman!

Lorber now turns to a familiar tactic - to confuse the concept of masculinity and femininity, and prove that they exist only in our minds. Instead of men and women, such feminists speak of masculinity and femininity. What makes us men and women? she asks. According to her, biological characteristics are not very significant in this aspect. Lorber writes that "Menstruation, lactation, and gestation are individual experiences of womanhood... but not determinants of the social categories 'female' or 'woman.' Similarly, 'men' are not always sperm-producers, and in fact, not all sperm producers are men" (Lorber 39).

The last statement is utter nonsense. Just because some men may have breast milk does not make them women; and just because some women have a lot of male hormones does not make them completely male. These exceptions only help us establish what the norm for masculinity and femininity is exactly.

Lorber herself again cites research that disproves her "gender as self-identification" theory. Here is what she writes: "Sociobiologists have argued that inexorable workings of the genes create markedly different male and female behavior." This is the state of affairs in science today. But here she disagrees with the results of these studies: "Sociobiological and biosocial research designs and interpretations of data have been extensively criticized as inadequate proof that biological sex alone produces gendered behavior" (Lorber 40). However, it is not clear from what position she can deny the fact that genetics, to some extent, determines our behavior. Lorber is not a specialist in genetics or in the natural sciences at all.

After all these failed proofs on her part, Lorber comes to her conclusion - a revolution is needed that will not only liberate women but also equalize the two sexes. This will be done by removing "gender stereotypes" and by allowing for the possibility that biological sex is different from cultural sex. But let the reader note: Lorber is still not talking about "the right to choose one's gender."

The great pain of this feminist is the supposed oppression of women: women have always been subordinated, even in revolutionary societies. She notes the following: "The French revolutionary government gave women, who fought in militias and in the army, some of the civil rights they had demanded, but not the right to vote or to be a member of any governing body. As the revolution became more repressive, women's societies were banned" (Lorber 260). Therefore, she believes that such a revolution must be carried out by women with precise and clear goals; a social revolution is not enough (and this is her criticism of Marx).

Lorber herself realizes that this new era will not represent an earthly paradise (unlike the vision of communism). People will still have problems, worries, emotions. Neither marriage nor the state will disappear. However, people will be different, and women will have more opportunities ahead of them: "Free of gender, race, and class inequality, what might we all be? Perhaps culturally identified women, men, heterosexuals, homosexuals, citizens of different countries, adherents of different religions, members of different occupations and professions" (Lorber 302). It will be a world with many different personalities, possibilities, identities. We can even say that in this world there will be no clear and fixed identity, but only talents for people to develop. How beautiful!

But all this is (non)science fiction. Identity is very important to personality. The latter is unthinkable without the former. We cannot develop without knowing who we are and what our place is in society as well as in the world.

Here we will leave aside the assumption that a person can choose their own sexual orientation or even gender. The problem with Lorber's concept is that it almost completely denies the role of nature and biology. It is true that she does not go to such extremes as today's feminists do.

The idea of radical feminists is to turn women into men, while at the same time women keep all their privileges (maternity leave, priority in all spheres, careful treatment of them). But why do women have to lose their femininity? Why should they lose their femininity just to have a higher income? Even the last statement has not been proven. It can be disputed, because in the 21st century women's wages have increased significantly, and more and more women are occupying important positions in business. And all this takes place without any "gender revolution" or "feminist revolution"!

6.3 In defense of nature

Summary:

The Bible shows clearly that God created the world as it is, and we should not attempt to modify it. To be creators is not our job. The feminist revolution, the LGBT revolution, genetic engineering- all these forms of onslaught on nature will do harm to man and the world as a whole.

After the shocking ideas of Judith Lorber and her fellow feminists, it is time to turn to common sense and logic. Let us see why they attack so fiercely the idea of the natural essence of man, and of nature in general.

As we have seen so far, the Logos is the universal law that governs the world. There are objective regularities in the world that do not depend on our will or desires. Things in the world exist as controlled by the Logos. Likewise, man exists only within the law that the Logos determined. Man has a stable, fixed natural essence. This essence is almost immutable - of course, as we have already shown, some of its elements may change in the course of history. But all this is taking place because we are getting closer to the end of history, therefore, we are getting closer to the truth, to God.

This is the basis of essentialism - or the concept that things have their essence. We have already shown the origins of essentialism in Plato and Aristotle. In their dispute with the Sophists, they prove that things have their essence; not everything in our world is a product of convention, of agreement between people. Not everything in our world is the work of human thought.

In our current analysis, we will first address the problem of "gender reassignment," as radical feminists and LGBT activists call it. Then we will move on to the more serious problem - that of the rejection of nature and the attempt to describe the world as a product of our imagination.

The Bible undoubtedly shows that there is a natural difference between men and women. There is no way to blur or eliminate this line of separation between the two sexes. It exists whether we want it to or not. Yes, there are men who are "more feminine" and women who are "more masculine," but that does not negate the fact that this line is real.

In the book of Deuteronomy we read the following passage regarding travesties:

> A woman must not wear men's clothing,
>
> nor a man wear women's clothing, for
>
> the Lord your God detests anyone who
>
> does this. (Deut. 22:5)

This prohibition refers to clothing, but we can also apply it to "changing one's gender" - something that God does not like and does not recommend. Elsewhere, in the book of Leviticus, we see the prohibition of homosexual practices:

> 'If a man lies with a man as one lies
>
> with a woman, both of them have done
>
> what is detestable. They must be put to
>
> death; their blood will be on their own
>
> heads.' (Levit. 20:13)

The reason for this severe punishment was not mere cruelty; this is about the violation of the natural laws on which our morality is based. Homosexuality is denied because it is against nature. It is evil to go against nature because it will destroy our world.

The need for men and women to live together is repeated in many places in the Bible. God has decided that a man needs company - in short, a family. Two men are unable to start a family. That is why a woman is necessary - she is not something superfluous, nor should she be seen as inferior to a man. Proof of this is a scene where the Pharisees ask Christ what he thinks about divorce. He replies that divorce is against the nature of things because God intended that man and woman should always be together:

> "Haven't you read," he replied, "that at
>
> the beginning the Creator 'made them
>
> male and female,'
>
> and said, 'For this reason a man will
>
> leave his father and mother and be
>
> united to his wife, and the two will
>
> become one flesh'?
>
> So they are no longer two, but one.
>
> Therefore what God has joined together,
>
> let man not separate." (Mat. 19:4-6)

These words demonstrate that man and woman complement each other and this should not be changed. But we can also take them like this: the border between man and woman can be overcome only through their mutual love. Thus they become one being - but it is not androgynous! If a woman wants to be equal to a man, she must enter into a marriage relationship and thus ensure this unity of the sexes. But there is no way for a woman to become a man, nor for a man to become a woman!

Here we also come to a passage that is frequently quoted by feminists, which they say insults women and describes them as "lower creatures." In fact, this passage from St. Paul affirms the natural boundary between man and woman and shows the importance of fulfilling our roles according to God's commandments. Here is what we read in the First Epistle to the Corinthians:

> As in all the congregations of the
>
> saints, women should remain silent in
>
> the churches. They are not allowed to
>
> speak, but must be in submission, as
>
> the Law says.
>
> If they want to inquire about something,
>
> they should ask their own husbands at
>
> home; for it is disgraceful for a woman
>
> to speak in the church. (1 Corinth 14:34-5)

This is not to say that woman has no opinion at all; but the wife must listen to her husband in matters of religion. It is not true that these words degrade women! It is a fact that women are more emotional in the realm of faith; they believe and feel more than analyze. Therefore, the man's opinion is critical here. But the more significant conclusion we can draw from this passage is that men and women should stick to their nature and natural roles. It is these roles that, according to Lorber, were once "invented" by someone.

We could add many more quotes about the nature of the two sexes. In all of them we find the fact that both sexes exist according to the laws of nature. There is no such thing as "I can define myself sexually." Gender, unlike religious belief, cannot be "self-determined." There are other things we can choose - where to live, what church to attend, what profession to choose. However, gender cannot be *chosen*, because it is a *given*.

Who needs this attack on nature? How does it support modern liberals and feminists?

We can assume that all this is the result of the development of modern (left) liberalism. Marxism's ideas of workers' revolution and universal equality are utopian today. There is no need for such a revolution because workers in the US live in good enough conditions. Therefore, the left camp must find other causes to work on and make a noise.

However, it cannot be denied that some capital and businesses are behind these ideas. There is a lot of money behind the idea of "gender reassignment" - these are doctors and medical institutes who will gain a lot from such "operations." These are psychologists, psychiatrists, as well as grantees of LGBT promotion programs. All of them will gain some financial benefits.

This hypothesis cannot be fully confirmed, at least for now. It is clear that someone is behind all this propaganda, but their goals are not entirely clear. It is possible that this is a more serious plan - a plan to destroy the foundations of our society, which will simply disintegrate. Something else will be created in its place, according to the rules the masterminds will set. One thing is clear - moving in this direction will not bring us anything good, so we must react quickly and powerfully!

But it is not only moral degradation that is the danger we see in the near future. Genetic engineering, which some want to apply to the human species, is such a threat.

In the case of genetic engineering, it is extremely important to define what is nature and what is not nature. Engineering, by its very definition, is an act of modification, of changing something. How is a living thing modified? Such actions have already been realized, and since the time of Sparta. This type of engineering was done by killing the malformed babies, thus the Spartans thought they would have a healthier future generation (healthy babies will become parents that would beget healthy and strong children). However, this was only a partial form of eugenics that does not threaten the entire human race.

Our natural state derives from biological factors that can only be purposefully changed by human intelligence. These are factors that are a kind of compulsion over us. Nature is what is forced upon us from "outside," by an "agency" that exists beyond the limits of human possibility. Nature opposes what we always want, desire and strive for.

We are created in such and such a way; we appear in the world in such and such a way - this is our nature. Any human intervention in the way we are conceived or come into being can be called unnatural.

Here comes the question: should we ban genetic engineering altogether? What if we can cure some dangerous diseases by employing genetic engineering? For example, by eliminating certain genes even before birth, we can prevent certain diseases.

This is a trap. What seems easy is usually associated with some kind of loss and will eventually make our lives more difficult. By gaining "security," we will lose our connection with nature. If we allow genetic engineering to take place for some reason, we will no longer be able to stop it! And this is exactly the goal - we ourselves ask for this type of activity to be implemented in our lives, because that way our lives will be "easier." Fewer diseases; longer life; less aggression - and all this will happen through genetic engineering! Can you imagine how beautiful the world will be!

The entry of technology into our lives will have its effect. The opposition between nature and technology will become stronger and will lead to negative results. In one way or another, nature will try to compensate for what we have changed in it. Despite our enormous scientific progress, we cannot cope today with some simple diseases such as malaria and tuberculosis. Moreover, trying to eliminate some diseases, others appear. Oncological diseases, mental diseases are increasing even though we live "better" today. It is the result of our attempt to control nature. Therefore, it is highly unlikely that genetic engineering will help us make our life better- perhaps the opposite will take place- more problems instead of more solutions.

6.4 Conclusion

As we can see, the attacks on essentialism come from different directions. However, the ultimate goal is one - to build a new world that will supposedly be better for all of us. This is a goal that is very reminiscent of communism and its ideal of a utopian world where we will all be equal and happy.

Social constructionism in itself is not harmful to society. Insofar as it deals with matters such as learning or education, it explains some processes well. But when we apply it to purely biological, natural concepts such as sex, then it already becomes an absurdity. Trying to deny nature here leads to the absurd idea that we can choose our own gender and that gender characteristics are actually something that exists only in the human mind. As we have shown, this position has nothing to do with science, and experience itself disproves it - even the evidence that Lorber herself gives denies her anti-essentialism.

The other strand, the technological strand in this quest to deny nature is today called transhumanism. We will not deal directly with this current, but we will take it upon ourselves to see what the dangers of the introduction of artificial intelligence are. If we can reject the objective reality of gender, why not repudiate the concept of man in general as well?

Transhumanism and the development of artificial intelligence follow the path already walked

by radical feminists and LGBT propagandists.

Chapter VII: A Human-made Logos

Our analysis of the universal and omnipresent Logos cannot be complete without addressing the problem: Are we the only rational beings? Could there be others in this universe?

No, that is not the alien life problem. Here we will talk about artificial intelligence, which is developing more and more seriously recently. What is his role? What is the part of technology in our lives? Can they replace man? Can man, in turn, be transformed into technology, into a robot?

7.1 An introduction to the moral dimensions of AI

Summary:

This is a short overview of the history of AI and the way sci-fi depicts it, with some examples of what is AI and what is robot, or android, according to sci-fi writers.

Artificial intelligence is a product of our quest to create a machine that can work with information. It has been a quest that goes back at least 350 years, since Blaise Pascal first attempted to create such a machine in France. The original idea was to create a machine to help us calculate. This is how calculators were born, and after them, computers.

In the early 1990s, it was still hard to even imagine that people would have computers in their homes en masse. A little later, however, this became a fact, and the majority of people had access to the Internet. At the beginning of the 21st century, it seemed improbable that computers would be replaced by tiny phones that could take pictures, surf the Internet, and handle data. But today, half of the world's population possesses mobile devices or computers.

Artificial intelligence appeared in connection with the development of computer technology. This kind of intelligence is capable of imitating the activity of the human brain - it is able to calculate, analyze, give an opinion on certain issues. Today, work is being done to make this intelligence have access to sensory data through sensory devices. Thus, we are gradually creating an intelligence that can collect sensory data and analyze it on its own!

Moreover, today AI is already being developed to give its opinion on abstract questions. This was considered impossible only half a century ago - back then we thought that computers only dealt with specific, practical tasks. Today, however, we can enter into a dialogue with AI about questions such as the meaning of life, freedom, morality, etc.

AI is practically applied in several fields today - automatic means of transport (cars and drones), services (deliveries, serving in hotels), medicine (as an assistant in diagnostics), military affairs (autonomous weapons, for example drones). However, can we imagine the end of this whole process? What else awaits us here? Are there limits to all this?

It is important to clarify that AI is not the same as computer programs. These are two different levels of complexity. The programs have a precisely established algorithm. The program cannot go beyond its original intent. It has certain limits and operates within those limits. At the same time, AI does not have well-defined parameters; yes, it is a collection of different programs, but it has the freedom to go outside of them as long as it access enough external data. AI is more of a process than a device. Unlike a computer, you can never be completely sure how the AI will answer your question.

Another difference is AI shows its own behavior. A computer has no behavior. The computer always acts the same way. However, the AI is capable of making decisions and changing them! For this purpose, it acquires certain data. The more data we provide, the more confident the AI will be in its decisions. The plan of scientists today is to create an autonomous AI that is able to collect data on its own, process it, and make decisions.

Here the reader may object that the AI is actually a pure robot. And it is true - even 100 years ago, science fiction writers presented humanoid machines that performed human-specific activities. After the Second World War, authors such as Asimov and Clark, in particular, took up this topic, describing the existence and behavior of robots in a wonderful way. Therefore, we can say that the history of robotics is also history of artificial intelligence.

Science fiction writers are the first theorists of the philosophy of artificial intelligence. They are the first to ask a number of moral questions. Here we will take Isaac Asimov as an example, who dedicated many of his works precisely to the interaction between humans and robots.

Isaac Asimov was a versatile talent who showed himself as a specialist in the fields of physics, biology, chemistry, and at the same time a very productive science fiction writer. In his short stories, as well as in the story "I, the Robot," he describes a future world in which robots have a significant role in human activity. These robots not only help us but also live with us. According to Asimov, the beginning of robotics will be set at the end of the 20th century, and in the middle of the 21st century, robots will coexist with people en masse. Robots will thus replace the appliances we all have at home today.

Because of the enormous capabilities of robots, Asimov proposed the creation of a special Code. It should be implemented in every robot, without exception. This Code includes three basic laws (as Asimov calls them). In short, these laws mean that a robot must always obey a human unless it results in harming a human (i.e., a robot shall not kill); a robot must always protect and preserve itself, unless it conflicts with the first law and if it results in injury to a human.

Here, Asimov already foresaw a serious moral dilemma: what happens to a robot that is ordered to harm a person in order to protect its owner? What order, what law here will have authority over his decision? In several places in Asimov's works, there is such a situation where the robot fails to make a decision. When the three laws conflict with each other, the robot's circuits overheat and it stops its activity.

Still, let us imagine this situation. A thief breaks into the home of a robot owner. What will happen? The robot has no right to kill him. He can only react if the thief points his weapon at the owner. But then it will be too late!

There is a way out here - the robot can be programmed to warn its owner and protect him without killing the thief. After all, its role is not that of a policeman or a security guard! Robots are designed to help us, not to serve as soldiers or police officers. Or at least it should be.

This is how Asimov envisages the robot affairs. But why shouldn't it be possible to use AI, or robots, as police officers? And what would happen then? AI is already being used in the military, i.e., it is a process that has already begun. Can an AI make the decision to kill a person instead of sparing them? And if so, is it moral?

These are all theoretical questions. Unfortunately, today it is rare for any business to consult moral philosophers or representatives of the Church before starting a new technological development. The moral point of view remains apart from the production of a given device. Thus, here we will talk more theoretically, about how things should be instead of what they actually are.

Another question that Asimov and his colleague Silverberg ask in the story *The Positronic Man* (1992) is the identity of robots. Can a robot have consciousness? And if so, does it have its own identity? Can we treat the robot as a person? In this book, this question is answered positively - yes, it is possible to create a robot in which consciousness of its own identity appears! It will be a robot that realizes itself that it is a robot. This quality we call reflection is unique to man. Therefore, such a robot will actually be a hybrid between a machine and a human. Even in the book, he acquires certain legal rights, no longer as someone's property, but as a person.

This is how things look from a science fiction perspective. Robotics today is not developing exactly the way Asimov, Silverberg and Clark envisioned it. They missed the giant leap with the development of computers. It is not really the exterior, the body of the robot that is most important; we must pay attention to what Asimov called positron schemes. The "brain" of the machine, i.e., artificial intelligence, is important. It does not have to be "incorporated" into the body of an android (a robot that looks like a human). But moral problems and dilemmas remain: what is the limit of artificial intelligence development?

It is clear that AI and robots should serve for the benefit of man. This is the common understanding - all technology should serve us, not lead to our destruction. At first glance, it seems so, but is this realistic today? Not at all. Let us just look at what nuclear technology has led to - instead of serving us, it has led (during the Cold War) to us living in fear almost every day. Many new developments today are first used in military affairs (for example, the Internet started as a military project). Genetic engineering poses new problems for us - can it be used to turn us into "limited humans" or "programmed humans"? As we see, it is not entirely true that technologies serve man - they serve specific people (primarily those who buy them).

As we have seen, AI demonstrates some cognitive abilities and decision-making resembling human thought. At the same time, it is rooted in programming. This is the limitation that we intentionally put on AI. But its ability to take decisions is impressive and it is time we turned to it now.

Thus, we continue our analysis, turning now to specific proposals and situations related to artificial intelligence. Finally, we will discuss these questions through the lens of Christianity and the problem of whether we are trying to create an imitation of the universal Logos.

7.2 Moral dimensions of AI

Summary:

AI provokes serious moral debate on how we can make use of it without doing harm to mankind. What about "sentient AI"? Could we coexist with an android that resembles us not only in its appearance but also in its intellect? Some solutions were offered by writers such as Isaac Asimov. We will also turn to the Catholic Church and its attitude toward AI in the opinion of Paul Tighe.

Things look different today than the science fiction writers thought. Instead of android robots, we now encounter automated cars, couriers, and even weapons. Still, the principle remains the same - an AI must make decisions based on (1) sensory input and (2) its program.

Travis Lacroix, a researcher on moral dilemmas related to AI, points out how important it is for AI to be able to make moral decisions on its own. In recent years we have seen some situations where AI makes a wrong decision and kills (unintentionally) a human. As Lacroix notes, "In 2018, a self-driving vehicle in Tempe, AZ apparently alternated between classifying a pedestrian, Elaine Herzberg, who was walking her bicycle in the street, as 'vehicle', 'person', and 'other object.' The result was that the vehicle struck and killed Herzberg" (Lacroix 4).

At first glance, this seems absurd - a machine should be well programmed and easily distinguish a person from other objects. But for an AI, it is not that easy. There are strange situations, such as a person on a bicycle or a scooter. To the AI, it is just an item. That does not mean the autonomous car has to hit that person; but there is such a risk, because in this case the "First Law of Robotics" (according to Asimov, this is the prohibition to injure a person) does not work.

AI must not only be programmed but also face real situations where it is forced to make decisions. We can say that it also needs to gain experience. This will help AI in making the right decisions. But what about moral dilemmas? According to Lacroix, a machine can make moral decisions without being human.

There is no way to avoid these moral dilemmas - we expect that these technologies will develop even more: "As autonomous vehicles become more prevalent on society's roads, it is supposed that it will become increasingly likely that an individual vehicle will need to be programmed to make decisions in situations that carry significant moral weight" (Lacroix 5). These decisions should be made based on the advice of experts from various fields, including the moral one. Although it is rare, these machines will still have to decide in some situations how to cause less harm and how to injure fewer people: "We suppose that an autonomous vehicle is about to crash and has no trajectory to save everyone. Is it better, for example, to hit a group of pedestrians on the road or swerve into a barrier, killing the driver?" (Lacroix 6).

Such a "moral machine" will make a decision in a specific situation based on specific propositions that are programmed into it. We cannot think that the machine will rely on abstract moral standards. As already mentioned, computers are typically only able to make concrete decisions - although AI may still be capable of grasping some abstract concepts, such as good and evil. That is why Lacroix states the following: "As noted above, what is actually being measured is how well the machine accords with some set of humans on average, not how ethical the machine actually is| relative to some meta-ethical standard" (Lacroix 16).

Is it possible for a moral machine to do the right thing? Can it make the right decisions? Let us think carefully - even a person is not always capable of this. Of course, if we take the First Law of Robotics (Azimov) as a given, then an autonomous car will always avoid harming human beings. This probably means a limited speed, a limited route, and (perhaps) external control by another computer (sort of a transport control center). But the big problem is this: what if these machines suddenly decide to harm people? It does not matter what the cause is - can we stop them? How will we control them?

According to science fiction writers like Asimov, sooner or later we will face a similar problem. The more autonomous robots become, the more likely they are to defy our will. How could we stop human-directed aggression?

Let us think about the history of cars in general. At first, they moved at a low speed and were believed to be unable to cause damage. As the speed increased, so do the crashes. In the very beginning, the inventors believed that cars would bring only benefit to mankind. However, over time we have realized that these means of transport are not safe at all. Could it be the same with artificial intelligence?

The moral conflict here is due to the question of what it means for a technology to act "in our interest." What is this interest - of all people, of a specific nation, of a given group of people? It is clear that not all people in the world will be able to afford to have a robot at home - just as today not all people have access to the Internet or a car. How will AI help all of humanity? And if it helps, for example, only Western societies, won't this lead to a dangerous competition between the West, on the one hand, and Russia and China, on the other?

At first, it seems as if AI actions "in our interest" are not so universal; this already casts doubt on whether the benefits outweigh the risks. Is the risk too great?

An article by Jonah McKeown sheds some light on this matter. Engineer Blake Lemoine "made headlines this week after raising concerns that Google's artificial intelligence system, Language Model for Dialogue Applications (LaMDA), may have developed sentience — in other words, it is no longer a machine, but a person" (McKeown par. 1). At one point, this AI replies that it is actually a person – i.e., we see something like a thought process working in it!

The engineer insists that this AI really possesses consciousness: "Lemoine says he concluded that LaMDA was a person — based on his religious beliefs, rather than in his capacity as a scientist. He publicly spoke out against it, creating several posts online explaining why he believes the AI has achieved consciousness" (Mc Keown par. 3).

This poses exactly the question that Asimov asks in his works: what will we do with a robot that is aware of its identity? Will it have rights like ours? How, after all, shall we distinguish it from man? Does artificial intelligence have a tendency to imitate humans? Yes, perhaps it is only an imitation; we have no way of knowing if this AI is truly aware that it is a machine (it has self-awareness). Maybe this is just one part of its algorithm? In any case, we should not underestimate this problem, which is equally important with that of AI actions "in our interest."

Given the explosive development of AI in recent years, the Catholic Church has called on scientists around the world to hold a dialogue on the moral dimensions of artificial intelligence. As McKeown writes, "In November 2020, Pope Francis invited Catholics around the world, as part of his monthly prayer intention, to pray that robotics and artificial intelligence remain always at the service of human beings — rather than the other way around" (McKeown paragraph 7). As we have shown, this is the basis of AI's moral development; but can we guarantee it? And more precisely, will scientists comply with the opinion of moral philosophers and the Church?

The Catholic Church has already come up with proposals for how robots can serve for our benefit. Six ethical principles were announced: transparency, inclusion (non-discrimination), accountability (someone must be in control of the machine), impartiality; reliability, and security and privacy (not to disclose personal data) (McKeown par. 9). These principles could be "translated" into something more particular, such as the principle of not harming a human, or the principle that AI should always obey the human.

Now we turn to an interesting conversation between researcher Brian Green and the Irish bishop Paul Tighe, Secretary of the Section of Culture of the Dicastery for Culture and Education. This interesting conversation shows a different perspective on the Vatican's attitude toward technology. Instead of denying it and severely limiting it, Tighe suggests we use technology to our advantage. His conception about our relationship with AI should be based on a positive approach, on the idea that AI could be useful to us.

Tighe explains that in recent decades there have been various ethical issues related to technology - first with the use of computers, and then with the Internet. In many cases, the Vatican was first highly critical of what was happening, suggesting from the outset that we should be cautious. According to him, this is not the right approach. He describes how his colleagues did not take the digital space seriously at all years ago, so he had to work with them a lot on this issue. As he puts it, "A whole process of learning had to happen in order for people to understand that these are very important spaces in which the Church needed to be present." For example, today we have access to important Church materials online; we can even watch the masses online. This is how we see the digital entering our physical space. But for Tighe there is nothing terrible here: "We had to overcome a tendency to make a distinction between the 'real' and the 'digital,' as if the digital were somehow secondary or less important or not serious" (Green 216).

Here, some critics may state that the digital was never real because it was man-made. But in a sense, Paul Tighe is right: digital is a way of perceiving and representing reality. In this space there can be many representations, many perceptions. However, we should never forget that human thought is behind it – the digital would not have appeared without human intervention. This is perhaps the only serious boundary between the physical and the digital - but both realms are part of reality today.

Bishop Tighe continues with something else positive related to artificial intelligence. Its development makes us ask ourselves various questions: "But I surmise that the really interesting thing AI is doing is to incite us to think again about what makes us human. What are the values that make us human?" (Greene 216). This is exactly what we described: how to distinguish a robot from a human person? If we and the robot have intelligence, how do we differentiate that intelligence?

Undoubtedly, by seeing ourselves against the background of machines, we understand better what we are. This has happened since the time of Descartes, who declared that animals are machines, but humans are not. While machines are pre-programmed and only act accordingly, we have free will and can always do something different. Of course, Descartes is seriously mistaken when he calls animals machines. And later philosophers like Julien Lametrie and also behavioral psychologists would call man a "machine" or "mechanism."

All of this AI development can make us wonder: Aren't we also programmed the way we program these machines and programs? A little later we will turn to this argument, which proves a Creator's existence. The fact is only intelligence can create intelligence!

Certainly, we see more and more similarities between our intelligence and AI. This is noted in an article by John Nosta. He is the founder of NOSTALAB, a think-tank dealing with issues in various spheres of life. In an article from October 2023, Nosta observes some similarities between our way of cognition and what we see in AI. According to him, "our sensory input may be directly informed by cognition and suggest a more 'integrated' processing between sensing and cognitive processing." As he sees it, "this perspective aligns with advancements in artificial intelligence, which are blurring the lines between perception and cognition, potentially facilitating a more integrated, fluid experience of reality" (Nosta par. 2). In short, our cognition and perception are an integrated whole; it is not true that we first start with the senses and then proceed with the processing of this data by the brain.

Nosta makes an important point: AI should not completely replace our intelligence. According to him, "Far from diluting the uniqueness of human cognition, AI serves to enrich it, taking what is already a nuanced interplay of sensory and cognitive functions and elevating it to new heights" (Nosta par. 7). Artificial intelligence helps us understand more about how our mind works; our aim should not be to use AI in the place of our mind. This remark should be taken as one of the basic principles of AI engineering. Given some of the bizarre ideas that have emerged recently - for example, that of merging the human brain with AI - this principle would prevent such experiments. Certainly, we still do not fully know how our brain works and what abilities it possesses that are still unknown to us. But even if we knew everything about our brain and our organism, we still shouldn't try to replace our intelligence with that of a robot. This is morally wrong - machines should serve us, without us becoming machines or machines controlling us!

These moral principles should be discussed with specialists from different fields. We need to include the businesses and laboratories that develop artificial intelligence. Without them, all these discussions will have no meaning. As Paul Tighe explains, "AI is such a complicated issue that what ethics has to do is to provide a framework and a language allowing different disciplines to talk to each other and understand each other's concerns, in order to be able to determine what is actually going to be best for human beings" (Green 221).

If we exclude AI developers from this conversation, then these developments will overtake our conversations. But that is why it is crucial to include the legislators - without them, our conversations will remain unproductive. Let us not forget how legislators reacted after the first operation of cloning a living creature in 1997 - they reacted in a flash to ensure that this experiment would not be conducted with a human. Therefore, we also need to clearly show what moral principles the development of AI should be based on, as well as where the limits of this development are.

Certainly, these conversations should not be limited only to Church leaders and, in general, to people of faith. We cannot go without contact with people who are atheists. In this case, it is not important whether we believe in God or not, but what the principles guiding our relationship with artificial intelligence will be. A little further on we will analyze the matter from the point of view of Christianity; we will not dwell on it specifically here.

As Paul Tighe mentions, AI helps us get to know ourselves better. It is possible to reach some conclusions that show our weaknesses and limitations: "I think there are ways in which AI will teach us to be more alert to the limitations of our freedoms, as it can predict patterns of behavior. But it will also raise huge challenges. For example, if it can tell in advance which men are likely to abuse women?" (Greene 223). This already raises a new series of moral questions - can we use AI to control people? The answer depends again on our definition of the phrase "in our interest." Does this interest apply to all people? Without exception, or only to certain people? Shall we exclude aggressive persons, alcoholics, drug addicts, and other such individuals from it? Do we have the right to direct AI specifically at such people in order to "tame" or control them?

Moral philosophers have long considered the use of machines and robotic devices controversial. It is true that transhumanists believe that the development of AI is a necessary stage of "human evolution." Transhumanists are representatives of a trend according to which machines will already be a part of our lives, and we ourselves must change so that we get used to living with them. Posthumanism sees the world of the future as dominated by technology, and man as merged with artificial intelligence. It believes in genetic engineering, in the possibility of man being modified and "changed." Therefore, it is not entirely true that all moral philosophers are against the lack of limitations in AI developments. There are philosophers who believe that we should not stop this development in any way.

Therefore, we can formulate three different approaches to the development of artificial intelligence: (1) total denial - or the idea that we should stop this development as quickly as possible; (2) a moderate approach - we can allow this development as long as it is not dangerous for people in general; and (3) full validation of AI, no matter how far that progress extends. Moral philosophers are entitled to argue about which of these approaches is morally correct.

We must keep in mind that the limitation of our own resources will not allow the development of AI to infinity. Today, for example, we see how the Internet and computer technology progress more slowly. Those "jumps" we used to see years ago are gone. Computers today look a lot like the computers of 5-6 years ago. Even mobile devices are not changing significantly. This is not to say that the advance of computers is at a standstill; but we no longer see that rapid pace of development which was at times frightening. Computers are getting a little more powerful these days, but you can easily buy an old computer and not see a big difference. Perhaps the only major difference is that computer technologies are more widespread - they are now widely used not only in military affairs, aeronautics and transport, but also in medicine and education - which was not the case until recently.

As reported by Paul Tighe, engineer Christof Koch attended a conference on AI. According to Koch, artificial intelligence is unable to acquire consciousness and cannot be considered a person: "AI and robots could performatively seem human, but he was very reluctant to ascribe any form of consciousness to artificial intelligences. In other words, you may end up believing you are interacting with a human, but ultimately, the question is: 'Is it actually human?' " (Green 225). Of course, the hypothesis that an AI could gain something like consciousness remains only one hypothesis. But if we recall Nosta's words that AI resembles the way our brain works, then we will understand that things are not so simple. Indeed, AI imitates our intelligence; it is severely limited. But if AI has (in some strange way) emotions and feelings, impressions, passions - then are we to assume that it has no consciousness? All this is said with the proviso that this cannot happen without affecting the biological state of such an AI - it will turn into an android, and it is quite possible that engineers will come up with a way to imitate even the human organism!

This idea is hinted at in *The Positron Man* (Asimov and Silverberg), where the main character himself wants to be modified so that he fully resembles the human organism. Could such modifications lead to the emergence of emotions and feelings? This is a complicated question, but according to physiological reductionism (which is a form of materialism), it is quite possible. According to this approach to biology, the physiological dimensions of an organism give rise to its psychic dimensions. In short, matter "produces" the soul. Thus, an android would have a "soul," although not quite human-like.

Coming to the question of the "soul" of robots, we cannot help but look at it from a Christian point of view. What should the Church's concept of AI be? Can we really afford to be "positive" about it, as Paul Tighe wishes?

7.3 Human helper, not another Babylon tower

Summary:

Artificial intelligence should serve mankind, not vice versa. We have to put some limitations on its development. Here we will discuss some essential points to be followed and kept by developers and legislators. We will also refer to several Bible passages to demonstrate the need to be modest and not to replace God with an artificial Logos.

There are some points of commonality between Christian teaching and the problems related to artificial intelligence. As Paul Tighe notes, "I think the Vatican is also following and listening to the secular debates and learning a huge amount from those, because many of the basic concerns raised in even quite secular contexts are issues to which we can relate—concerns about bias, privacy, inclusivity, etc." (Greene 217). As we said earlier, we gain more knowledge about man by comparing ourselves to machines, and specifically to AI. By realizing what it means to be human, we also understand how our relationship with AIs should be based on human morality, not on morality viewed from the perspective of a machine. For the machine, man is not necessarily the highest being in the world, apart from God. For the machine, moral anthropocentrism may not apply. We cannot expect all rational beings in the universe to think like us (as Immanuel Kant believed) - because we always see the world and life from a human perspective. For us, the person is the basis of our worldview. It does not matter whether we believe in God or not; but human life is always the highest value. However, for a robot man is not necessarily the highest form of life.

A machine will not believe anthropocentrism, even if it is programmed in the machine itself. If artificial intelligence goes too far, it will probably think that human life is not the highest value. This can lead to moral dilemmas when the AI will have to decide whether to save a human life or prefer another living being. Let us imagine the following case: an AI decides that a human community is polluting the environment too much, and this poses a greater threat to life on earth. Then this AI will immediately decide to eliminate the threat to nature, i.e., mankind! Such a hypothesis is not only imagination. It is a potential situation because we cannot be certain of what an AI would think about human beings in, say, ten years.

There is no way to be sure that our programming will prevent such a way of thinking. This AI can then decide to reduce that community or limit it so that it can no longer pollute the environment! This is a hypothetical example, but it demonstrates well that we may run the machines out of control at some point.

What should be the reaction of the Church community to the development of Artificial intelligence? In the interview with bishop Paul Tighe, we have already seen that we should not approach it entirely negatively. It is not right to deny all the achievements of technology and science just because they seem "strange" to us. As Tighe states, "despite the Church's efforts to speak positively about science and technology, there is a perception, not just among some scientists, but culturally, that somehow there is an opposition" (Green 218). It usually comes from the older generations who are not well acquainted with new technologies and do not use them much. This negativity is easily explained by the fact that not all people are good with computers and even with the Internet.

We would like to make two points here: a positive and a negative. First, we will start with the negative and then we will continue with the positive one. The latter is also very important to our solution to the problem of where we should draw the limits of AI development.

We have already mentioned a critical argument: the existence of AI is due to human intelligence. AI to some extent copies our intelligence; of course, it also has many limitations - these are due to the fact that we ourselves do not know enough about our intelligence. And now let us imagine: one day AI-controlled machines decide that they have appeared out of nowhere. Or they decide they have nothing to do with the given person and deny their relationship with him. This argument is slightly reminiscent of the Watchmaker argument, but not quite. Now, we are not just talking about a mechanism that was created by some intelligence; and we are discussing the fact that there is a similarity between artificial intelligence and man!

If we could see this artificial intelligence talking now, we'd have a good laugh. But do atheists not talk the same way? Here it is: according to them, our intelligence emerged after "tens of thousands of years of evolution." One million years ago, the first humans appeared who did not have any of our intellectual traits. Then their brains began to develop. About 50,000 years ago, Neanderthals and Cro-Magnons men appeared, who stood very close to us in a physiological and intellectual sense, but not quite. They manifested some abilities to draw simple pictures and even had something like a religion, but their language was very primitive. Therefore, only 50,000 years ago, human intelligence as we know it today did not exist!

How exactly did language come about? Why is it so complex? Why can we communicate so easily through it? Why, for example, did a chimpanzee not evolve so well as to be able to communicate like we do? Will chimpanzees have something like human language in 50,000 years, or even 500,000 years? This is very illogical and even impossible!

Intelligence begets intelligence. Our intelligence came from somewhere. It did not develop "as a result of long evolution." There is no such thing in nature - we do not see such a development anywhere! But even in human civilization we do not observe it - how can we say that Plato was less intelligent than we are! On the contrary - today we can derive a variety of ideas from the ancient Greeks, Chinese, Indians, Egyptians, Mayans, and other peoples. The fact that many civilizations have disappeared without a trace does not mean that they were not civilizations! Just because we fly airplanes today does not mean the ancient Chinese or Egyptians were any dumber!

All this does not seem "unscientific" or "anti-evolutionist." Here we do not aim to reject evolution entirely - surely there is such a process in nature which might be called evolution. But it certainly did not realize in the way that today's evolutionists claim - a blind development "by chance," without any intelligence to stand at the beginning of it. Moreover, the data about "primitive people" itself does not prove the fact that they were... people. Therefore, evolutionists today need to rethink their views.

And yet, we are not here to start an argument about evolution. Our aim is only to show how absurd is the claim that our intelligence appeared "out of nowhere" in the course of "random evolution." The development of artificial intelligence shows that someone else is behind it. The further we go into the realm of AI, the easier it will be for us to see the truth: we are created by a Supreme Creator endowed with supreme intelligence!

In this sense, we should look positively at AI. It only demonstrates that there must be a necessarily existing connection between two different intelligences. This does not mean that one AI gave rise to another AI, but rather that an AI is begotten by another type of intelligence.

Here, the atheist would respond like this: artificial intelligence is something completely different from a human. AI is a machine, a mechanism. It is programmed and this can be easily seen. We are living beings and that puts us in a different position. The difference is qualitative, not quantitative - as Georg Hegel would say.

But why not apply this conclusion to man as well? Why shouldn't human intelligence be created from something qualitatively different from man? Why should the Creator not be a higher intelligence that cannot be comprehended by our thoughts? Why not see our intelligence as complexly programmed software? After John Nosta demonstrated the similarities between AI and human intelligence, why not go further - to a Creator we are similar to?

And here - after many years, the "fool" (AI) will say: "There is no man! Man is a fiction" (similar to Psalm 14). How will it be explained to it that it is not so? How will AI come to the conclusion that man created it?

These are not purely hypothetical problems because they have to do with theology. We can only welcome the development of AI because it proves our relationship with the Creator even more visibly!

There are many more ideas to discuss in relation with the progress of AI in the future. How should the Church relate to AI? How should believers treat it?

Our answer here will refer to a biblical scene. A long time ago, people decided to build the Tower of Babel. They had the ambition to reach all the way to heaven, all the way to God. This is what the book of Genesis says:

> They said to each other, "Come, let's make bricks and bake them thoroughly." They used brick instead of stone, and tar for mortar. Then they said, "Come, let us build ourselves a city, with a tower that reaches to the heavens, so that we may make a name for ourselves and not be scattered over the face of the whole earth." (Gen. 11:3-4)

God punishes them by dividing them through the tongue. Instead of one language, they now have hundreds of languages so the people cannot understand each other and stop building the tower.

The tower is an important symbol here. This is the human attempt to reach God, to become God. This aspiration is always present in our nature; we cannot blame the man for that. Man seeks infinity; he tries to overcome all limits.

The problem arises when we are unable to control this passion for infinity. Then it degenerates into something else - the desire to be gods. Isn't the development of AI an example of such a desire?

We can say that it is part of our nature to overcome various difficulties, to deal with problematic situations. Man always moves forward, albeit at the risk of getting lost in the jungle of adventures that life on this earth offers us. The construction of the Tower of Babel thus reflects this element of our nature. We create, we explore, we take risks - this is an important part of our being in this world. It has always been this way as long as there has been humanity. In this light, we can also look at the development of AI - this is a project that leads us to an unknown place; it connects the past with the future of humanity. Perhaps this is the path to our exit from the sphere of planet Earth? Maybe we will colonize the outer worlds? Because robots could easily adapt to life on, say, Mars (if that makes sense at all). Certainly, the appearance of androids, or robots with the appearance of humans, will seriously affect human development.

However, all this is also a big risk. We can see the Tower of Babel as a metaphor showing that excessive risks lead to failure. The lesson of this Bible story is: no matter how much we aspire to the heavens, we will not conquer them; but there is a risk of losing the favor of our Creator. Man is also a limited being; before us there is always a limit, an end. We must know when to stop moving toward that end.

If we are less proud, it would help us realize exactly where to stop. Pride makes us foolish and ready to reach the gods, to conquer the heavens. Modesty is an important

Christian value; it helps us to realize our finitude and seek God. For example, in the Epistle of the Apostle James we read the following:

> Submit yourselves, then, to God. Resist
> the devil, and he will flee from you.
> Come near to God and he will come
> near to you. Wash your hands, you
> sinners, and purify your hearts, you
> double-minded.
> Grieve, mourn and wail. Change your
> laughter to mourning and your joy to
> gloom.
> Humble yourselves before the Lord,
> and he will lift you up. (James 4:7-10)

This message indicates that it is always better to take life seriously. We should not be proud just because we have money or power or fame. These are transitory phenomena that always come to an end. We should think more about our salvation, our life after the end of earthly existence, because in this way only we will be better prepared for the moment when we stand before God's judgment. Our excessive attachment to the earthly makes us haughty. That is why we read the following in Proverbs: "When pride comes, then comes disgrace, but with humility comes wisdom" (Prov. 11:2).

Pride is a grave sin; this is one of the reasons for our separation from God. The wicked man is haughty, as we read in Psalms:

> In his arrogance the wicked man hunts
>
> down the weak, who are caught in the
>
> schemes he devises.
>
> He boasts of the cravings of his heart;
>
> he blesses the greedy and reviles the
>
> Lord.
>
> In his pride the wicked does not seek
>
> him; in all his thoughts there is no room
>
> for God.
>
> His ways are always prosperous; he is
>
> haughty and your laws are far from him;
>
> he sneers at all his enemies.
>
> He says to himself, "Nothing will shake
>
> me; I'll always be happy and never have
>
> trouble." (Ps. 10:2-6)

This arrogance will one day be destroyed in the most unpleasant way. But why do people continue to be haughty, to value only earthly things? Is it not in our very nature? Maybe we will never stop being attached to the material, to the earthly?

Man is blind on this earth to the extent that he thinks that it alone exists in the whole world. This blindness makes us believe there is no God, there is nothing beyond the earthly world. But owning too many things also blinds us. The less we own (and the less we realize we own anything), the better for our salvation. Possession itself is not the problem; the greater difficulty is attachment; but usually these two phenomena are related. We also see this in John's First epistle:

Do not love the world or anything in

the world. If anyone loves the world, the

love of the Father is not in him.

For everything in the world— the

cravings of sinful man, the lust of his

eyes and the boasting of what he has

and does— comes not from the Father

but from the world. (1 John 2:15-16)

That is why we must make our choice: either we are with the Father and then deny our

attachment to the world, or we are with the world and then deny our relationship with God!

There seems to be no middle ground here, no other option that is a compromise. The more

material possessions we accumulate, the more we will become attached to the earthly world.

Perhaps these verses are too extreme - still, it is more important not to be arrogant. It is

possible (at least theoretically) for a person to be both wealthy and humble. The point is not to

think that we become gods; we cannot take the place of the one, all-powerful Creator!

Therefore, the Christian point of view regarding the development of artificial

intelligence should be based on the following principles:

1. At any moment, this development must be preceded by the dissemination of

information - what exactly will be done and why. This development should not be kept secret

from the public.

2. Businesses involved in IT and AI development must by law consult with religious

figures, moral philosophers, and other people with potential influence in the field of ethics.

3. It must be clearly stated when AI shall not replace humans - in which activities this CANNOT happen (by law). For example, AI can replace humans in the field of education or services, but not in the military or police (this can give it dangerous power in its hands).

4. Absolute legislative ban on the development of a hybrid between a human and AI - here we refer to the recently appeared idea of Elon Musk to connect the human brain with AI. This is the most direct path to creating a humanoid robot. Such a hybrid is very dangerous for the future of humanity because it calls into question the existence of mankind at all.

5. Legislative prohibition of considering AI as a person. In no way can AI acquire rights equal to human rights; nor can it be regarded as the owner of property.

6. Legislative prohibition of potential reproduction between AI and a human being - this is a point similar to number 4.

7. Constant dialogue between AI developers and the Church; involvement of the Church in these developments and their service in the interest of the Church.

A positive approach will go a long way in realizing these seven points. Otherwise tensions will appear, and then the dialogue between AI-producing businesses and the Church will be very difficult to achieve. Both sides must be open.

We want to emphasize the extreme importance of points 3 and 4: (3) AI should not and cannot be military or police; shall not acquire arms; it shall not even go near a weapon. Unfortunately, today we see a good prospect for exactly that - drones with AI are already in use, the idea being that such a drone will be able to find its targets more easily, instead of destroying civilian infrastructure and civilian lives. No one consulted the moral philosophers or the Church on this matter. What do we do when such an AI drone turns on us? What will happen when he refuses to obey our orders? What will we do when terrorists employ military drones?

To this, the military would respond: we must develop such weapons because, anyway, Russia and China will also produce them. But this way of thinking is wrong - the point is not to develop them, but to have a dialogue about their use. There is no such dialogue today - as a society, we stayed away from this process. We learn from the news that such weapons exist! What are their test results? How well do they know ours from the enemy? Can they turn against the one who uses them? Do the military plan to use them even more massively? And police officers with AI - what are the plans regarding their production? Many questions remain up in the air.

Regarding point (4), it is obvious that a hybrid between an AI and a human could lead to the mass hysteria of humans to be "enhanced" by AI. It will be a desire similar to our ambition today to have a car or travel by plane. We will be prone to accepting such a procedure because many humans around us are becoming AI- hybrids. Similarly, our society has been pressed to accept LGBT "values," but this was a kind of "soft pressure." The most powerful way to make us accept this new hybrid is to promote it and advertise as something that would change our life forever. And it will do it, indeed!

After some time, such a hybrid will seem normal. Science fiction will be implemented in reality. Therefore, we must think about the consequences of this possibility. Let us look at legislation, which is one of the ways to prevent such an experiment. Do we have the capacity to create a hybrid between a human and, say, a dog? Such attempts today are prohibited by our legislation, and rightly so. Such phenomena will only lead to mankind ceasing to exist and their replacement by something else. From a technology perspective, this is not a problem; but from man's point of view, this is unacceptable!

Passing beyond the Christian point of view, we will notice one fact. Whether we accept the Logos as identical with Christ or not, we know and see that the Logos rules the world. And now that we are developing AI, we are actually aiming to replace the logos with an artificial Logo! Why do we need it? This advance is probably due to our ambition to control nature; and so, we now want to control not only nature, but that which controls it - the Logos! These are natural laws, reasonableness, regularities, wisdom. *We believe that we will succeed in creating our own laws of nature*, we will master nature in our own way. Tomorrow we will create a human-AI hybrid; in some time, we will create an artificial planet; and someday, we may even create artificial life! Here we indicate not only how things seem from the perspective of man, but also from that of the Logos.

A warning needs to be issued here. It will be a false Logos, just as the world of consumerism, hedonism and materialism is a false reality. This ambition of ours will crumble and bring a great cataclysm to humanity. Even the internet reality we have created so far can very easily disappear. Only one day without electricity all over the world, and our virtual reality will be over! No one knows what would happen after that. Will this be a world disaster, or will we rebuild our internet reality again? Not only are we fragile; our devices produced by us are fragile as well!

And even the lack of electricity is not the only possible difficulty. All it takes is an extremely strong magnetic storm. *We must never forget that reality is not what we create but what is forced upon us from the outside*; reality is what is forced upon us despite our wishes and dreams. The Logos is objectively existent, and we have no possibility of either eliminating it or replacing it with something else.

Yes, some readers would say that our artificial intelligence is an attempt to imitate the Logos, and there is nothing wrong with that. We respect the laws of nature and the wisdom available in the world. But is it really so? Where do we see this reverence and respect in this rapid development of technology? Where do we see the moral debates? In a society where it is claimed that nothing natural is real, and everything is almost "human fantasy" or "social construction," there can be no respect for the Logos. Those who want to change their gender because "gender is a social construct" will never respect the Logos. They will always argue that the Logos is also a "human invention" and that we have the right to see the world as we wish. Their tendency to deny nature simply because God created it will lead them to bitter disappointment. This is not our problem, it is not the problem of people who look at the world realistically. But if this ideology is imposed on us, it will be a catastrophe for all mankind.

7.4 Conclusion

Artificial intelligence is a huge opportunity that has opened up to our humanity. For many centuries we have imagined communicating with beings of our own making. We are now close to the moment when we will be able to see with our own eyes what such communication will be like. It has its advantages and disadvantages.

From a Christian perspective, the creation of AI is not unique. The very creation of man with his intellect is a miracle that we should often think about. Only intelligence can create intelligence! *It is impossible for intelligence to appear by chance* - the development of AI by man today proves this.

The Church is not categorically against these developments. They can make our lives easier, to some extent. Like the Internet today, AI can also help attract and communicate with more believers. As Bishop Tighe comments, we should not be negative before we know what it is about. We need to give these new technologies a chance.

At the same time, we need to set moral and legal limits to AI developments. They must be based on respect for the person and our values. Man is a person; the machine is not. Man is endowed with free will; the machine's will does not exist. Man can make the decisive choice in given situations; the machine cannot and should not be allowed to!

Our hubris could lead us to try to place AI above humans. Then we will say: Here, look, we are also Creators! And we are gods! But this arrogance will be fatal. One day, these projects of ours will destroy us. Therefore, the warnings we cited in this chapter are not accidental. We should approach them seriously, not with laughter and mockery. The Logos should be respected, not replaced or eliminated. The world will exist as it was created by God - whether we like it or not; whether we want to change it or not. The Logos is a universal power which governs and directs our world. It would be better to follow it instead of being proud fools rejecting this universal Wisdom and reason.

Conclusion

The publication of this work was provoked by the disturbing tendency of late to deny nature, to deny essence. This is a tendency characteristic of contemporary leftist liberalism, which, unlike classical liberalism, tends to describe the world as one vast social construction, i.e., as a fantasy that depends on human will. While the classical liberalism of John Locke, Thomas Paine, Benjamin Franklin, and other philosophers perceived the world as governed by reason and the laws of reason, modern leftist liberalism denies these laws and replaces them with human desires.

Thus, the present work is one answer to the question: what is this thing we call nature? Is there a human nature that is fixed and stable? Is it true that we are what we want to be? Is it true that our will is stronger than nature?

According to our interpretation, human nature is governed by the universal wisdom we call the Logos. This is wisdom that has been known to ancient peoples and cultures. It has been recognized and admired by all cultures in their own way. However, the pagan concept of the Logos is incomplete and therefore incorrect - it perceives the Logos as an impersonal force that sometimes spontaneously (without much visible logic) makes decisions about our lives. For the ancient Greeks, the Logos is a Universal Law, but chance and spontaneity have a place in it. We cannot command this Law, we have no claim to it.

The Christian understanding is more complete and shows the Logos in a different light. The Logos is not only divine; he is God himself. In the Holy Scriptures we see how Christ is called the Word, or Logos. It is the Living Word that not only rules the world but also saves human life. The Word saves us, and our salvation is the Word, the Logos, the Wisdom, the Law.

We must not forget that philosophers also perceive this Logos as a natural law. Even if they do not recognize the divine origin and essence of this Law, many philosophers recognize its existence. Logos and natural law are actually the same thing - no matter what we call them. Nonetheless, today the concept of Logos is characteristic of Christian theology; this is also the reason why some philosophers consider them as something separate - but this is a serious mistake.

The existence of the Logos itself, of the laws that we can easily perceive and realize, demonstrates that these laws were created by one Intelligence, one Mind. This fact we have shown in one of the chapters of the present work, where we explain that our universe could not have arisen by chance without the intervention of such an intelligence. In this way, the concept of artificial intelligence also leads us to God - because we are created in a similar way (though not the same way).

Whatever an atheist does, he must deny the obvious - the existence of natural laws and the wisdom we see around us. The atheist's attempt to hide in the shelter of scientism is unsuccessful - *science is not the enemy of religion, and scientific theories do not obviously deny the existence of God.* There is no way we can strive for the truth about the world and completely deny the existence of a Supreme Power endowed with intellect and will. These two things are mutually exclusive. Militant atheism is today marginalized in scientific circles. As we have shown, even ardent atheists are forced to admit that there are enough clues in the scientific data today that lead to a Creator.

At the same time, we do not reach a state of ultimate rationalism in this book. As we show, the Logos is also a mystery. It is attained to not only through reason, but also through faith, hope, love. Thus, reason is not the only way to reach God; nor is it a complete way in itself. This fact is well seen in the course of the Holy mass, which we have taken here as an excellent example of the manifestation of the Logos. The mass points to our Creator, but also to the Law of Life, the law that governs this world. The liturgy is an emanation of God's wisdom, God's reason and God's mystery.

Atheism's last attempt to deny God is by rejecting human nature altogether and natural principles in general. According to the extreme form of social constructivism that we see in Judith Lorber, gender is just a "social construction" that is deprived of objective reality. Therefore, we have whatever gender we want. Lorber herself did not go that far, but her followers some thirty years later already reached and claimed quite clearly that socio-cultural phenomena are the only real phenomena in this world - everything we call nature is an "illusion."

In Lorber's conception, we see a fierce attack on essentialism, or the approach according to which there are fixed stable entities in the world. Of course, essentialism does not deny change and development - we have already looked at this, drawing on some theological material. The very course of history after the appearance of the Son of God on earth confirms this - we are moving toward the end of history, and therefore nothing is completely fixed and stable. But it means that we are getting closer to the truth, we are getting closer to God, which is why we have more knowledge about the world, about Him and about ourselves.

Man is also immutable, insofar as he was created in the image and likeness of God; and at the same time, he is changing as he is part of the history while it is moving toward its end. The natural law, the Logos, does not really change, but we come to our full knowledge of it gradually. Our ancestors living 3000 years ago knew much less about the Logos than we do today. This does not mean that the Logos changes, but that only our concept of it expands and enriches.

Therefore, we could assert that we change, and we do not change at the same time; we are ourselves, and at the same time we overcome ourselves. But our nature is our human nature. We cannot claim that nature is an illusion or that entities are fiction. Any attempt to create such a concept will crumble and be destroyed like the Tower of Babel. *The de-naturalization of the world will kill itself by its own weapons.* And after all this, only common sense will remain, which sees the obvious - the reality of the divine Logos.

Works cited

Anselm of Canterbury. "Proslogion." *Complete Philosophical and Theological Treatises*, pp. 88-112. Minneapolis, Arthur Banning Press, 2000.

Asimov, Isaac. *I, Robot*. HarperCollins Publishers, 2018.

Asimov, Isaac and Silverberg, Robert. *The Positronic Man*. London, Victor Gollancz Ltd, 1992.

Von Balthasar, Hans Urs. *Cosmic Liturgy: The Universe according to Maximus the Confessor*. San Francisco, Ignatius Press, 2003.

Berger, Peter, and Luckmann, Thomas. *The Social Construction of Reality*. Penguin Books, 1991.

Holy Bible. New International Version.

Catechism of the Catholic Church. https://www.vatican.va/archive/ENG0015/_INDEX.HTM

Çimen, Ünsal. "Francis Bacon and the Relation between Theology and Natural Philosophy." *Synthesis Philosophica* vol. 67, issue 1, 2019, pp. 105–123.

Daly, Cahal. Natural Law Morality Today. *Catholic Culture*. Lecture from 1965 https://www.catholicculture.org/culture/library/view.cfm?recnum=2744

Dawkins, Richard. *The Selfish Gene*. Oxford UP, 2006. 30-th Anniversary Edition.

Eddington, Arthur S. *The Nature of the Physical World*. Macmillan Company, Cambridge UP, 1929.

Eliade, Mircea. *The Sacred & the Profane*. New York, Harcourt, Brace & World, 1963.

Epictetus. *Discourses*. New York, D. Appleton and Company, 1904.

Green, Brian. "The Vatican and Artificial Intelligence: An Interview with Bishop Paul Tighe." *Journal of Moral Theology*, vol. 11, Special Issue 1, 2022, pp. 212–231.

Greengrass, Mark. "The Theology and Liturgy of Reformed Christianity." In: R. Po-Chia

    Hsia (ed.) *The Cambridge History of Christianity*, vol. 6: Reform and Expansion, pp.

    104-124. Cambridge UP, 2007.

Gregg, Benjamin. "Against Essentialism in Conceptions of Human Rights and Human

    Nature." *Human Rights Quarterly*, vol. 43, issue 2, 2021, pp. 313-328.

    https://muse.jhu.edu/article/791094

Hoblik, Jiri. "The Holy Logos in the Writings of Philo of Alexandria." *Communio Viatorum*,

    vol. 3, 2014, pp. 248-266.

    https://www.academia.edu/31369233/The_Holy_Logos_in_the_Writings_of_Philo_of

    _Alexandria

James, William. *Pragmatism: A New Name for Some Old Ways of Thinking*. New York,

    Longmans, Green, and Co, 1907.

Jammer, Max. *Einstein and Religion: Physics and Theology*. Princeton UP, 1999.

Justin Martyr. "First Apology." In: Philip Schaff (ed.), *Ante-Nicene Fathers*, vol. I, pp. 423-

    501. Grand Rapids, MI, Christian Classics Ethereal Library.

    http://www.ccel.org/ccel/schaff/anf01.html

Kant, Immanuel. Groundwork of the Metaphysics of Morals. Cambridge UP, 1997.

Lacroix, Travis. Moral Dilemmas for Moral Machines. *AI and Ethics*, vol. 2, 2022, pp. 737-

    746. https://doi.org/10.1007/s43681-022-00134-y

Lefebvre, Gaspar. *Catholic Liturgy: Its Fundamental Principles*. New York, Benziger

    Brothers, 1924.

Lockwood, Thornton C. "Physis and Nomos in Aristotle's Ethics." *The Society for Ancient

    Greek Philosophy Newsletter* vol. 6, issue 2, 2005, pp. 23-35.

Lorber, Judith. *Paradoxes of Gender*. Yale UP, 1994.

Lorenz, Edward. *The Essence of Chaos*. Taylor & Francis e-Library, 2005.

Louth, Andrew. *Maximus the Confessor*. London and New York, Routledge, 1996.

St. Maxim the Confessor. "Difficulty 10." In: Andrew Louth (ed.). *Maximus the Confessor*, pp. 91-152. London and New York, Routledge 1996.

McGrath, Alister. *Re-Imagining Nature: The Promise of a Christian Natural Theology*. John Wiley & Sons, 2017.

McKeown, Jonah. Sentient AI?: Here's What the Catholic Church Says about Artificial Intelligence. *Catholic News Agency*, 15 June 2022. https://www.catholicnewsagency.com/news/251552/sentient-ai-heres-what-the-catholic-church-says-about-artificial-intelligence

Mitsis, Philip. "Stoicism". In: Christopher Shields (ed.) *The Blackwell Guide to Ancient Philosophy*, pp. 253-267. Blackwell, 2003.

Mwania, Patrick. "The Justin Martyr's Concept of Logos Spermaticos and its Relevance to Theological Conversation in Africa Today". *Roczniki Teologiczne* vol. LXIV, 10, 2017, pp. 189-204. DOI: http://dx.doi.org/10.18290/rt.2017.64.10-14

Nosta, John. The Symbiosis of Perception and Cognition. *Psychology Today*. 25 October 2023. https://www.psychologytoday.com/intl/blog/the-digital-self/202310/the-symbiosis-of-perception-and-cognition

Paley, William. *Natural Theology*. Cambridge UK, 2009.

Plantinga, Alvin. *God, Freedom and Evil*. Grand Rapids, William B. Eerdmans Publishing, 1977.

Plato. *Protagoras*, (translated and edited by C.C.W. Taylor). Revised Edition. Oxford University Press, 1990.

Premier Christian News. Celebrated Cosmologist, Sir Roger Penrose, is Challenged to Believe in the God that Stephen Hawking Denied. 4 October 2019.

https://premierchristian.news/en/news/article/celebrated-cosmologist-sir-roger-penrose-is-challenged-to-believe-in-the-god-that-stephen-hawking-denied

Saleem, Amna; Kausar, Huma; and Deeba, Farah. "Social Constructivism: A New Paradigm in Teaching and Learning Environment." *Perennial Journal of History* (PJH), vol. II, issue II, July-December 2021, pp. 403-421.

Smith, Leonard. *Chaos: A Very Short Introduction*. Oxford UP, 2007.

Smith, Tom. What is God's Economy in the Bible? *Holding to Truth*, 20 November 2019 https://holdingtotruth.com/2019/11/20/what-is-gods-economy-in-the-bible/

Taylor, C. C. W. "Nomos and Phusis in Democritus and Plato." *Social Philosophy and Policy* vol. 24, issue 2, 2007, pp. 1-20.

Thomas Aquinas. *Summa Theologiae*. Christian Classics Ethereal Library https://www.ccel.org/ccel/a/aquinas/summa/cache/summa.pdf

Walsh, Anthony. *God, Science and Society. The Origin of the Universe, Intelligent Life, and Free Societies*. Vernon Press, 2020.

Webb, Clement C. J. *Studies in the History of Natural Theology*. Clarendon, Oxford, 1915.